The Friday Afternoon Club

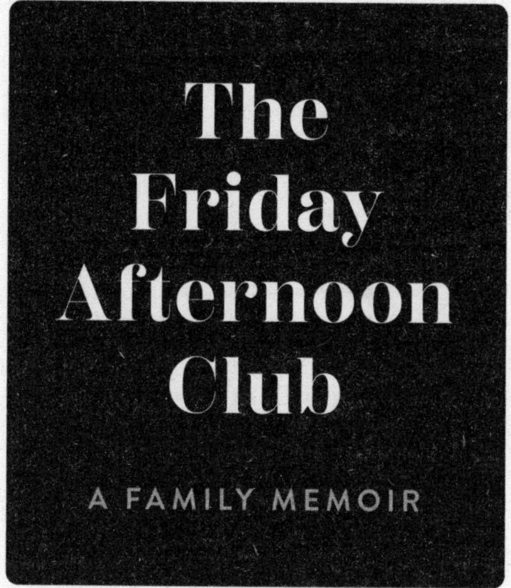

Griffin Dunne

PENGUIN PRESS
NEW YORK
2024

PENGUIN PRESS
An imprint of Penguin Random House LLC
penguinrandomhouse.com

Grateful acknowledgment is made to Copper Canyon Press and The Wylie Agency (UK) Limited for permission to reprint an excerpt from "Snowfall" from *The Second of Four Books of Poems* by W. S. Merwin (Copper Canyon Press) and *The Carrier of Ladders* (Atheneum), copyright © 1971 by W. S. Merwin. Reprinted by permission of The Permissions Company LLC on behalf of Copper Canyon Press, coppercanyonpress.org, and The Wylie Agency (UK) Limited.

LIBRARY OF CONGRESS CATALOGING-IN-PUBLICATION DATA

Names: Dunne, Griffin, author.
Title: The Friday afternoon club : a family memoir / Griffin Dunne.
Description: New York : Penguin Press, 2024.
Identifiers: LCCN 2023030129 (print) | LCCN 2023030130 (ebook) | ISBN 9780593652824 (hardcover) | ISBN 9780593652831 (ebook) | ISBN 9780593833315 (international edition)
Subjects: LCSH: Dunne, Griffin. | Dunne, Griffin—Family. | Actors—United States—Biography.
Classification: LCC PN2287.D848 A3 2024 (print) | LCC PN2287.D848 (ebook) | DDC 791.4302/8092 [B]—dc23/eng/20240212
LC record available at https://lccn.loc.gov/2023030129
LC ebook record available at https://lccn.loc.gov/2023030130

Printed in the United States of America
1st Printing

Designed by Amanda Dewey

Some names and identifying characteristics have been changed to protect the privacy of the individuals involved.

To my brother, Alex,
who was there through it all

Belmont Books
79 Leonard Street
Belmont, MA 02478
(617) 932-1496
6/14/2024 10:18:12 AM

REG #: 27 CLERK #: 39 TRAN #: 100159

1@ $30.00 9780593652824 $30.00T
FRIDAY AFTERNOON CLUB: A FAMILY MEMOIR

Sub-Total: 0000119449 $30.00
Tax $1.88
Total: $31.88
Tendered: MASTERCARD $31.88
XXXXXXXXXXXX6955 mmyy APPROVAL 10018Z
Transaction ID: MASTERCARD
Reference No: 212580
Transaction Type: Sale

BC/Member Award Status
3 units $90.31

RETURN POLICY: Store credit only. Must be returned within 30 days of purchase. Item must be in new condition.

It's very difficult to escape your background. You know, I don't think it's necessary to even try to escape it. More and more, I start to think that it's necessary to see exactly what it is that you inherited on both ends of the stick: your timidity, your courage, your self-deceit, and your honesty and all the rest of it.

—Sam Shepard

Hey, kiddo, what can I say?
I'm a work in progress.

—Dominick Dunne

The Friday Afternoon Club

Prologue

At 3:00 a.m., during the early hours of Halloween 1982, Detective Harold Johnston of the West Hollywood Homicide Division rang the doorbell of my mother's house in the flats of Beverly Hills. Marina, her live-in housekeeper, woke to the sound and let the detective in. She expected she'd have to disturb Mrs. Dunne's sleep, but when she led Johnston into her bedroom, the lights were on and Mom was already sitting up in bed, bracing herself for news that is never good at that time of night.

The first thing that caught Johnston's eye was my mother's wheelchair. He was a tough Irish cop who'd made countless house calls like this before, but never to a lady like Mrs. Ellen Griffin Dunne of 528 Crescent Drive North. He took in the wheelchair, the collection of glass hippos lining the shelves of an overstuffed bookcase, a bowl of rosebuds floating in water, and a black cat lying protectively on her lap, both waiting for the detective to get to the reason for his visit. The closest murder had ever come to this house was in the pages of the Georges Simenon novel the detective clocked on Mrs. Dunne's bedside table.

Detective Johnston gently informed my mother that her daughter had been strangled by a man named John Sweeney. At this moment Dominique Dunne was still alive, though she had been placed on life support at Cedars-Sinai hospital. Glancing once more at Mom's wheelchair, the detective asked if there was anyone she'd like to call.

My father was the first and only person who came to mind. She reached for the phone but it fell to the floor, scaring the cat off her lap. Her hands trembled so much she fumbled the numbers on the rotary dial. She gave up and handed the phone to the detective and told him Dad's number in New York City.

"Thank you," she said when he handed it back. "Nick, I'm here with a homicide detective named . . . I'm sorry, I forgot your name . . ."

"Detective Harold Johnston. Would you like me to speak to him?

"Yes, please. Thank you."

That's another thing Johnston noticed about my mother that was unusual in his line of work: even when told that her daughter was on life support, she was unfailingly polite.

After delivering the news to my father, he handed her back the phone.

"Nick," she said, "I need you."

"I'll be on the next plane."

After they hung up, Dad's next call was to me at my apartment, three blocks from his.

"I can't tell if I'm dreaming now or what," he said after relaying his conversation with Johnston.

I'd had two hours of sleep and the taste of cocaine still lingered in the back of my throat, so it took a moment to focus.

"Wait . . . did you say *homicide* detective?" I asked, bolting out of bed.

"Griffin, get over here now. I need you."

I was twenty-seven years old but never felt more like a lost little boy.

Part One

One

My mother was the only child of a cattle rancher. Her father's thirty-thousand-acre ranch was called the Yerba Buena, situated in Nogales, Arizona, a border town just north of Sonora. Tom Griffin chose to raise Santa Gertrudis cattle, a risky venture for a city slicker from Chicago, but at last he'd fulfilled his dream to return to Arizona's high desert, where as a child he was sent to cure his weak lungs.

Tom was born into a socially prominent family that had made its fortune in the Griffin Wheel Company, which manufactured wheels for all the Pullman train cars that crossed America. His uncles were playboys and philanderers whose shenanigans often found their way into the gossip columns of the Chicago dailies. In the mid-1920s, my great-great-uncle George Griffin died of a heart attack while in bed with his mistress aboard his yacht off the coast of Palm Beach, Florida. The mistress was Rose Davies, sister of the movie star Marion Davies, who happened to be the mistress of the publishing magnate William Randolph Hearst, so elaborate measures were taken to prevent a national scandal.

Ms. Davies was snuck ashore in the dead of night and caught the next sleeper car to Los Angeles, with actual Griffin wheels whirling beneath her berth. Meanwhile, George Griffin's steadfast crew dressed him in pajamas, loaded him onto a tender, and checked his corpse into the Breakers Hotel. After tucking him in, the vice president of the Griffin Wheel Company solemnly called George's wife to say that her husband had just died peacefully in his sleep.

His wife, my great-great-aunt Helen Prindeville Griffin was no stranger to wealth, having been a doyenne of Washington, DC, society who summered in Newport, Rhode Island. At the moment when Mrs. Griffin had been notified of her husband's death, she was in bed with her lover at the Hotel del Coronado in California, and took the news that she was a widow rather well. She untwined herself from the arms of Admiral Paul Henry Bastedo who served under Secretary of the Navy Franklin Roosevelt, and proposed they get married in the morning so he could be her date at her late husband's funeral. To the tabloids' delight, the newlyweds took Helen Prindeville Griffin Bastedo's private railway car to Lake Forest, Illinois, to attend the service. The act so outraged the Griffin family that they used their juice with Union Pacific to divert the train and the unlucky passengers coupled to Helen's private car. The train choo-chooed deep into Wisconsin, denying the newlyweds their grand entrance to the funeral. The family were less successful trying to have Helen cut from George Griffin's will, and she inherited every cent of his enormous fortune.

Scandal visited the next generation of Griffins a decade later, on the day of Tom's wedding to a woman from an equally prominent family. Approaching the church in the back of a limousine, he watched the crowd of guests and photographers awaiting his arrival and told the chauffeur to keep driving, all the way to Chicago Union Station. Once there—still in top hat and tails—he boarded a Pullman car (on Griffin wheels) and headed westward to begin his new life as a rancher in Nogales.

As KIDS, we loved when Mom took us to Nogales. My younger brother and sister and I used to cross the border into Mexico on foot with a pack of cousins, as easily as going through a subway turnstile. We rambled up a hill to reach a restaurant called La Roca, set on top of a large rock. At the bottom of the rock, a cave, once a prison, used to shelter a cantina called La Caverna. La Roca was built above only when La Caverna burned down under suspicious circumstances. Tom Griffin was long dead by then and was spared the demise of his favorite haunt, where he famously sat at his usual table, with a parrot on his shoulder who'd bite anyone who got too close. As much as he tried, he never mastered Spanish as well as his parrot, but he made up colorful words that sounded like the language, and locals always got the gist.

One of my grandfather's favorite requests was for the mariachis to play "El ternero perdido," or "The Lost Calf." The song required the alto trumpeter to go outside the bar and way down the block, to toot his horn as the lost calf. A chorus of mariachis sang as the worried cows calling out for their lost calf, and then there was a solo, presumably the mother of the calf, who pleaded, "Oh where, oh where is my little lost calf?" The tension would build, and suddenly the audience would hear the lost calf somewhere far off. His trumpet sounded like a child, crying for its mother. When the patrons of La Caverna heard the lost calf, they'd go apeshit and Tom's parrot would squawk at the top of its tiny lungs. Then the door would burst open and the alto trumpeter would wail, "I'm here, I'm here, I found you at last." Everyone in the bar, drunk on tequila and elated that the little calf had finally found its mother, would cry in relief.

On one trip to La Roca, everyone danced on top of the rock that once housed La Caverna. Mom tried to stump the mariachis, knowing the lyrics to every cancion, which impressed the band, though they were never stumped. My little sister, Dominique, started to yawn around two in the morning, and Mom took the hint and gathered us to cross back over the border. When the mariachis saw that Mom was leaving, they begged her to stay a little longer. One of our cousins said in Spanish to the musicians, "Why don't you guys come with us?"

We went back through the turnstiles into the United States, no questions asked, followed by the mariachis, who had to lift their giant guitarróns over the twirling bars. Our group marched on to my cousin Eddie Holler's house, where we were staying, just across the border.

Mom put us to bed when we got there, and somehow we managed to sleep through the ruckus downstairs. Early, but not too early, the next morning, I went downstairs for something to eat and stepped over mariachis asleep on the floor, still in sombreros, clutching their trumpets and harps.

ONE LATE NIGHT in Los Angeles, in my early teens, I was watching a movie on television with my mother, as we often did back then when Alex and Dominique were asleep.

On the screen was an old Western about settlers traveling the frontier in wagon trains. They were under such constant attack from Sioux warriors that one of the homesteaders went mad, leapt from the wagon, and shrieked across the plains. His wife, not missing a beat, calmly took over the reins and snapped the horse along to keep up with the train. "That woman," my mother said to me in the glow of the television screen, "is exactly like your grandmother."

My mother, Ellen Beatriz Griffin, was given the middle name of her mother, Beatriz Sandoval. My grandmother—Gammer, as we called her—was one tough cookie. It was said that she'd been stung so many times by scorpions that she was immune to their pain.

The Sandoval family had been in Mexico for over two hundred years and were raised to consider themselves Mexicans, not Spaniards. Beatriz's grandfather, José Sandoval, owned silver mines, fishing and pearl concessions in the Sea of Cortez, and major real estate in Hermosillo and Guaymas. The Sandovals were on the wrong side of the Mexican Revolution, so as the rebels closed in to seize their property, my relatives fled to the safety of Baja California, before eventually settling in Nogales, and in time managed to build their fortune all over again.

Beatriz's family was not without scandal either; her brother Alfredo did serious time in prison, not once but twice, for embezzling from a bank the Sandovals owned. His grandfather forgave him the first time, but after the second he demanded that Alfredo's name never be mentioned, an order Beatriz followed to the end of her life. I was perversely proud to have a jailbird in the family and tortured my grandmother with my curiosity about him, oblivious that her shame was on par with being the sister of John Wilkes Booth. My mother finally pulled me aside and told me to knock it off.

Tom Griffin met Beatriz shortly after moving to Nogales and swept her off her feet, even though she was engaged to an aristocrat from Mexico City. Tom courted and badgered her to dump her fiancé and marry him instead, and after she gave in to his charms, they soon eloped. However, her previous intended was already on an overnight train from Mexico City to Nogales for their wedding, so to be sure he didn't arrive, Beatriz sent a telegram to every stop the train would make—and there were many in those days—to inform him that the marriage was off.

PLEASE DO NOT COME. STOP read the first message he received as the train was pulling out of San Juan del Rio. THE MARRIAGE IS OFF. STOP. By Zacatecas he held twelve more. I PLAN TO MARRY THOMAS GRIFFIN. STOP. At Hermosillo, Señor Sad Sack had a neat pile of about thirty telegrams before finally taking the hint and turning back to Mexico City.

Though my mother romanticized her parents' relationship, she was a lonely child on the Yerba Buena, pained by her father's absence during World War II, when he served in the Pacific as a captain in the navy. She once told me, after one too many Pinot Grigios, that when she was a little girl, she walked into her parents' bedroom and thought her father had come home because an officer's uniform was crumpled at the foot of the bed. Gammer shrieked in alarm as her daughter slipped out of the room, neither ever mentioning the moment except to me that night.

"Who was the officer?"

"He was an admiral."

"The Griffin gals sure had a thing for admirals. Who was he?"

The television was on as usual in her bedroom. John McCain had just been released from the Vietnamese POW camp known as the Hanoi Hilton, and his painful walk on the tarmac to his waiting family was playing on the late-night news. She pointed to McCain, the young naval pilot on the screen, who had also been raised in Arizona, and said, "That guy's father."

The draft was winding down but still in effect, and since my eligibility was fast approaching, I followed the Vietnam War closely.

I knew enough to know that the future senator's father was Admiral John S. McCain, commander in chief of Pacific Command.

"You're kidding!"

The next day I brought up what she'd told me the night before and expressed my amazement.

"I never said any such thing," she insisted.

"Yes, you did, Mom."

"I don't know what you are talking about."

I knew not to pursue the subject and, like Mom and her mother, the sister of an embezzler, never mentioned the subject again.

MOM WAS SENT to Miss Porter's School for girls in Farmington, Connecticut, a year before Jacqueline Bouvier would graduate. Miss Porter's was a proving ground for young ladies to perfect their penmanship for dinner invitations and provide a suitable résumé for future husbands out of Harvard or Yale who were bound for greater things. Its theater program gave Mom the acting bug, and after graduating, she briefly attended the University of Arizona before heading to New York to follow her dream to be on Broadway.

Like most proper girls newly arrived to Manhattan, she began her stay at the ladies-only Barbizon Hotel, where curfew was enforced and men were not allowed beyond the lobby. (Her future sister-in-law, Joan Didion, also a native of the west, would find a room in the Barbizon a decade later to begin her life as a writer.)

Mother's olive skin and dark hair were out of step with what Broadway had in mind, so she didn't land many acting parts, though she photographed well and appeared in a few advertisements modeling designer clothes.

The longer she stayed in New York, the less likely it seemed she would ever be on Broadway or, even less likely, the cover of *Vogue*. But she loved the city, and she also loved children, so she felt being a mother would be the next best thing she'd be good at. If Ellen Griffin were to give up her ambitions and follow the trodden path of most young women in the 1950s, she wouldn't just give in to the first beau who fell in love with her. She would wait, as long as it took, for the right man, which didn't take much time after all.

Two

My father's father was a beloved doctor in West Hartford, Connecticut. He was something of a local hero for performing the first open-heart surgery in recorded history. The patient was an eight-year-old boy who had caught a bullet, fired accidently by his father when the kid stepped between him and a twelve-point buck.

In those days, anyone brought to an emergency room with a gunshot wound to the heart was considered a hopeless case and left to bleed out rather than risk such a daring procedure and the lawsuit certain to follow. Why Dr. Richard Dunne chose this day or this boy to hold a beating heart in his hands is unknown, but his Hail Mary pass was regarded as a watershed event in coronary medicine and encouraged the advancement of open-heart surgery.

When I was about six, my grandmother, whom we called Gammer Do, brought me up to the attic of her house on Albany Avenue in West Hartford. She opened a footlocker filled with black-and-white portraits of long-dead ancestors and explained their history and how we were related. I was bored silly until she took out a little silver nugget from a yellowed envelope and placed it in my hands. It was the bullet that had killed the little boy.

At least I thought she said it killed him.

I remember her telling me that it was the first surgery of its kind, and though the boy died soon after, the operation was considered as much a success to medicine as the brief flight of the Wright brothers was to aviation. That made perfect sense to me and was the first time I considered that failure could also be looked upon as success, an insight I would draw on for encouragement when faced with future disappointments. But at the time, I just thought how cool it was that an old lady kept the bullet from a dead kid. It wouldn't be until I was in my sixties that I found out, to my dismay, that the operation was a total success and the boy lived to a ripe old age.

When Dr. Dunne wasn't mending hearts, he was breaking my father's, with routine beatings from a Brooks Brothers belt. Dad was a sensitive kid and a passionate fan of movie stars, whose pictures he pasted on his side of the bedroom he shared with his older brother. The other side of the room was adorned with athletic trophies and football pennants.

My father once recalled to me that during a particularly brutal beating, when he was about the age of the kid who caught the bullet, the Doctor had worked up a sweat, calling him a sissy between blows, stopping only when their maid interrupted to say his hospital was on the phone. Dr. Dunne left the room and went into the hallway, where telephones were jacked in those days, to take the call.

"Ten ccs of corticosteroid budesonide should do the trick,"

Dad heard him patiently instruct the attending nurse on the other end of the line.

"Well, thank you, Sister Shannon, for the update. Feel free to call me anytime," said the Doctor, whose son was at that moment prone on his bed, immobile with pain and shame. The Doctor then returned the phone to its cradle, came back into the room, and picked up where he'd left off.

These bedtime assaults usually started after family dinner, likely because Dad had been warned to stop explaining the plot of *Becky Sharp* or whatever recent picture had moved him, which no one else at the table gave a shit about.

"And Miriam Hopkins *finally* gets invited to the ball—"

"All right. Enough, Nicky," warned the Doctor.

"But they don't know she's from a different class—"

"I said *enough*!"

"But when they find out her life is ruined, and she gets so sick that—"

"Shut up!"

Dad couldn't help himself. Tears filled his eyes and his voice broke, but he kept on in defiance and disbelief that the plot, costumes, and Ms. Hopkins's luminescent performance would never mean as much to his family as it did to him.

Only his maternal grandfather, Dominick Burns, appreciated my father's passion for a story well told. In the mid-nineteenth century, when he was ten years old, Burns escaped the famine in Strokestown, Ireland, and made the crossing with a card tied around his neck so his relatives on shore might recognize him. He went right to work sweeping out a grocery store in Frog Hollow, the Irish slum of Hartford. Within twenty years, he would own that grocery store and earn the nickname the Saint of Park Street for never letting a penniless immigrant leave his store empty-handed. As his wealth grew, he opened a bank that offered loans to newly arrived immigrants no other bank would dare give money to, and his philanthropy got the attention of Pope Pius XII, who made him a papal knight.

Dominick Burns was a literature lover and autodidact who compensated for his lack of education by insisting his grandchildren be well read. Dad was his prize student, though the fifty-cent pieces awarded for reciting a Shakespeare sonnet from memory was incentive enough. My father and his younger brother John would become well-known writers, and both credited their "poppa" as a major influence. Like Dominick Burns, I also lacked formal education, and though I can't blame a famine for not getting past the tenth grade, I can credit my becoming a voracious reader to my shame as a dropout.

Dad was the second oldest in a family of six children, four brothers and two sisters. Their mother, Dorothy, was a devout Catholic and doting mother who worshipped her husband despite the routine beatings upstairs that she pretended not to hear. There was a six-year age difference between my father and John, and far more serious differences in their future, the first being that John never fully believed that their father beat Dad at all. John's memories growing up on Albany Avenue were wistful, and though he agreed the Doctor was strict, he never considered him to be cruel.

Toward the end of World War II, Dad was drafted into the army in the middle of his senior year at Canterbury, a boarding school run by Benedictine monks. John F. Kennedy had left the year before he arrived, much like his future wife, Jacqueline Bouvier, had left just before my mother started at Miss Porter's.

The monks were tough on my father, but they were tough on

everybody, and he enjoyed not being singled out for discipline as he had been at home. Dad had been in a few plays and decided he'd like to be an actor, but with the war still raging in Europe and Asia, he feared he might not live long enough to get the chance. He was only seventeen when he was given an early diploma and sent to boot camp until he turned eighteen, when the army could ship him overseas.

His older brother, Dick, the Good Doctor's namesake, had already enlisted in the navy and was attending Officer Candidate Training School. Richard E. Dunne Jr. was his father's favorite and a football tackle so fearsome his nickname was Tarzan. He was everything my father was not. But while Dad couldn't catch a football if it were stapled to his forehead, Dick didn't know Bette Davis's last line in *Now, Voyager* or how to write a cogent fan letter to Tyrone Power.

After basic training, Dad boarded a troopship called the *Mariposa*, bound for Southampton, England. The Germans had just killed eighty-four American POWs, in what was known as the Malmedy massacre, not far from his company's destination in Belgium.

The first action he saw was when a train transporting him and the 95th Infantry to the front lines was strafed by a Messerschmitt. My father's terror brought on hysterical laughter he was helpless to stop, even when his sergeant slapped him in the face, yelling at him to shut the fuck up. This caused the soldier next to him also to burst into horror-filled hilarity, and while bullets ripped into the train, the two of them hooted convulsively, each taking turns getting slapped and punched by men in their company to snap them out of it.

The other soldier was named Hank Bresky and would become

Dad's only friend while in the service. He was also the only other man whose masculinity was called into question, prompting their sergeant to nickname them the Golddust Twins.

As forward observers, Dad and Hank's job was to go behind enemy lines in the Ardennes forest and report activity. One night, in what would come to be called the Battle of Metz, the 95th met such intense fire that they were forced to retreat. The order passed down the line, but by the time it reached Dad and Hank, they'd heard two soldiers crying for help deep into the enemy's position. Without a word between them, they headed in the opposite direction from their retreating platoon. The soldiers were seriously wounded and possibly dying. Dad and Hank had no idea who they were or how they'd gotten there, but each put a man on his back and carried him for miles through the dark forest, lit only by shells exploding all around them. At daybreak, they finally came across a unit loading their wounded into an ambulance. When they tried to hoist the men they'd been carrying all night into the back, they were told there was no room. My father lost his shit, calling the medic every name in the book until the guy relented and let the men they'd brought join the rest of the wounded. The soldier Dad carried had not uttered a word the entire night, but as Dad loaded him into the ambulance, the wounded man reached out and squeezed two of his fingers in gratitude. Dad never knew if the guy made it, but suspected he probably did not.

The Golddust Twins rejoined their company at a German castle the army had requisitioned and were awarded Bronze Stars in front of the men who'd mercilessly mocked them. Those same men had to sleep in pup tents on the grounds while Hank and Dad were given opulent bedrooms in the castle, which had been reserved for officers.

To the astonishment of Dr. Dunne, the wrong son came home a war hero. His eldest and favored son served dutifully as an officer in the navy but never saw combat. The *Hartford Courant* placed Dad on its front page, praising "Corporal Dunne's courageous performance and devotion to duty." The household on Albany Avenue filled with his parents' friends, eager to shake his hand, and young ladies wanting to see his Bronze Star.

A dinner dance was given in his honor at the country club Dominick Burns had founded as an alternative for Catholics restricted from Protestant clubs. Dr. Thomas Hepburn, the father of the blue-blooded Katharine Hepburn, lived across the street from Dr. Dunne, but neither wealth nor their common profession could overcome centuries of prejudice, and the two families never spoke. Those early years of being snubbed, or "high-hatted," as Dad used to say, laid the groundwork for a social insecurity that never placed him in the right club, but just across the street from the swells who "belonged." Horatio Alger tales embarrassed him, and he preferred to describe Poppa Burns as "a wealthy banker" rather than a grocer who fought his way out of an Irish slum.

During the dinner dance in his honor, which also celebrated his entry into Williams College, Dad looked up from a conversation he was having with a debutante to see his old sergeant, who had once cruelly christened him a Golddust Twin, busing plates from his table. When their eyes met, they both quickly looked away in mutual shame. The sergeant quit his job the next day.

When Dad came home with a medal, he sensed a grudging respect from his father, but after dodging incoming artillery, he no longer feared his Brooks Brothers belt or even cared what he thought. I once asked him if he ever felt like shoving that medal in his father's face, yelling, "What do you think of your sissy son now, old man?" He said he didn't feel that, because after many years, he'd finally let go of his anger toward him. I'd grown up hearing him rage against his father, but if he was feeling sanguine in that moment I didn't want to spoil it, and I let the answer slide.

When Dad turned nineteen, his father died quite suddenly. The Wright brother of coronary exploration was felled by a heart attack that left my father numb. Rather than mourn with his family at the wake, he disappeared with a boy his age to Poppa Burns's golf course and had sex in the back of Dr. Dunne's Buick. The war had taught him to be reckless with his life and take risks with his reputation, especially at a time when one's sexual preference could get you killed. This was only the beginning of a game of chicken he played all his life.

Dr. Dunne's casket was in the living room, as was the custom, where it lay in state during the wake. When the guests had left after a boozy evening of reminiscence and song, my grandmother stood with her children over the coffin, gazing down at her husband, lost in grief. After a respectful silence, she softly said, "I wish . . . I wish we could have him stuffed."

The Dunne siblings collapsed in laughter, rolling on the floor in hysterics as Dorothy begged them to behave themselves. If I ever wonder where my dark sense of humor comes from, I look no further than that moment.

Forty-five years after the war, Dad had become a famous bestselling author who used to gripe, half in jest, "I have to pick up another goddamn award." He was never shy about recounting his latest accomplishment, or gleefully repeating a fawning compliment from a cabdriver, talk show host, or movie star. He once called me in New York in a fit of excitement. "You are not going to fucking *believe* who just recognized me in the elevator at the

Chateau Marmont . . . the rock star Bone-O! Bone-O knows who I am. Do you believe it?"

So I was not only more than a little surprised to find out my father was a war hero but shocked it took until 1998 for him to tell me.

We met at one of his favorite overpriced restaurants, where the waiters always fussed over him. The day before, he'd asked to see me with such urgency that I canceled whatever I had planned. He'd recently been diagnosed with prostate cancer, and I feared he would tell me that it had spread.

After our drinks arrived, a Diet Coke for him, a martini for me, he took a breath and I braced for what he was about to say.

"Yesterday, I saw the movie *Saving Private Ryan*."

"Okay," I said.

"Did you see it?"

I had. The movie had just come out, and I was impatient to discover where this was going.

"You know, I fought in that war."

As someone who considered himself a bit of a history buff, I suddenly realized I knew more about the evacuation of Dunkirk than I did about that part of my father's life. I'd examined Robert Capa's photographs and cried during *The Best Years of Our Lives*, but I couldn't recall asking my father a single question about the war. I think when I was very young I sensed it was a subject best not brought up, and then, as I got older, I simply could not imagine him in uniform.

"Griffin, that movie was *exactly* like what it was to be in combat. I sat alone in the theater and relived every terror I ever felt then. I was sent overseas for eight months, and for every one of those days I was so . . . *afraid*. I remembered all the bodies and the blood I had managed to forget. I didn't forget it, I just put it somewhere, and that movie brought it all roaring back."

His hands were shaking, but he managed to pull something out of his blazer pocket. It was the Bronze Star.

"Did you know your old man was given a medal of honor?"

Then he told me how he got it: the two wounded soldiers, the bombardments, Hank, being called the Golddust Twins, the squeezing of his two fingers. His voice cracked and then found its footing, and cracked again throughout his telling. I thought of getting out of my seat to hug him but didn't want to interrupt his flow.

"I don't know where that came from, Griffin," he told me. "That impulse to run toward the enemy for those guys, but Hank and I didn't give it a moment's thought. I can't believe that was me . . . but it was. I *did* that. That was me . . ."

I picked up his medal and he watched me. The ribbons were crisp, the colors still vibrant, and the thick bronze metal weighted with the gravitas it deserved. I pictured my father as a boy half my age and two inches shorter, surviving in conditions I knew only from novels by Vonnegut and Mailer.

How could I have been surprised that he would defy an order to retreat to save a wounded comrade? His reporting had brought him death threats and blackmail attempts. He was an Irish terrier in a Turnbull & Asser shirt, who struck fear in the hearts of those who had it coming. An image crossed my mind so absurd that I smiled. As Dr. Dunne tries to beat the sissy out of my father, the defiant little boy yells out the last line of *Now, Voyager*: "Don't let's ask for the moon, we have the stars."

"What are you smiling about?" my father asked.

"I was just thinking how nobody fucks with a Golddust Twin."

Three

After Williams College, Dad's first job in the early years of live television was stage-managing *The Howdy Doody Show*, a popular children's program starring an overly cheerful puppet named Howdy. Dad won over the tough New York crew by doing filthy things to Howdy moments before the show went on the air. If his timing to the countdown was off by mere seconds, children all over America might be treated to watching Howdy fellate himself or get boned in the ass by my father.

Lenny, as Mom was known, was dating Dad's best friend Howard Erskine, a Broadway producer who brought her to see his out-of-town run in Hartford of a now forgotten play called *Late Love*, starring Arlene Francis. Howard and my father knew each other from Williams College and were in the same acting club with Dad's other best friend Stephen Sondheim, who played opposite him in Clifford Odets's *Waiting for Lefty*. Howard asked Nick (Dad's nickname) if his gal, Lenny, could stay the night at his mother's house on Albany Avenue. The couple took the New Haven Railroad (with Griffin wheels), and my father met them at the station. The moment Nick laid eyes on Lenny stepping off the train, he was a goner.

After showing Lenny the guest room, my grandmother pulled Dad aside and whispered, "That is the woman you are going to marry." I don't know how his best friend Howard felt when my parents did just that a year later, but the two men remained close to the end of their lives.

Nick was a born raconteur and very funny fellow whose stories kept Lenny in stitches. His sexual harassment of Howdy both shocked and charmed her because she'd never known anyone to go to such lengths to get a laugh. When Nick told her he wanted to be more than just a stage manager in the burgeoning television industry, Lenny knew this was a dream he didn't share with just anyone.

He was as different as could be from the boys she knew from Arizona, and that made her feel sophisticated. Her last boyfriend had wrestled steers in rodeos, but Nick could tell a Givenchy from a Cassini, describe the sexual perversions of Wayne Lonergan, a notorious murderer in the 1940s, and claimed to know the whereabouts of Ingrid Bergman, still in hiding after leaving her husband for Roberto Rossellini. He was her tour guide on their long walks through Manhattan: there is the subway grate where Marilyn's skirt blew up in *The Seven Year Itch*; that's the spot where a Genovese capo was gunned down; there is the love nest where the Duke of Windsor began his affair with Wallis Simpson. Nick had dated other women from swell families who considered him a catch, but he'd never followed through on their advances, leaving them hurt and confused. It wasn't until Lenny that he met the girl who finally understood who he was and what he wanted to be. He found someone he could open his heart to, all except the part about his sexual attraction to men, which he closeted her from knowing.

Within months of the out-of-town opening of *Lost Love*, now playing to full houses on Broadway, Nick asked Lenny to marry him. She replied that she needed a week to think it over. A letter arrived "in her Farmington handwriting," as Dad wrote years later, saying, MISS ELLEN BEATRIZ GRIFFIN ACCEPTS WITH PLEASURE THE KIND INVITATION OF MR. DOMINICK DUNNE TO BE HIS LAWFUL WIFE. His proposal had been another Hail Mary pass, and he couldn't believe she had not turned him down. He chose to overlook the fact that she accepted a lifelong commitment as if agreeing to attend a dinner party, but in the next decade would see her reply as a perfect yet cruel metaphor for their marriage.

The week of their wedding, Mom brought Dad to the Yerba Buena to meet her parents. What a rancher who judged rodeos and his future son-in-law had in common, Tom Griffin was determined to find out, and he took Dad up in his new Cessna 140 from his own landing strip for a man-to-man talk. I have no idea what they discussed high above the Sonoran Desert, but I imagine my father charmed the hell out of him, just as he had his daughter.

The wedding flowed with liquor, and the Irish Catholic Dunnes from Hartford got on famously with the rancheros and cowboys of Nogales. Tom Griffin had secretly been diagnosed with a brain tumor that would kill him soon after I was born, but on that day, he was in fine form and grateful his health allowed him to give his daughter away.

Mom quickly became pregnant and readied their classic-six apartment on the Upper East Side for my arrival. Dad had left the puppet show for the far classier *Playhouse 90*, a groundbreaking live television series that started the careers of people like Arthur

Penn, Sidney Lumet, Paul Newman, and James Dean. The Eisenhower years were a time of hope and expansion for many postwar Americans, and none were more hopeful than the young couple who would soon be my parents.

THE MORNING I WAS BORN, Dad was a wreck. Having gotten Mom safely to Doctors Hospital, he was told that she required an emergency C-section, and to sit in the waiting room until he was called. Five hours later, he'd gone through a pack of Luckies, and after making a nuisance of himself to every nurse who passed, he went to buy more smokes at a deli across the street. Walking back to the lobby, he saw the surgeon who was to perform the C-section about to step into a cab. He ran to him and practically grabbed the doctor by the lapels.

"What happened?"

"What do you mean, what happened?"

"My wife! Is she all right?"

"Which one is your wife?"

"Lenny Dunne, for God's sake!"

"Oh, Mr. Dunne, my apologies, didn't anyone tell you?"

"Tell me what?"

"We did the C-section hours ago. She's fine. Baby's fine. Someone should have told you, but it's been a crazy day. I've done three since."

More relieved than pissed, Dad let the man get in his taxi. Before it pulled away from the curb, the doctor yelled out the window, "Oh, and don't worry about the foot!"

On the long walk back to the maternity ward, Dad pictured me growing up in a wheelchair or with a prosthetic leg, but while my right foot did curl inward when I was a newborn, it turned itself out by the time I could walk.

From the moment I was born, my father told me I was always trying to get somewhere else. My first word was *taxi*. I had a toy suitcase that I'd carry around the living room and raise my hand to hail a cab, yelling, "Taxi, taxi," as if late for an important meeting.

Elizabeth Montgomery, who later played Samantha in *Bewitched*, was my first babysitter. She was a struggling actress with a small part in *Late Love* when she met my mother, and though Elizabeth was her employee, my mother and she became close friends. Elizabeth once told her, while changing my diapers, that I had a bigger dick than her husband. That marriage was, needless to say, short-lived.

There is a kinescope from an early episode of the *Today* show in which Arlene Francis, also from the cast of *Late Love*, interviews my mother, billed as the "typical New York housewife," while a camera follows her on a routine day. (The daughter of a rancher who went to Miss Porter's was hardly a relatable housewife, but somehow Dad got her the gig through his connections at NBC.) There wasn't much content in the early days of morning talk shows, so this segment is a mundane, fifteen-minute blow-by-blow of the life of a young family. It begins with Dad heading to work like a character out of a John Cheever story, while Mom does household chores, runs errands, and takes me to Central Park to feed the ducks. At one point in the clip, she enters a shoe store on Lexington Avenue and leaves me in my pram on the sidewalk, as if we lived in Grover's Corners.

When she tries to lay me down in my crib at the end of the day, I nuzzle into her neck, not wanting her to leave. Anyone tuning in that morning would have seen a little boy who loved his mother more than anything in the world. When the camera cuts back to Mom in the studio, having just watched the segment she narrated, she looks lost in the moment, as if still savoring my affection. Arlene Francis ends the interview by saying to her viewers, "We wish Lenny, Nick, and Griffin all the luck in the world as they begin their bright future."

As it turned out, we were going to need it.

Four

If it wasn't for Humphrey Bogart, we'd never have moved to Los Angeles. *Playhouse 90* was going to do a live remote show of *The Petrified Forest* from Hollywood, and Dad was needed to stage-manage the broadcast. Bogie had specifically asked that my father be hired, based on a recommendation from Frank Sinatra, who'd worked with him earlier in New York. Dad had been to LA once before, as a child with his aunt Harriet, who shared his love of movies. They took a guided tour of movie stars' homes, and he never forgot seeing Spencer Tracy walk a little unsteadily into the Brown Derby.

At the end of a rehearsal at CBS Studios, Bogie asked my father if he had any dinner plans. If he didn't, he'd like to take him to a party his friends were throwing in Beverly Hills. They'd bonded over going to boarding schools when Dad told him he went to Canterbury and was surprised to learn Humphrey Bogart went to Andover. Who would have thought Sam Spade was a preppy?

That night, the kid who pasted stars' pictures from *Photoplay* on his bedroom walls was paralyzed in awe as Bogie introduced him to Grace Kelly, Jimmy Stewart, Ava Gardner, and his wife, "Betty" Bacall. Judy Garland sang a piano duet with Frank Sinatra, who nodded to Dad in recognition.

"Lenny, we gotta move here," Dad woke Mom to say when he got back to his room at the Beverly Hills Hotel.

"But Nick, we just got our apartment in New York."

"Fuck that. We're moving."

When my parents left New York for California, Dad rented a beachfront house in Santa Monica from the silent movie star Harold Lloyd. Marion Davies, the sister of George Griffin's mistress, Rose, had built the house next door as a folly to entertain guests with William Randolph Hearst, who had finally made her an honest woman. On the other side of the Dunnes lived Pat and Peter Lawford, the sister and brother-in-law of the president-to-be. When Mom first saw the seven-bedroom house her husband had rented sight unseen for their small family, she asked, "Were you drunk?" My mother had recently given birth to my brother, Alex, so now there were four of us, but still, the house, which Harold Lloyd called a "cottage," was ridiculous in size and well beyond the means of a stage manager.

One of my earliest memories from the Santa Monica years is of a morning I still see only in flashes. It's a jumble of details I was told and things I remember, but the images from that day remain vivid and I can't distinguish between the two.

Alex and I had a nanny named Mrs. Leasing, who was very old. She'd been with us for only a week, but I remember her as plump and stern. In my mind's eye she looks like Maureen Stapleton as Emma Goldman in the movie *Reds*. One early morning when I was four years old, I got out of bed and went into the bathroom for a tinkle. Mrs. Leasing was lying on the floor with a girdle around her ankles, so I had to step over her to reach the toilet. I hadn't yet mastered how to pee standing up, so I sat on the seat wondering why Mrs. Leasing chose to sleep on the bathroom floor instead of her own bed. I decided she'd probably want to be woken, so after finishing up and flushing, I gave it a shot, but she wasn't moving. I know now that she'd had a heart attack while sitting on the toilet and the red pool forming at her mouth was blood mixed with broken teeth from the fall, but at the time I was more worried she might be angry that I woke her from such a deep sleep.

I trotted down the hall and into my parents' bedroom. Ashtrays on both sides of the bed were filled to the brim, and an empty bottle of wine was on the floor. The air was stuffy with the stink of stale smoke and my parents were out cold, half-covered under the sheets.

"Mommy, Daddy," I called out to the two bodies. No response.

"Mommy, Daddy, Mrs. Leasing is on the bathroom floor, and she has strawberry jam all over her mouth."

"Go back to bed, Griffin," groaned my father through his hangover.

"But there is strawberry jam on her face."

"Honey, please go to bed," begged Mommy.

I was exonerated for my intrusion by a bloodcurdling scream from our housekeeper, who had just discovered Mrs. Leasing's corpse.

A policeman was assigned to take me to the beach to distract me from seeing my nanny leave our house in a body bag. But I saw her anyway. That I remember clearly, though I also have a memory of what immediately followed that can't possibly be true. The uniformed policeman tried to sit on the sand with me like an overgrown kid, but his holstered gun made that difficult, so he unclipped it from his belt. Clocking my interest in the weapon, he said, "You want to see it?"

"Can I hold it?" I asked.

"Sure."

He took the gun out of the holster and handed it to me as if I'd said "Pass the butter." No safety warning, no lecture about never pointing it at people—just, *Here, kid, hold this.*

The barrel was long and the pistol so heavy I needed two hands to lift it. I pointed it toward the ocean and pretended to get off a few shots at flying seagulls. It's an incredibly happy memory, but I don't see how it's possible a policeman would let a four-year-old play with his gun. Maybe the sight of a dead body was a trauma I replaced with the comforts of strawberry jam, friendly policemen, and a little boy's fascination with guns. Whatever the details of that morning, Mrs. Leasing was my first run-in with death, though far from the last.

MY BEST FRIEND'S UNCLE had just been elected president of the United States. Christopher Lawford was the son of our next-door neighbors, and his mother was the sister of the newly elected president.

Every morning his nanny or mine (I had a live one by then) drove us to kindergarten at a Catholic school called Marymount, which was run by nuns. It was also an all-girls elementary school, and we were the only boys on campus. I don't know why the sisters made an exception for us, but we were fine with the arrangement. One of the things Chris, the new president, and I had in common was a robust attraction to the opposite sex.

The girls fussed over us, and we fell in love with a different one every week. My earliest erotic memory was a game I played with a mischievous cherub named Wendy. She told me to lie down on the lawn so she could turn me into "grass soup." She kneeled over me and gently closed my eyes.

"I have to add the ingredients," she whispered in my ear.

"Here comes the salt." I felt her fingers lightly dance on my forehead and cheeks.

"This is the pepper"—followed by more finger dancing that made my brain warm and fuzzy. Next came blades of grass that she sprinkled on my face and in my hair.

"Next, we add the grass to the soup," she said, "and we cook it all together."

Wendy then swept the blades around my face as if she were stirring a pot. I couldn't keep from looking at her any longer and opened my eyes. We were in the shade of a jacaranda tree, and I gazed up at her and her bossy little smirk in a corona of purple and was in heaven.

Besides our affection for five-year-old girls, Chris and I also worshipped the president of the United States and his First Lady. We talked about him constantly. Of course, Chris had been to the White House for the inauguration, and I grilled him about every detail.

One day he brought a model of a navy warship for us to play with. On its bow was written PT-109, the name of Lieutenant John F. Kennedy's torpedo boat.

Chris told me about the moonless night the PT-109 was cut in half by a Japanese destroyer that sailed past, unaware of what it had done. The collision nearly broke "Uncle Jack's" back, but despite his agony, he managed to swim some of his seriously injured crew to the shore of a deserted island, where they would be stranded for over a week. Chris showed me a picture of a coconut that Uncle Jack carved an SOS into, that a Solomon native gave to the navy crew who finally rescued them.

Another photo was of the shirtless Lieutenant Kennedy in aviator shades at the helm of the PT-109. I thought he was the most handsome grown-up I'd ever seen. I loved the way his hair got thick on the top of his head and how, in other photographs, he put his hand in the pocket of his blazer with one thumb sticking out. I asked for a rocking chair for Christmas and complained of a bad back, the inference being that I, too, suffered from an old war wound.

That night I talked my head off about President Kennedy's bravery to Mom and Dad. They were well used to my idol worship but kept their politics to themselves. What I didn't know was that before Jack won the election, my parents campaigned for Nixon and wore straw hats with NIXON FOR PRESIDENT printed on the brim. My father even headed a group called Catholics Against Kennedy.

His feelings for the Kennedy family were a complex mingling of envy and animus. In Dad's childhood, his family were considered "the Kennedys of Hartford," and the Dunnes would concur. Both had large Irish American families with competitive and athletic children, both ruled under fearsome patriarchs with passive wives who were deeply religious. The big difference was that while the Dunnes were compared with the Kennedys, the Kennedys had never even heard of the Dunnes.

Before Dad moved next door to the Lawfords, there had been two interactions, one indirect, the other tenuous, that placed his family in the orbit of the Kennedys.

At the onset of the war, his older brother, Dick, was courting Jean O'Leary, to whom he would be married for fifty-nine years. When Dick brought her to meet his family, Jean held them spellbound over dinner about her father's friendship with Joe Kennedy, which had ended in betrayal. During Prohibition, the men had been business partners running Dewar's scotch out of Canada. When the Volstead Act was repealed, Joe sold their piece of Dewar's to Seagram's behind O'Leary's back and kept the money for himself.

"What a bastard," said Dr. Dunne, shocking his children, who had never heard him utter a profanity.

The other interaction was in 1950, when Dad was a plus-one to Robert Kennedy's wedding to Ethel, after a young socialite invited him at the last minute. He rightly assumed he was not her first choice. He got all dolled up but was never close enough to the bride and groom to be introduced, furthering a theme of his feeling snubbed by people he loathed, yet yearning for their respect.

That bitter sensation came roaring back to Dad when Peter and Pat Lawford gave a party for the president-elect and didn't invite him and Lenny. The sounds of raucous hilarity coming from the party next door seemed to mock my father, who watched the glamorous goings-on from the window, his face literally pressed against the glass. Once again, he fought back a nauseating anxiety that the crowd he longed to run with might never let him join. You'd think spearheading a caucus called Catholics Against Kennedy might have something to do with his not being invited, but to him, that didn't seem reason enough.

Next morning the gossip columns said the guests included Marilyn Monroe, whom Dad had always wanted to meet, and Robert F. Kennedy, who didn't want to meet him. The *Herald Examiner* shook in his hands, and an inchoate storm stirred in my father that would climb to category five in the following decades.

THE FIRST TIME I ever laid eyes on Mrs. Kennedy was on the cover of *Ladies' Home Journal*, which my mother subscribed to. For a moment, I thought this graceful woman was my mother. I was an unabashed five-year-old mama's boy who thought her the most beautiful woman in the world. Mom's friends compared her with Elizabeth Taylor in *A Place in the Sun* and Jennifer Jones in just about everything.

When the First Lady gave birth to John-John, I told Mom I wanted to send them a cane so she and the president could spank John-John when he cried too much. In lieu of a cane, Mom tore off the rubber band of my bounce-back paddleball paddle and gave me tubes of oil paints from one of her short-lived hobbies. My only explanation for wishing the president's son to be beaten so soon after being born is that I was sucking up to his ravishing mother. I imagined Jackie admiring the pains I took to color the paddle red, white, and blue, and being charmed that I wrote John-John's name on it in my mother's nail polish.

Mom had something else in common with Mrs. Kennedy: they both had come home empty-handed from the maternity ward. Twice. In 1955, the year I was born, Jackie miscarried a boy and, a year later, delivered a stillborn little girl the couple had planned to name Arabella. A few years after that, Mom lost two little girls, the first stillborn, the other an infant named Dorothy who lived for only twenty-four hours.

I was with Dorothy the last morning she would be floating in my mother's amniotic fluids. On that day in 1958, I was a bossy three-year-old pushing food around my plate and making my mother get up and down for more milk. She was in a white peasant dress that barely covered her enormous belly. When she got up with a groan to reach the fridge, I saw a big red spot on her backside.

"Mommy, you sat in catsup."

"What?" She felt the back of her dress with fingers that came back stained with blood. Her world seemed to stop for the longest time.

"Honey, get in the Bug. We gotta go. Right now. Okay?"

When Mom shifted her weight in the seat of our VW Bug, blood that had seeped into the upholstery sprayed up in a fine pink mist. She worked the gearshift in bare feet and passed slowpokes at breakneck speed. Only four miles away, St. John's Hospital was a place she was all too familiar with, having delivered her stillborn a year before. The Bug's horn sounded like a trained seal honking for fish, which must have made our arrival at the emergency room unintentionally cheerful. As someone came running toward us with a wheelchair, my mother grabbed my hand, even finding time to kiss it, before saying she had to rush inside but would send a nurse to come get me.

"I'm going to be okay, honey. Don't worry. Daddy will be here soon."

While Mom was being prepared for surgery and Dad fought his way through traffic from the 20th Century Fox lot, a young resident doctor and I played a game, where I hid under his white gown by standing on his feet and holding his legs like stilts. He would walk back and forth to the nurses' station asking, "Where is the little boy who was just here?"

"I don't know," a nurse would say, "he was just here a minute ago." They would search and search for me everywhere, and I couldn't stop giggling.

I was still under the young doctor's gown when I heard Dad's voice, demanding to know where my mother was. He sounded cross but I don't think he meant to. I came out from my hiding place, and Dad knelt and pulled me close. Behind him was our nanny, who'd rushed from the playdate with Alex to take us back to the beach house. The Bug was still parked right where Mom had left it.

A day after surgery, Mom surfaced from an induced coma to see a priest administering her last rites. Complications had led to more complications, so somebody had thought to send him over, just in case. He sprinkled her face with holy water and babbled in Latin as Dad stood dumbstruck at her bedside. She looked to her belly and noticed it no longer blocked the sight of her toes. She could tell by her surroundings that she was no longer in a maternity ward and knew, without asking, what had become of Dorothy.

"Get him out of here" were her first words.

For a moment, neither the priest nor my father knew which of them she meant. "Him," she said, pointing at the priest. "Get him the fuck out of here."

Dad had never heard her say the word *fuck*, let alone in the presence of a priest. Mom was so unfailingly polite that you'd think she might consider disrupting her own last rites, even if not dying, to be the height of rudeness. Parking attendants and bellhops were so charmed by her courteousness that they often refused her tips. But this two-bit priest, who represented the same God who'd killed Dorothy and left her for dead, was the last straw. Mom swatted the New Testament out of his hand and didn't stop shouting until he left.

When she returned home from the hospital, drawn and frail on the arm of my father, she tried her best to place my pint-size sorrow before her own, but we both knew that after our journey to St. John's, we shared something that would hold us together forever.

"You were so brave taking me to the hospital, Griffin," she said. "I'm sorry I didn't bring back Dorothy."

"That's okay, Mommy." She looked so pretty.

Dad tucked my mother into bed and made sure Alex was asleep before joining me downstairs. He heated alphabet soup and we ate off trays in front of the TV watching a *Million Dollar Movie* about a couple who adopted a little girl.

"But Daddy, how did her parents die?"

"I don't know, Griffin. I've never seen this movie."

"But *how did they die?*"

The question gave him an opening to address the daunting subject of death with his three-year-old, and he began to explain to me how beautiful heaven was and how lucky Dorothy was to get in, as if she'd been drafted by the Dodgers. My fiercely Catholic grandmother had told me about a place called purgatory, where babies who weren't christened lived in limbo. I worried that Dorothy had gone there instead but kept it to myself. I tried turning my focus back to the TV but couldn't stop thinking about orphans.

"You know, I went in to see her," Dad said during the commercial. Tinker Bell was flying around a jar of Peter Pan peanut butter, and I wondered if Never Never Land looked like purgatory.

"Who?"

"Dorothy. The doctor let me say goodbye . . ."

The singsong tone in which he had been speaking dropped so abruptly I thought another grown-up had entered the room. I looked around, but we were alone.

"What did she look like?" I asked, not quite sure I was following him.

"She was blue."

"Blue?"

"Yeah," he said finally, pushing around the letters in his soup with a spoon. "Bluish. Like the color of a Tiffany's gift box. She was wrapped up on a metal table . . . I kissed her."

A gift-wrapped baby came to mind. Then more images rushed in, like a cartoon that zipped around faster than Wile E. Coyote: baby Dorothy all tied up in ribbons and bows, her skin baby blue as an Easter egg, and Tinker Bell buzzing over her body like a huge mosquito.

"Griffin . . ." Dad had to say my name twice before I heard it. His eyes were moist and glassy, and his voice had a scratch in it. He reached out and pulled me onto his lap.

"I'm sorry, kiddo. That was wrong for me to say. Let's not tell anybody that, okay?" He smelled like lemons and cigarettes, which I kind of liked.

"You know, Jackie lost a little girl. Same age as Dorothy," my father said softly.

"You mean Mrs. Kennedy?"

"Yes, Mrs. Kennedy," he said, properly chastised for being overly familiar with the woman I loved.

"Hmmm . . ."

"These things happen, Griffin. Bad things we don't want, but sooner or later, they happen to everybody. Even your mommy. Even the president. Even his wife."

Five

A year after Dorothy died, Dad moved us out of Santa Monica and into a house on Walden Drive in Beverly Hills. He'd been made vice president of Four Star Television, named after its four elegant stars, David Niven, Dick Powell, Charles Boyer, and Joel McCrea. Four Star was considered a classy production company with an output deal at CBS, or the "Tiffany Network," as its CEO William Paley called it. But prestige television was no match for motion pictures, and a vice president's salary was no match for a five-bedroom house in Beverly Hills, so inherited money from the Griffin Wheel Company stepped in to pay the mortgage.

The Georgian house on Walden Drive was sturdy and austere, white with black shutters, reminding my father of his childhood home in West Hartford. It stood between a Spanish colonial and a hideous structure that looked like a branch of a Lincoln Savings and Loan.

Our first week on Walden, Johnny Stompanato, strongman for gangster Mickey Cohen and boyfriend of Lana Turner, was stabbed to death around the corner. As the sirens wailed, my father woke to have a "looky-loo" in just his bathrobe behind the yellow tape that wrapped the crime scene. He knew who Stompanato was because mobsters fascinated him almost as much as movie stars. When he'd lived in New York, he used to sneak into open-casket viewings at the Campbell Brothers Funeral Home to peek at whichever Genovese capo had recently been clipped.

Dad returned home at the crack of dawn to shake my mother awake to hear his theories and motives about an actual murder that had happened only a block from where they slept. He predicted, even before the *Los Angeles Times* or *Confidential* magazine hit the stands, that Lana Turner did the stabbing, but her teenage daughter, Cheryl Crane, would take the fall since she was too young to go to prison. His excitement bewildered my mother, neither of them realizing that his fascination with crime stories would one day make him famous.

In 1959, my mother was pregnant again, for the fifth time, but now with more dread than hope. Each delivery had been a life-threatening episode with caesarean sections, so she could expect, once again, to be ripped open like a piñata filled with infants, some dead, some alive, not knowing which until she'd risen from the anesthetic. Mom would have been happy with just the two of us, but her husband had hopes for six, like his fiercely virile and heterosexual father.

As his wife's belly grew, Dad's first order of business was to plant her a rose garden in consolation for previous losses, and to express his gratitude for giving it another try. He remembered how much she loved the roses in her parents' garden at the Yerba Buena, and Lenny was touched by his failed effort to cheer her up.

They had kept on the gardener from the previous owner, and

when Dan dug up the earth to plant the roses and spread the fertilizer, I never left his side. He was a huge man of about fifty who worked in a sweat-stained T-shirt and a rumpled fedora and who reminded me of the tough guys I'd seen in black-and-white movies. I made myself as useful as a four-year-old could be, thrilled to jump in and out of the back of his '57 Ford pickup to fetch a rake or wrestle a hose to the flower bed. I was fascinated by the cracks and calluses on his hands and fingers, where decades of dirt were so imbedded that no amount of Lava soap could ever clean them. Holding a shovel, I'd grip it tightly, willing that over time my baby-smooth hands would become tough as leather like Dan's. He kept a thermos of coffee in the cab of the truck, and when he took a break from the sun, we'd sit inside and have soulful talks. He once told me about the time it snowed in Los Angeles and Walden Drive was covered in a layer of white. I knew snowfall in Los Angeles was unlikely but longed to see it so I could make a snowman on our front lawn. Dan had fought in the Pacific and still hated "the Japs," so I did as well, appalling my mother when I told her so over breakfast.

One day, I followed Dan into the basement to find a set of sprinklers he'd left before we moved in. The house was still so new to us that the basement was empty and smelled damp from the beads of moisture on the pipes overhead. Dan pointed to the thickest one that traversed the ceiling.

"The lady who lived here before your family moved in, she tied a rope around that and hung herself."

He said this as if he were telling me the name of a rare flower. "That's why her husband sold the house."

Far from thinking this morbid bit of history was a perverse detail to tell a child, I found it fascinating, like a surprising twist in an otherwise mundane story. My imagination was shaped by the television shows I watched, and the soundstages I wandered onto when visiting my father at his office at Radford Studios Center. He produced a series called *The Big Valley*, starring Barbara Stanwyck, a once great but now aging movie star whose time had come to surrender to the boob tube. She played the tough matriarch on a large ranch who thought nothing of stringing up cattle rustlers on her land. When I pictured the woman who lived in the house before us, I imagined Barbara Stanwyck tossing a rope over the sturdy pipe in the basement to hang herself instead of a horse thief.

I was by then a self-conscious kid in a new preschool, desperate to be noticed, and realized that an old lady who'd been found swinging from a pipe in our basement would make a helluva impression on my classmates. First, I tried out my material on my father.

"Daddy," I said before he left for the studio, "did you know that the woman who used to live here killed herself?"

"*What?* Where did you get that idea?"

"Dan told me."

"Who the hell is Dan?"

"Our gardener. I helped him plant the rose garden."

That afternoon I sat on the front lawn waiting for Dan's truck to come rumbling up the street. The young rosebushes had all been bedded, so there was nothing left to do but watch them grow. But the backyard could have used a trim, and I expected to soon be following Dan's deafening lawn mower that spit blades of overgrown grass into a basket it was my job to empty. I looked forward to the smell of cut grass and holding clumps of it in my hand. I waited and waited but I never saw Dan again.

ALEX AND I FIRST laid eyes on our sister, Dominique, from the top of the stairs. Mom had just come back from St. John's, but this time she came home holding a sleeping baby. Not that she had been spared yet another life-and-death drama. Mom's delivery was a week late: her pulse slowed to such dangerous levels that the hospital feared she might not pull through, so they kept her for observation. St. John's didn't allow children to visit (despite the exception for me two years earlier), and Alex and I yearned to see her, a problem Dad solved by bringing us outside her window, since her room was on the first floor. He had to lift Alex up, but I could see her just fine, and despite the kisses she blew us from her bed, she looked exhausted and frail. I was confused why her baby wasn't in the room and feared something bad might have happened, but kept my worries to myself.

When Alex and I watched from the top of the stairs as our mother walked gingerly through the front door of our house with a brand-new baby in her arms, we felt shy and unsure of the protocol for greeting a little sister.

As Dad brought in her luggage, Mom looked around, wondering where her little scamps might be, until she saw us at the top of the landing.

"There you are," she whispered. "Come say hi to your sister."

I held Alex's hand to help him down the stairs, descending on tiptoes, fearing I might wake her. Mom held Dominique on her lap so we could get a good look at the sleeping creature, and Alex suddenly reached out to touch her.

"Careful, honey," Mom said softly but still causing Alex to draw back as if touching something hot.

"It's okay. Just be gentle, like this," she said, lightly touching the baby's patch of dark hair. Alex slowly put his hand out and landed it gently on her crown. He looked so happy, as if someone had finally arrived whom he could say stuff to that he'd never tell his big brother.

"Can I kiss her?" he asked.

Mom nodded and held Dominique up to him, and when he kissed her, she opened her eyes and smiled as if waking from a wonderful dream. In that moment a connection between them was born and, in me, a worry that I might never be included.

"You can give her a kiss, too, Griffin," Mom suggested. I did, but Dominique's gaze never left my brother.

"I finally got my daughter," my mother said, no longer exhausted and frail, but beaming. She'd lost two little girls, but at long last one had survived.

DAD'S LOVE FOR MY MOTHER was unabashed. He never missed the chance to tell me how beautiful she looked when she entered the room, or how smart and well read she was, how lucky he was to have married such a "class act."

I was seven when Dad was fretting about the perfect thing to get Mom for her birthday. One Saturday, as he was heading out the door to run errands, our eyes connected, and he gave me the slightest nod to join him. I knew the invitation was for me alone, so I got up from a coloring book I was scribbling in with Alex, as if going to pee, and instead snuck out the front door. Dad and I giggled like a couple of kids farting in church as we pulled away from the house. He told me that he'd decided to buy a ring for Mom and needed my opinion. I couldn't have been more awestruck if John Glenn asked me to sit on his lap in *Friendship 7*.

At Tiffany's, we looked at a range of possibilities. Dad passed me an eye loupe to study the gemstones for imperfections, which I did with the gravitas of a Talmudic rabbi. The bands were gold or silver, and the stones were just diamonds, and all seemed to look the same after a while. Bored, I scanned along the glass counter with the loupe, enlarging the other rings on display until I encountered a huge sapphire surrounded by diamonds. I pulled away the loupe and pointed. "What about that one?"

"Your son has a good eye," said the dealer. He took out the ring and showed it to my father.

"It looks like a ring Richard Burton gave Elizabeth Taylor," Dad said breathlessly. Burton's extravagant gifts and bad behavior on the set of *Cleopatra* had been in the news almost daily.

"Well, it's certainly not that," scoffed the dealer, who suddenly sounded like an asshole. "That was a diamond, this is a sapphire. And it's certainly not the Hope Diamond, which I must get asked about a hundred times a day."

"I didn't ask you if it was the fucking Hope Diamond," Dad said.

My bowels clenched. Oh shit, a scene. Whenever Dad said "fuck," it was in a flash of anger that always shot needles of dread up my armpits. I braced myself against the glass counter. "That ring was called the Blue Rock," Dad continued in a death warrant tone, "and I know the difference between a diamond and a sapphire."

"Of course, sir."

"Gift wrap it. We are in a hurry."

"What an asssssshollllle," Dad bellowed on the way home in his brand-new Mercedes-Benz. He was one of the first in Hollywood to buy the führer's favorite car after the war and was often screamed at by Jewish motorists on the streets of Beverly Hills. Vindication came soon after, when the Benz became the de rigueur automobile of talent agents and studio heads.

Dad laughed so hard, he had to hock a glob of phlegm out the window, sending me into hysterics. Suddenly he was overcome by a fit of coughing and clenched his chest in pain.

"Oh no, Griffin, I'm having a heart attack. Take the wheel, kid. Get us home."

"Don't worry, Dad, I got it."

I hopped onto his lap, grabbed the wheel the size of a sundial, and steered us through a light at Roxbury and Little Santa Monica.

"Give it some more gas!" I cried, which he did, all the while groaning in pain. Dad worked the gas pedal, and I steered the car until he took over the wheel to turn into our driveway.

This macabre little game had started when I first insisted, around the age of five, that he let me drive his car. He would just say, "Kid, if I die behind the wheel, it's all yours."

Dad assumed I could handle his dark humor from an early age, but he knew never to try out his morbid bits on my little brother.

The first sight gag he ever played on me was while reading the paper over his morning coffee. After placing his cup back in the saucer, he grabbed his eye in a panic, covering it with one hand while moaning in agony.

"Griffin, there is something wrong with my eye. I think it's falling out." I stood paralyzed, not knowing whether to get help or see where this was going.

"Wait, it's coming loose," he said, gripping his hand as if trying to get ahold of his eye socket.

"Hold on. It's coming out. Ow, this hurts. Wait . . . I got it!" he said, pulling his hand away from his face.

"Want to see?" He held out his hand, and there, in his palm, rested an eyeball. I stood dumbstruck, not so much scared as very curious. I got closer to inspect it, almost daring to touch it, when I realized it was fake.

"Daddy, that's not your eyeball," I said, already starting to laugh.

"I know! It's made of glass. Doesn't it look real?" He was delighted with himself, and I thought him the funniest man in the world.

My parents were giving a lunch the following Sunday, and we planned to repeat the gag, only with me in the starring role.

On Dad's signal I walked onto the patio with my hand up to my face, my fake tears commanding the attention of the grown-ups.

"What's wrong, son?" he asked, bringing all conversation to a halt.

"My eyeball is falling out," I said, acting my little heart out. "Wait, I think I got it."

I pulled my hand away from my face and held out my palm for the guests to see the eyeball. They looked not at my hand but at the disturbed little child before them. I could tell I was a flop, and to make matters worse, the glass eyeball fell from my palm and smashed to pieces on the paved patio. People just shrugged and continued with their talking.

Only Billy Wilder paid me any mind. In a clipped Austrian accent he said, "I think you gotta work on your act a little more, kid."

On Mom's birthday, Dad and I gave her the sapphire ring. She looked at us and started to open the gift with a "what are you boys up to" expression that had us snickering. But it took her forever to unwrap it. It was a little blue box with one ribbon, but for some reason she was dragging it out. Mom would stop after pulling one tail of the bow to say something inane that had nothing to do with the gift, until prompted by my father to continue. Then another train of thought would cross her mind, the ribbon in one hand and the box in the other. It didn't occur to me that she might not want to open it. That if she didn't see what was inside, she wouldn't have to pretend to be grateful for a gift from a man she was thinking of leaving. All I knew was that to be given a present and not want to tear it open was alien behavior. My father seemed oblivious to the absurdity of the moment and engaged her in grown-up talk about who called while he was out and some dinner party they might or might not go to on Tuesday, never looking at her hand that held something we had so much fun buying. I couldn't take it anymore and cried out—

"It's a blue sapphire ring and I picked it out!"

"Griffin, you ruined the surprise," Dad complained.

"Just open it!" I was on the verge of crying and peeing at the same time.

"All right, honey. Calm down. Jeez."

She opened the box and peered at the ring. An unreadable expression settled on her face.

Then, looking at me, not at my father, she said, "It's beautiful, Griffin. Thank you."

Her delivery and choice of words were exactly the same as when I'd given her an ashtray I'd made out of putty for Christmas.

"Well, I paid for it," muttered my father, the joy of our earlier adventure a thing of the past.

"It looks like the ring Richard gave Elizabeth," Mom said.

"Well, it isn't," Dad and I said in unison.

Six

If hero worship were a disease, my case would have been terminal. By the third grade I had so many idols I couldn't keep up with which fantasies went with which actor or pop star I imagined was my friend. My walls were covered with cutouts of the Beatles, whose first album I played incessantly in front of the mirror, air-guitaring and singing the chorus as if I were the adored fifth member of the band.

The actor I most worshipped was Sean Connery, though I only knew him as 007. The day he came to a pool party at our house, I was starstruck. I couldn't believe James Bond was doing laps in our pool, and was just as surprised to see on his head a huge bald spot that must have been covered with a toupee for the movies. In an effort to impress 007, I jumped in the deep end before I had mastered a decent dog paddle and sank like a stone. I saw the reflections of people smoking and drinking from below, like an underwater Hockney painting, oblivious to my efforts to reach the surface. I was certain I would drown and not be found until Tuesday, when the pool man came. Suddenly, in one swift motion, a hand lifted me by the butt and placed me at the pool's edge.

"A wee bit early for the deep end, sonny," said James Bond.

After school, I would go to my father's studio in the Valley and walk uninvited onto soundstages. *Gilligan's Island* was a favorite, though the pestilent lagoon where the castaways lived could give a mosquito malaria. Still, I thought it nature's most beautiful sight. Bob Denver, who played Gilligan, was an early idol, my fandom only tarnished when I saw him have a meltdown over a last-minute rewrite and upend a watercooler onto the floor of the soundstage.

An exception to my grown-up idols was a child actor who starred in a comedy called *McKeever and the Colonel*, set in a military school. He played McKeever, who got to wear a uniform and be a smart aleck, and I was desperate to be his friend.

One day while shooting hoops by myself on a playground, I saw McKeever running flat out in my direction. I thought my prayers had been answered and was going to ask him to play a little one-on-one, when I saw that he was being chased by a small mob of angry kids. McKeever whizzed past me at breakneck speed followed by taunts of "I'm going to kick your ass" and "you're a dead man."

Running to catch up with the mob, I fantasized that he and I would take our last stand against them, throwing knuckle sandwiches side by side, like Johnny Ringo and Curly Bill. By the time I caught up with them, McKeever had climbed to the top of a chain-link fence out of reach of the kids, who howled below like a pack of rabid dogs. McKeever just looked down at them and smiled, and I thought him the bravest boy I'd ever seen. Until he opened his mouth.

"Fuck you," he yelled from his perch. "I make more money than all your loser parents put together!"

That McKeever was a bit of an asshole came as a surprise. He came down a few notches on my idol chart, right alongside Bob Denver.

The only star who would never disappoint me was John F. Kennedy. Shortly after the Bay of Pigs, I'd begun a mostly one-sided correspondence with the president. I was about six at the time, and the whole idea of a bay filled with pigs was both disgusting and oddly erotic, details I chose not to share with the commander in chief. My letters were chatty and breezy about everything from the guest list for an upcoming birthday, to how much I hated a kid named Bobo Lewis, even confessing that my parents voted for Nixon. Over time, I received two very nice responses from the president's secretary, Mrs. Lincoln, who married a descendent of my second favorite president, and though I lost the first one, the second one read:

Dear Griffin,

The President wanted you to know that he wishes you all the very best on your upcoming birthday and hopes you have a wonderful party. He also thanks you very much for the paddle.

Sincerely,
Evelyn Lincoln
Personal Secretary to the President

When the Kennedy family attended Sunday Mass at St. Francis Xavier in Hyannis, we would go three hours later in Beverly Hills to "Our Lady of the Cadillacs," so dubbed for the extravagant cars in its parking lot.

One Sunday morning I just didn't feel like going to church. Yes, the rituals of a Catholic service bored me silly, and I hated the monsignor who gave me my first Communion, but neither played into my refusal. For no particular reason I told my parents that I was staying home and they should go without me. Until then I hadn't been an especially rebellious kid, and my father was taken aback by my militant refusal to get my ass in the car.

"Fuck it," he said when it was clear I wasn't budging, "we are out of here." And off they went.

Once alone, I roamed the empty house, growing restless and lonely, crashing hard from the thrill I felt from confronting my father. Just as I was regretting my temper tantrum, my family returned from Mass, bursting through the door in a fit of excitement.

"*We sat behind the Kennedys!*" screamed my brother and sister over each other. "They were at church, and we got to meet them."

No, God no, I thought. *This can't be.* I listened in shock as they described in agonizing detail how beautiful Mrs. Kennedy looked, what the president wore, and how bright his smile was.

"He didn't know who you were," offered my brother.

I had clearly hurt Jesus's feelings, but how petty of him to punish me for missing one stupid day of church.

By the third grade, I had fallen into a dangerous habit of telling whopping lies at school. I said them impulsively, relishing the rush of unearned attention, lording my unique experience over classmates to make their lives seem dull. I once wore an Ace bandage to school and told everyone I had sprained my wrist after parachuting from a plane. When a kid said his parents got him a German shepherd, I said mine were going to get me a baby lion.

To have to say I was the only one in my family who *didn't* meet the Kennedys was a story I was incapable of telling.

The first group I lied to about meeting Mr. and Mrs. Kennedy was a cluster of scary girls during recess. Almost every kid in my school was Jewish, so chances of witnesses were slim.

"Too bad you guys are Jewish, I could have introduced you to Kennedy."

"He doesn't like Jews?"

"No, he loves 'em, he loves everybody. But he's a Catholic and so am I, so we got to hang out."

"You are such a liar."

How could they tell? I hadn't even warmed up yet.

"It's true. We sat right behind the president and Mrs. Kennedy, and when they came back from Communion, I said hello."

"Are those the vanilla wafers?"

"No, it's the body of Christ and they don't come in vanilla. Anyway, when they sat down, I just leaned over and said, 'President Kennedy, my name is Griffin Dunne. I don't know if you remember my letters.' The president then turns to his wife and says, 'Jackie, this is the kid who wrote that letter I showed you.' Then she looked at me and said, 'Are you the boy who sent us the paddle?'"

"Why did you send them a paddle?" one of the scary girls asked. Oops, I hadn't intended to bring up the paddle.

"I'm not allowed to say. Anyway, he tells me he is going to see Sandy Koufax pitch that afternoon, and just when he's about to invite me Jackie shushes him because the monsignor was talking, so he whispers, 'I'll tell you later.' And then the service finally ends, he waves me over and says, 'I don't like the sound of that Bobo Lewis.'"

"You told him about Bobo?"

"You bet I did. And then we walked out of the church together and all the photographers took our picture."

The story was a huge hit, and I was made to tell it over and over, each time coming up with new and convincing details. Bobo Lewis transferred to another school soon after.

I was in Mrs. Dillard's third-grade classroom when the principal gravely entered with tragic news. Taking a moment to compose himself, he announced: "The president of the United States has just been assassinated in Dallas, Texas."

In the silence that followed, I heard myself say to no one in particular: "But . . . I *knew* him."

President Kennedy's murder should have put an end to my telling my whopper, but instead, I only tailored it to fit a post-assassination audience. I kept the folksy access a child might have to a global figure but pared down most of the dialogue and added the presence of the Secret Service. It became an anecdote about a starstruck kid meeting his idol, and the idol, not wanting to hurt the kid's feelings, not only tells him he remembers his letters but reminds his wife about them too. I had heard that Kennedy had a silent buzzer on the floor under his desk, and if he was stuck in an obligatory meet and greet with someone like a Boy Scout, he would step on it and an aide would rush in to say Khrushchev was on the phone sounding upset. "I gotta take this call," he would tell his guest with regret. That was the Kennedy in my story: polite and gracious till the very end of his life at Dealey Plaza.

When I was nineteen, I moved to New York to study acting (fittingly enough) at the Neighborhood Playhouse. After our first day of classes, I joined a group of students for coffee, and we got around to telling each other about our backgrounds. I was in the middle of the life-changing, oft-told story that never really happened.

"Jackie, this is the kid"—hold for laughter—"who wrote that letter I told you about."

The sentence echoed back to me in a tone of mockery I'd not heard before, and abruptly, I stopped talking. My new friends looked at me quizzically as I gathered my thoughts.

"So, yeah," I said after a long moment, "this was this kid." I stopped again. It was my first week in New York and the beginning of my new life, and I realized I couldn't lie any longer.

"Wait a minute, this didn't happen. I'm about to tell a lie. I never met Kennedy or his wife. I wasn't there. It didn't fucking happen."

"Okay, man, that's cool," someone said, sounding a little confused.

"I never met the motherfucker," I gasped, now short of breath.

"Okay, okay, nobody's saying you did."

I called my brother in California that night to come clean with him as well.

"I was so angry with myself for choosing that day of all days to skip church, and my jealousy and rage toward you guys was so intense, I had to insert myself, barge my way into your experience, just to feel *worthy*."

"I'm not following you."

"I'm talking about the day you guys met the Kennedys. How could you not remember that?"

Alex thought for a moment before saying, "Oh wow . . . I know what you're talking about. We never met the Kennedys."

"What?"

"Dad told us on the way home to pretend we did to get back at you for refusing to go to church. I remember he was really pissed."

So, all that time, I was telling a lie based on a lie. This should have come as no surprise, as I had been brought up on stories told by people who loved to tell stories. I would become a person who played fictional characters on the stage or screen in other people's stories, raised by a family who wrote books and produced movies about people with stories to tell. My father's fake heart attacks were no more real than his glass eye or my family sitting behind Jack and Jackie at Our Lady of the Cadillacs. They were stories, not lies, and encouraged to be repeated.

But prolonging the whopper about my meeting the Kennedys was a bridge too far, even for me. That day in the coffee shop, I parted with that synthetic memory like passing an old lover on the street without saying hello, and never told that story again.

Seven

My uncle John brought his fiancée to meet my parents in the spring of 1963. John met Joan Didion in New York when he was working at *Time* magazine and she at *Vogue*. When Joan's love for Manhattan had run its course—achingly described in her essay "Goodbye to All That"—John suggested they quit their jobs and move to Los Angeles. She needed no convincing.

He introduced her to my mother over the phone with hopes she might look at a house they'd found for rent in the want ads. The two women had only the tone of their voices to go on, but each recognized that the person on the other end of the line would be a significant part of their lives. Joan felt more at ease with the daughter of a rancher than with the Irish Catholics on John's side, most of whom she felt disapproved of her. Mom was only too happy to look at the house for them, which was all the way in Palos Verdes, an hour's drive from Beverly Hills. When she called Joan back with a positive review, John rented it sight unseen.

My parents invited John and Joan to lunch soon after they

settled in Palos Verdes. Now that Mom was to meet her future sister-in-law in person, she was surprisingly nervous, puffing away on low-tar cigarettes and fussing over the table setting she'd arranged by the pool. My mother was a voracious reader, had followed Joan's articles in *Vogue* and had consumed *Run River*, her debut novel, in one sitting. Joan was a "serious writer," Dad explained to his children, "not like the hacks" he'd hired to write at Four Star. A novelist living in Los Angeles was then a novelty, and my parents showed more attention to the details of this lunch than they ever had entertaining Hedda Hopper or an out-of-town viscount. Dad made Alex and me change outfits several times before deciding we'd look most impressive in matching red swim trunks, each with a gold buckle.

When John and his fiancée arrived, I was in the pool and Dad ordered me out as if he'd seen a shark. Mom and Joan hugged on sight, relieved their first impressions of each other formed over the phone would prove correct. Dominique and I fell into position according to size, like we were the Trapp family about to meet our new nanny. Dominique curtsied before Joan, who giggled, thinking it was a joke, which it was not. Dad always made Alex and me bow when meeting adults, but our wet swim trunks took the pomp out of that circumstance, so we just solemnly shook her hand.

"How do you do," I said, as I'd been trained. Joan looked at me through sunglasses and smiled warmly. I was struck by how she was not much taller than me and just as skinny. I was too young to have a girlfriend, but I remember thinking, should I ever go steady, I'd want to be with someone who looked just like Joan.

"Umm, Griffin," said John, "I think you got a little something sticking out down there." From a broken seam in my trunks, a lone testicle had parted from its twin, poking out like a lonely grape. John's and Dad's laughter roared in my ears, and my face flushed hot with shame. The one way to rein in my embarrassment was to remain focused on Joan, the only person not finding me hilarious. She looked more embarrassed for the cackling Dunnes, telepathically conveying to me, *I'm not with those guys.*

Within the decade, Joan would be famous for taking positions contrary to popular opinion, accepting the vitriol that followed, and not straying from an inner strength she called "character."

THE HOUSE MY MOTHER had found for them was on a bluff called Portuguese Bend that looked over the Pacific. Not long after our lunch by the pool, I saw the movie *It's a Mad, Mad, Mad, Mad World* at the Cinerama Dome. To this day I have never laughed so uncontrollably in a movie theater. It opens with Jimmy Durante, slowly dying from a car accident, telling five motorists who stopped to help that he buried "three hundred fifty G's under da big *W.*"

"The what?" the motorists ask, hoping to get more information.

"Undah da big dubuya," he says in his last gasp of breath. He then kicks the bucket, and I mean an actual bucket that happened to be at his feet, sending it down a canyon, and me into a fit of hysterics. The five motorists then embark on a mad, mad road trip to find the money buried under the *W.* For weeks I would annoy anyone in earshot with my impression of Durante by croaking, "Undah da big dubuya."

The first time I went to John and Joan's house *I* nearly kicked the bucket when I saw, in their backyard, four slanted palm trees in the shape of a *W.* The same *W* where Jimmy Durante told the five lunatics he'd buried the cash.

"Look! It's the big *W*, I tell ya," I screamed in my best Jonathan Winters. "It's the big *W*!"

"What are you going on about?" asked John.

"Those are the palm trees from the movie *It's a Mad, Mad, Mad, Mad World*!"

"Yeah, I heard they shot some movie here before we arrived."

"*Some movie? Some movie?* Only the funniest movie on the face of the earth!"

"All right, calm down," said John, far more amused than annoyed. My passion for movies tickled him, and we often compared notes on what we'd last seen.

"*A Shot in the Dark*. Hilarious," I'd once told him.

"*The Pink Panther*, I heard it's a piece of shit."

"You heard wrong. I also saw *Goldfinger* last week. Amazing. Did you know the girl they painted gold died?"

"I'm more of a *Dr. No* man."

"You're crazy! This Bond is much better. You know Sean Connery saved my life?"

"You've brought that up more than once. You're a worse name-dropper than your father."

We had established early on a sort of Irish Rat Pack shtick, where ribbing and gossip was our currency. The delight we took in each other's company would in time torment my father, but in those early years, Dad was proud to see his smart-ass son keep pace with his little brother.

By the midsixties, my parents were well immersed in the social frenzy of Hollywood, and for a time were the "it" couple, invited to every party and hosting their own, big and small, about twice a week. Dad compared himself and Lenny with Gerald and Sara Murphy, socialites who entertained the great artists of the Lost Generation on the French Riviera, and on whom Fitzgerald based Nicole and Dick Diver in *Tender Is the Night.* Their parties were lively affairs with up-and-coming stars like Warren Beatty and Dennis Hopper, and old dependables like Joseph Cotten and David Niven. Dad always made sure to invite John and his serious writer wife, proud to introduce them around. John was then known as "Nick's brother," though by the end of the sixties, Dad would be known as "Joan Didion's brother-in-law."

John's ambitions as a journalist were as cunning as my father's for social climbing. His first book was called *Delano*, which followed Cesar Chavez through the Central Valley of California, organizing exploited grape pickers to strike. (The only time I ever saw John cross with my mother was when she set out a bowl of grapes from Safeway that had been picked by scabs.) *Delano* was serious reportage and well reviewed, but sold few copies. The subject that fascinated him next was not the social life of Hollywood, like his brother, but the business of Hollywood. He wanted to write about the people who decided what movies got made and, someday, write movies for them as well.

At one of Dad's parties, John met Richard Zanuck, president of 20th Century Fox. John earned the studio head's trust to write the first behind-the-scenes account of what goes on in a dream factory. He hung out on the set of the disastrous *Doctor Dolittle*, sat in on story meetings for future disasters, and pinpointed, in brutal detail, a time when studio executives had no idea what their young audience wanted to see.

The result was *The Studio*, a scathing and hilarious takedown of 20th Century Fox in 1968, their worst financial year. Zanuck not only didn't take offense at the book but gave John his first screen-writing assignment. John would later write several more screenplays for Zanuck, who, by then, no longer took my father's calls.

WHEN I WAS A BOY, I feared I might never become a man. Tonka toys bored me, and I didn't collect baseball cards or even follow sports. I was the first in my third-grade class to like girls, and they liked me, but I worried my disarming personality meant that I might be made of more chick than dude. Calling people "sissies" and "fairies" was what rowdy boys did to anyone who wouldn't double dare or agree that girls were stupid. I could throw those terms around with the best of them, but, deep down, I felt like the fearful kid who cuts the cheese in class and deflects his humiliation by blaming others.

At my elementary school, boxing was a mandatory sport, and a ring was set up in the middle of the playground. Starting from first grade, we were pitted against equal-size boys and duked it out without protective headgear. I hated boxing, but I hated pain more, which made me surprisingly aggressive in the ring. Yet even if I hit a kid with an uppercut so hard it made him cry, I still felt weak and unmanly.

Lassie was a TV show I followed weekly without fail, and I longed for Timmy's country life and his loyal collie so much it pained me to watch. Instead of having a brave dog that would get me in and out of adventures, I had two groomed poodles with shaved chests and pom-pom tails. I'd pestered my father for a German shepherd, but what he brought home instead were a couple of snobs who loathed children. He even named them for us: the miniature poodle was called Oscar, after Oscar Wilde, and the standard was named Bosie, Wilde's sobriquet for his doomed lover, Lord Alfred Douglas. I was too young to grasp the homosexual reference, but the sight of these silly fops mocked my idea of masculinity.

Whenever I tried to coax Bosie into a walk around the block, he'd look at like me like George Sanders in *All About Eve.* Many years later, when it came time to put him down, he seemed eager to get to the vet, grateful to be rid of crass Americans who couldn't tell the difference between a Burgundy and a Côte de Rhône. If he could have written a farewell to us, I imagine his manicured paws would have penned the same words George Sanders left before overdosing on Nembutal: **Dear World. I am leaving because I am bored. I am leaving you with your worries in this sweet cesspool. Good luck.**

The two best friends I grew up with until sixth grade were named Cody and Gunnar. (Yes, our names were Griffin, Gunnar, and Cody, and we paved the way for children who would later be christened Blanket, Apple, and Moon Unit.) Cody's dad was Jack Palance, who played the psychopath that gunslinger Alan Ladd kills in the 1953 Western *Shane.* Gunnar's dad was Howard Keel, who played everyone from singing lumberjacks to Wild Bill Hickok. Gunnar and Cody were brazen little fight promoters who taunted me relentlessly with the claim that either Howard or Jack could "lick" my dad with one hand tied behind his back. That both men were over six feet tall and Dad was only five foot four didn't stop me from throwing his name in the ring for an anytime-anyplace throwdown. I became so competitive about how tough my father was that one day I casually mentioned that he'd recently been arrested for robbing a bank. The lie spread through the school like smallpox, and the principal called our house in concern. My father answered and couldn't believe my whopper.

"Is that what you'd like . . . for me to be in prison?" he asked when I came home from school.

"No . . ."

"Is that something you would like me to do, rob a bank?"

I was speechless.

If my father being a bank robber was too much to ask, at least he could have been more like his tough Irish younger brother, who struck me as a fearless son of a bitch. Uncle John was one of the first journalists to report from Vietnam. He and David Halberstam whored around the Saigon Hilton and flew in country on Hueys while embedded with the army. He started fistfights with competing reporters in Manhattan watering holes and walked the streets of Watts during the height of the riots for *Life* magazine. My father, on the other hand, was producing a television show called *Adventures in Paradise* about a man who sailed through Polynesia in a shirt unbuttoned to his waist.

I don't think Dad would have gone to my school's father-son baseball game if I hadn't told everyone about his bank robbery, but something about the lie reflected a lack of pride on my part that he wanted to disprove. The weekend before the game, he asked if I wanted to play catch in the backyard. I couldn't have been more shocked if he'd invited me to stick up a liquor store, which I would have loved, but his effort to connect through sports made me uneasy.

"Do you have a mitt?" I asked, as if that might end the activity.

"I thought you might have an extra," he said.

"Yeah, but I'm left-handed."

"Then fuck it."

"No, wait." I retrieved the extra mitt and handed it to him. "You can just wear it backward."

He wore my left-handed mitt on his right hand with surprising aplomb. He was far less graceful when it came to catching anything with it. Grounders rolled gently between his legs, and even my softest lobs plopped out of his glove. Our practice came to an end when Bosie snatched the ball away from my father, unwilling to witness his incompetence a moment longer.

The day of the game, when it came time to pick teams, Dad was chosen last from the lineup of fathers. The Gunslinger and the Lumberjack were the first two picked. Positions were volunteered or assigned, and Dad was sent to right field, which I took as a minor comfort; only the rare left-handed hitter could manage to knock one out there. Also, as second baseman I could always drop back for a pop fly so he wouldn't have to run in. My major concern was how Dad would do at bat, but by the fifth inning I relaxed a bit. He was walked once, then tapped a little grounder that looked like it was meant to be a bunt, and was respectfully thrown out at first. So far, so good. Besides, the dad who played Wilbur in *Mister Ed* got most of the attention at the pitcher's mound for accidentally beaning the third-grade batter (whose father directed *Green Acres*) while the kid was taking a practice swing.

Who would have thought that the gunslinger Jack Palance was left-handed? He drew with his right in *Shane*, but I guess he hit left. I motioned for Dad to move even deeper into right field, but he was joking around with Natalie Wood, who'd brought him a hot dog to keep him company. By the time I got his attention, the crack off Mr. Palance's bat could be heard all the way to the Warner Bros. Ranch, and the ball was headed straight toward right field. Dad threw down his hot dog and grabbed the glove from Natalie, who'd been holding it for him while he ate. He got his glove back on, but the ball had already sailed over his head, and my only hope was that he'd chase it down and throw it to me to connect to third, which Mr. Palance was approaching like a runaway steer. But every time Dad got to the ball, it wiggled just out of his grasp and coquettishly kept its distance.

The groans and laughter from the stands were so loud that he couldn't hear my unconvincing encouragements of "You got this, Dad."

When he finally reached the ball, Dad managed to drop it one more time before hurling it for some reason at Natalie Wood, who jumped out of the way. By then, Mr. Palance had reached home base on the heels of the vice president of Paramount and the guy who wrote *The Nutty Professor.*

When the inning mercifully ended, I walked back with my team to the dugout, where kids were doing imitations of my father throwing the ball.

"Well, kid, I guess I fucked that up." Dad's voice came from behind me. I turned around and slowed down so he could catch up and not think for a moment that I was embarrassed to be seen with him. I'd spent so much time before the game anticipating embarrassment that when the moment actually came, I wasn't in the least embarrassed but felt . . . well, pride would be pushing it, but I was eager to challenge anyone who dared glance at my dad sideways. I looked around for Gunnar and Cody and readied my fist to punch them in their faces if they made even the slightest crack. I thought of a million lame insults about their fathers to use in a retaliatory attack. Had I known then what I know now, I could have said: *Well, my dad's a decorated war hero. What did yours do during the war?*

My fragile identity at that time was tied to a father who couldn't throw to third and gave me two French poodles named after famous homosexuals. What I secretly longed for was to have a father like my hotheaded uncle. It took me many years to understand what it meant to be a man, and by then I realized I'd been raised by one all along.

MY LITTLE BROTHER, Alex, bubbled with a passion so foreign to the rest of us, we joked that an absinthe-swilling poetess must have left him in a basket on our doorstep. Even Dominique, from an early age, was old enough to know Alex wasn't really abandoned, and wise enough to realize our brother was very different, not just from us but from everyone we knew. Alex's little fingers could turn pages of books meant for adults, and his curiosity for all things was voracious. He was an open-faced sandwich of feelings, able to cry with joy and pain in equal measure, sometimes within moments of each other. Dominique and I were in awe of his intelligence and sensitivity, but secretly I thought feeling that much must be exhausting.

Another trait that made our brother seem alien was his complete lack of interest in seeking the attention or approval of others. He never envied our father's praise for even the slightest of Dominique's accomplishments or shared my compulsion to charm every stranger. If Alex had to choose to be noticed for anything, it would have been his capacity to love everyone and expect nothing. His ambition was to be cleansed of all ambition. Where this ascetic gene came from is a mystery Dominique and I wondered about for years.

From the earliest age, Alex was a gifted writer who wrote stories for an audience of only one. Whatever he composed, and whomever he gave it to, was for those eyes alone and not to be shared.

I once broke his trust over a story he gave me about a boy who loved a girl so much "the change jumped out of his pockets whenever she passed." It was touching and hilarious and in a thoughtless moment I told my aunt Joan, no stranger to a good narrative, how brilliant it was and joked there might be some literary competition in the family. Later, when she asked Alex if she might read it, he looked at me in utter betrayal before coldly answering, "I don't think so."

"That was only for *you* to read," he yelled as soon as we were alone.

"But it's so good, Alex! Why won't you share it?"

"I want it back," he said. And when I gave it to him, he ripped it up in front of me.

Every eccentricity that Dominique, Mom, and I appreciated about Alex irritated my father for reasons that confounded and upset us.

When we ate with our parents, it was never at home and always in one of three restaurants: Chasen's, the Brown Derby, or the Bistro. One night at Chasen's, where we dined on Sunday nights, our father pointed out Jimmy and Gloria Stewart while Alex tried to recount the plot of *Lord of the Flies*, a novel he was currently enthralled by that failed to garner our interest.

"And these kids, all about my age, just *hate* this fat kid they named Piggy," Alex went on, oblivious that our attention had drifted to Alfred Hitchcock being led to his table.

"And they carried these sticks of bamboo with sharpened tips, so they were like spears."

"I'm going to have the chili," said Dad. Then to Dominique: "You should try it, it's what they're famous for."

"I know, Elizabeth Taylor had it flown first class to the set of *Cleopatra*," Dominique said. "But you know I don't eat meat."

Dad roared with unabashed delight.

"So, all the kids suddenly get sick of Piggy because he cries too much and misses his mother, which is understandable."

"I know, we saw the movie. Shall we order?" said Dad, cutting Alex off, he hoped for good.

"So, they surround him, with their homemade spears, and tell him to shut up, and one of them pokes him in his fat stomach, which draws blood—"

"Okay, we got it," said Dad, his attention on the menu.

"And the sight of the blood excites the other kids, so they jab him, too, and more blood spurts out of him, and everybody laughs."

"All right, Alex, *enough*, time to order."

The cruelty of the young castaways caused my brother to choke with emotion. I put a calming hand on his leg, but there was no stopping him.

"And Piggy tries to get away, but he's chased off a cliff and smashes on the rocks below—"

"*Enough already. Jesus!*" said Dad, loud enough to make the Jimmy Stewarts look over.

Alex didn't say a word for the rest of the meal.

Dad's indifference to his son bothered Dominique and me to such an extent that we decided that I, as the oldest, should tell him how hurtful he was being.

He wasn't in his bedroom, so I knocked on the bathroom door. When no one answered, I opened it to see that Dad was in the shower. Before turning to leave, I noticed through the glass panel that his eyes were closed, and he was talking to himself. His face was contorted in rage. I couldn't make out every word over the jets from the shower, but what I did hear was "You fucking asshole, I'm going to kill you. Oh yeah, well, fuck you too. Motherfucker . . ." I didn't know adults talked to themselves, I thought it was just me, like when I called myself stupid for leaving homework on the bus or pretended to be a sportscaster calling plays from an imaginary pitching mound. But watching my father muttering in rage, I felt as if I were eavesdropping on a terrible secret coming from a confession booth. Ashamed and embarrassed (for him or myself, I wasn't sure), I slipped out unnoticed.

When I was sure he was out of the shower, I knocked again, and he told me to come in. Dad wore a towel around his waist, and I took the time when he gargled and spit mouthwash into the sink to gather my courage.

"What's up, kiddo," he said after a while.

"Why do you treat him like that?" I asked.

"Who?"

"Alex. It's as if you don't even like him."

My father blushed a shade of shame, looking into the mirror of the medicine cabinet for a time before answering.

"It's because he reminds me of me."

Maybe he saw in his sweet, sensitive son the same little boy whose father beat him with a Brooks Brothers belt. The same little boy who was so alien to his father and brothers and sisters that they couldn't have cared less about the plot of *Becky Sharp*.

Eight

I think my mother enjoyed the constant socializing the first year or two after we moved to Walden Drive. My parents received several invitations a week—then sent by telegram—from the wives of studio heads, directors, and movie stars to dinner parties and premieres. My parents hit them all except for the nights they threw their own parties, which were always a hot ticket and lasted well into the night. If it was a small dinner for twelve, my father would summon his children to say good night to the guests before the booze took hold. Alex and I would bow in unison, wearing matching silk bathrobes, and Dominique would curtsy in a Victorian nightgown and mobcap to a chorus of cooing and "Isn't that adorable." (Years later, while I was smoking a joint with Dennis Hopper, my high was killed when he said, out of the blue, that our good night act was the "saddest thing" he'd ever seen in his life.)

If the party was larger and fell on a school night, a nanny would check my sister, brother, and me into a hotel in our pajamas, each carrying homework and an overnight bag.

Dad was less popular than my mother, seen by some as maybe too eager to belong. But his dark, ironic wit made him tolerable, even though he insisted on bringing his Rolleiflex camera to every party, snapping photos of powerful people who wouldn't normally comply. Later he'd feverishly paste them into big leather scrapbooks documenting his incredible life, as if that moment in time would never last. Which it wouldn't.

In 1964, Nick chose to overlook that his wife no longer wanted to hire Lew Wasserman's parking valets or the bartender who poured for Nancy Reagan, or perform any other social obligations. He instead chose that year to throw his biggest party ever—a "Black and White Ball" to celebrate the tenth anniversary of his marriage to Lenny. There would be no eleventh, as Mom would file for divorce before the end of the following year.

Dad loved the color palette Cecil Beaton used for the Ascot racing scene in *My Fair Lady* and hired an interior decorator to re-create a setting with the same vibrancy and joy. When he was finished, our home on Walden could be mistaken for a soundstage on a studio lot where an epic Edwardian ball was to be filmed.

Every stick of furniture was put in storage to make way for table settings with gilded bamboo chairs. Rose gardens and fountains were painted on flats and placed behind all the windows to create the illusion of moonlit gardens stretched an infinite distance. The backyard was tented over, with a dance floor for guests to swing to the sounds of Peter Duchin and his orchestra. Bottles of Dom Pérignon were delivered to the Beverly Hills Police Department and our neighbors to preemptively soothe their tempers when the band kept them up. A second meal, of scrambled eggs and Bloody Marys, was to be served at sunrise.

Nick labored over the seating chart for this heady group as if he were cracking the Enigma code. He had cannily placed Truman Capote between Natalie Wood and Tuesday Weld because he knew they all loved to dance and would be the first on the dance floor to get the party rolling. But at the last minute Capote brought along Alvin Dewey, the detective who solved the Clutter family murders, which *In Cold Blood* was based on, and his wife, so extra chairs were found and squeezed in to make room for the uninvited couple, ruining Nick's meticulous table setting.

The gossip behind Dad's back questioned how a *television* executive could afford such extravagance to entertain movie people, and it was widely assumed Lenny's trust from the Griffin Wheel Company had something to do with it, though no one declined his invitation to the ball.

When the police were summoned at daybreak to finally shut the party down, it took two officers to break up a drunken fistfight between John Huston and William Wellman on our front lawn. The handful of people who are still alive and had danced that night away would tell you it was an unforgettable evening.

Vogue featured an article about the ball, and *Women's Wear Daily* hired Don Bachardy, Christopher Isherwood's partner, to sketch the evening gowns worn by my mother and the ladies who reigned over Hollywood society. Glowing thank-you notes arrived from George Stevens, Billy Wilder, and a young Dennis Hopper. Dennis brought his wife, Brooke Hayward, who would later marry Peter Duchin, the bandleader of the music they danced to. The articles, gossip items, and thank-you notes from the party were all lovingly pasted by my father into his scrapbooks.

And he was right about Truman Capote bringing the fun to the dance floor. He cha-cha'd and caramba'd the night away, having so much fun that he decided to give his own Black and White Ball the next year. Nick Dunne was not on the guest list.

When I was in my early twenties and had my first starring role in a play, I received a glowing notice in *The New York Times.* It was a fantasy come true to even see my name in the Gray Lady, and for weeks after I would pull out the clipping to gaze at my picture and reread the complimentary paragraph.

Before the play had opened, I had been cheated on by someone I loved, and my suffering was so great I feared I might never get over it. Twenty-four words written by a stranger in a newspaper, read by thousands, vanquished my pain as if I'd never known heartbreak at all. My high from that review lasted as long as a first hit of freebase, but the crash that followed when I returned to my former self was worse than the day my girlfriend betrayed me.

My father's similar high off the praise from celebrities and gossip columnists for his Black and White Ball distracted him from an emptiness he'd usually top off with booze, but the house on which he'd built his inner life was in a Potemkin village, and all it took was a slight gust of self-loathing to bring the scenic flats, like the rose gardens he had painted, crashing down around him. He could no longer deny that the marriage whose anniversary he'd just celebrated was coming to an end. Like a husband who impregnates his unhappy wife so she won't leave him, he now knew that throwing my mother a big party was only to delay the inevitable. His drinking had become sloppy and so constant that he'd often black out, sometimes waking in terror from a recurring dream that he'd run over a child with his car the night before.

As their eleventh anniversary approached, and just before my tenth birthday, Lenny Dunne was done with Nick Dunne. The parties and name-dropping had grown tiresome, and even Mom's closest friends found the pluck to ask why on earth she stayed with him.

One night, on their drive home from dinner at Chasen's (or the

Brown Derby, or the Bistro), Dad relived who'd been sitting where, and as he warmed up to a bit of gossip, Mom interrupted to say, two blocks from our house, that she wanted a divorce. He begged her to change her mind, crying in our driveway and swearing he would do whatever it took to be a better husband. But when Mom said she was done—whether with a friendship, a restaurant, or now a husband—she only said it once. She was done.

When Mom and Dad jointly broke the news to us, we were seated on a couch in the library. My parents flanked a long coffee table propped up by four carved wooden knights that I used to confide in as a toddler. They had clearly come up with a plan to present their split in optimistic solidarity, professing their mutual love but admitting to insurmountable problems we were too young to understand. Their plan went quickly off the rails when Dad, who had the first line, burst into tears, exclaiming, "Your mother wants to divorce me!" We had never seen a grown-up cry before. Alex and Dominique immediately started bawling in tandem, and I, feeling empty and a tad guilty for not being devastated, decided to join in with some fake tears. I covered my eyes and made "boo-hoo" sounds, watching Mom through my hands as she also covered her face to hide her tears. Through the slits of her fingers, I saw one completely dry eye the same moment she caught sight of my parched one looking back at her. For a beat we both stopped our faux wailing midbreath and then picked it up again in unison. I understood the moment to be a silent pact that, from now on, I would be the man of the house.

MOM TOOK US TO SPEND the summer on Coronado Island, a ferry ride from San Diego, and where her grandmother, Helen Prindeville Griffin, had taken her as a child. Helen Griffin was first taken there by the admiral she brought to her dead husband's funeral the day they married. Admiral Bastedo was stationed at North Island, a naval base at the tip of the island, but the couple lived at the Hotel del Coronado, which Marilyn Monroe would make famous in the film *Some Like It Hot*.

That summer, Mom dated a pilot who was also stationed at North Island, and the house we rented was next to the landing strip where F-4s and B-52s took off and landed around the clock. For a boy my age, it was a warmonger's dream come true.

I worshipped the pilot because he would tilt the wings of his fighter jet in greeting when he flew over our house. My best friend in Coronado was a kid whose father was in the catapult crew aboard the carrier USS *Coral Sea* awaiting orders to go to Vietnam. We'd bicycle on our Stingrays to the naval base, wave to the MPs in their guardhouse, and wander around the *Coral* without ever being questioned.

One night, when the pilot was over for dinner, I asked him a million questions about combat and the sound barrier and if he liked the Monkees song "Last Train to Clarksville," which was playing on the radio. He turned to my mother and said, "What's it going to take to get this little runt out of here?"

Stunned with humiliation, I went upstairs and had a good cry. My mother dumped him on the spot and back he went to his base, because when it's over, it's over.

I think the only man Mom ever really fell in love with after the divorce was the writer Irwin Shaw, whom she met a year later while vacationing in Greece. When she arrived back in Los Angeles and the taxi dropped her off from the airport, Mom inexplicably rang the front doorbell to be let into her own house. My siblings and I were crazed with excitement at her return, and when we opened the door, we found her barefoot in a caftan, holding sandals in one hand and what looked like a laundry bag in the other. Her feet were dirty and still crusted with sand from the beaches of Mykonos. The three of us jumped around her begging for hugs, which were not soon reciprocated. She was clearly bummed to be returning to her life as a single mother of three, while pining for Irwin, who was a known lady-killer. We had to pull her inside and make her drop her bag in the hallway.

Alex said, "What's wrong, Mom? Didn't you have a good time?"

"Oh no, honey, I had the best time of my entire life."

"Then what's wrong?" Dominique asked.

"I had such a good time and I'm truly happy to see you kids, but I just wish I could have stayed a little longer. That's all."

"What was your favorite part?" I asked, slightly belligerent.

Mom thought about it for a long while. "Well, the food . . . and the donkeys."

"There were donkeys?" Dominique squealed.

"Oh yes, honey. We rode them everywhere. But you know what I miss the most? The music."

The movie *Zorba the Greek* had recently come out, and she'd bought the soundtrack in Athens. "You want to hear what I danced to every night in the tavernas?"

"*YES!*" we yelled, and jumped up and down.

She went to the hi-fi, put on the Theodorakis theme from the movie, and told us to line up and put our hands on each other's shoulders. As the song kicked in, slow at first but teasing mayhem, she moved one foot over the other, which we dutifully followed. The song picked up pace and so did our footwork, then faster and faster until the bouzouki was lost in a frenzy we exhausted ourselves trying to keep up with, and then we all fell on the floor in giggles. Alex and Dominique climbed on top of Mom, but despite my joy at her return, I felt too grown-up to join the pile-on. She hugged them tight, her mixed feelings a thing of the past, and looking at me, said, "Oh, how I have missed my munchkins so."

Nine

My school grades were never very good, but they were such a source of worry to my parents by the time I reached the sixth grade that there were concerns I might not even graduate from elementary school. I was diagnosed with what was then a little-known disorder called dyslexia. I found reading to be a stressful and insurmountable challenge. When I was nine, I'd come home with a Christmas ornament I'd made, a *Reader's Digest* folded so the pages looked like a tree, spray-painted in cheery colors. I was rather proud of it, until Dad said, "Now, if we could only get you to *read* the magazine instead of defacing it."

Besides the dyslexia, it was assumed I did poorly in school because I was so upset about my parents' divorce. This couldn't have been further from the truth, but I played along, looking doleful when the subject came up, preferring to be thought of as a sad sack rather than just plain stupid. Assuming I was either or both, it still strikes me as odd that my mother and father's solution was to send me away, at the age of eleven, to repeat the sixth grade at a strict boys' boarding school three thousand miles from home.

The change to a different school never improved my grades, but in the harsh Dickensian environment, *I* changed—learning how to cheat, steal, and lie under pressure with the steady pulse of a serial killer. I was like the kid who goes to prison on a minor charge and comes out more criminal than when he arrived.

In the last year of the Civil War, a couple of spinsters named Eliza Fay and Harriet Burnett founded the Fay School for Boys in Southborough, Massachusetts. The initial student body was made up of the sons of Yankee officers or wealthy civilians who could afford to send recently arrived immigrants to fight the Confederates in their place. The boys learned Latin, were caned when they misbehaved, and quarantined from the opposite sex. When I entered Fay in 1967, those three traditions were still firmly upheld.

The day my parents dropped me off, we rolled up to the school in a long black limousine that so embarrassed me, I had to be coaxed to step outside. My father had already leapt from the limo toward my new dormitory to announce my arrival like a vizier checking a crown prince into his floor of suites at the Plaza.

Mom wore a wool Chanel dress she called her "mommy suit" for the occasion and seemed far less excited than Dad to be leaving me behind. Maybe the reality of what they were doing, in which she was a silent partner, finally kicked in. The school *was* awfully far away, and I was quite young, and though not a great student, I was a kid more interested in pleasing others than causing trouble. Sensing my mother's growing regret, I made a lighthearted crack about her "mommy dress" to lift her spirits.

"I'm going to miss you, sweetheart," she said, closing in to engulf me in a hug.

I held up my hand. "Not here, Mom." The limo had already attracted enough attention, and I couldn't handle another public display. She understood and stopped herself from taking my hand as we entered the dormitory.

My barren alcove was identical to a long row of others with beaverboard walls that didn't reach the ceiling. A heavy cloth served as a door. Dad was totally pumped by our surroundings.

"I just met the father of a kid you should get to know. He's the chairman of Bethlehem Steel," he said in a stage whisper. "If you get yourself invited for the weekend to their estate in Bethlehem, I want a full report."

Not realizing that he meant Bethlehem, Pennsylvania, I had assumed that being from Hollywood, I was the student who had traveled the farthest, and felt irrationally enraged to be upstaged by a kid who hailed from the birthplace of the baby Jesus. Why my father wanted me to go to the Middle East for the weekend but wouldn't let me come home till Christmas was confusing. I was too young to recognize that my misplaced rage toward who I thought was a young Israeli was covering my bewilderment and fear of being abandoned.

A firehouse bell I'd seen only in cartoons clanged so loudly Mom nearly jumped out of her mommy suit. The bell signaled the parents to say their goodbyes, and in the following years would tell us when to wake, eat, and shit, and was the last sound we heard before lights-out. I got a handshake from Dad and a covert hug from Mom, so as not to embarrass, and off they went.

When the last of the parents filed out, a silence fell among a room full of newly abandoned youngsters. A boy from Japan, who couldn't have been more than nine and barely spoke English, retreated to his alcove to stifle a whimper. I looked at the kid from Bethlehem and pictured him dead in a manger.

My first week I was ordered to kneel for thirty minutes on the dormitory's hardwood floor for crying after lights-out. The kid in the next alcove was actually the culprit, but I took the rap, because if he'd had to kneel, his wailing would have kept the rest of us up all night. I didn't last thirty minutes. No one ever did. Like my knees, I soon became calloused to the conditions I had been dealt. Rather than succumb to self-pity, I was like a POW on the Bataan Death March, grateful there were no maggots in his tablespoon of rice.

The proctor who made me kneel on the floor that night had made me his "fag." (You read that right.) Not only was my school given the most effeminate name possible, but Fay was also one of the last institutions to still be influenced by the English boarding school custom of "fagging" that dates back to the eighteenth century, in which new students are "fags" to the older ones. The origin of the f-word was not in reference to the derisive term we know today, but to the bundle of short wood sticks, called faggots, that first-year Eton students were required to gather for their masters, who all had dorm rooms with their own fireplaces. Nine-, ten-, or eleven-year-olds would be in servitude to sadistic thirteen-year-olds, fetching them coffee, running their errands, and staying out of their sight lines before they thought of new ways to torment them. The fagging system served as the training wheels for future despots who would one day rule their corporations or seats in government with impunity. It was rumored that the older boys' unbridled power led to hushed incidents of sexual abuse. I was no stranger to their headlocks or getting swatted on the ass in the shower room by a rat-tailed towel, but as far as being molested, I was gratefully spared. At least from an older student. The only run-in I had in that department was with a teacher.

Mr. Silver lived in a little apartment on the same floor as our dormitory. He was probably in his thirties, an age so generic it seemed to boys my age that all grown-ups were born the same year. He favored a flat-top haircut, a style made popular by rednecks who yanked Black people off lunch counters during Jim Crow. The skin on his face was wax, and tightly pulled back, as if a plastic surgeon had tried to smooth over some horrible burns.

Mr. Silver had a beagle named Fanny, who one night wandered into our dorm looking for a little attention. I was eating red licorice and gave her a strand just to see how she'd react. My dormmates and I thought it hilarious to see Fanny trying to dislodge the licorice from her teeth, when Mr. Silver appeared and stopped our laughter cold. He demanded to know who had given the candy, and when I fessed up, he summoned me to his apartment.

He sat in a club chair and made me stand before him. His hand on the armrest was directly level with my crotch, a few inches away.

"Is giving Fanny licorice something you thought would be funny?" he asked with a touch of menace. A half-empty bottle of bourbon was on his side table.

"No, I just wanted to see what would happen. I'm really, really sorry."

"Did you think she would like it?"

"I didn't think, and I apologize."

"I don't take to people being cruel to animals. Especially mine."

I noticed that, as he spoke, his eyes never left my crotch. I'd outgrown my chinos since football season, which made my pants skintight, and I became aware that he was looking at the outline of my penis trapped to the side of my leg.

"I don't think Fanny liked it any more than if I did this to you."

He lifted his hand and ran a manicured index finger along the outline of my bulge, starting at the bottom of one side and rounding down the other. Silver repeated the motion two more times before speaking again.

"Is that something you like, or is that something you don't like?"

I looked at his face, still gazing at my crotch, and thought he might be the ugliest man I had ever seen.

"Don't like. Something I don't like," I said, swallowing away a stutter, enjoying the shade of self-loathing that crossed his burn-victim face.

"All right," he said finally, "go to your room."

Ten

My second year at Fay overlapped with my first brush with puberty. I was a twelve-year-old girl-crazy boy but till then found arousal in the smell of their shampoo or the coo of a feminine voice that made my brain tickle. Negotiating an ongoing erection throughout the day was my norm, but as I'd never heard of puberty, I had no idea a hormonal nature program was taking place in my pants. My first year at Fay, I tacked a poster of Raquel Welch in *One Million Years B.C.* to my wall because I thought dinosaurs were cool, but a year later all I wondered about was what was going on under that fur bikini. Having never had "the talk" about birds and bees and boners and semen, I had no idea what was happening to me.

Before my ninth birthday, my father thought it was time for me to be educated about sex, but he didn't get very far.

"Griffin," he began, "I think you're old enough to know what I'm about to tell you."

"That's okay, Dad," I assured him. "I already know."

"You do?"

"I've known for years. I've just been pretending I didn't."

"And what is it you know?" he asked, suddenly as nervous as a suspect to a crime ascertaining just how much the police have on him.

"That there is no such thing as Santa."

He didn't see that coming and groaned with disappointment that he was going to have to have "the talk" after all.

"Well, yes, that's true, Griffin," he began. "But what I wanted to talk about is how you were born. How we all were. You see, your mom has a vagina that is between her legs, where you and I have our penises. Before you came out of Mom's vagina, I put my penis inside her—"

I slapped my hands over my ears to cut him off, but words like "penis" and "vagina" managed to bleed through. I pictured a bouncing dick landing on every disturbing word like they were lyrics to a sing-along, and silently begged someone to turn off the music. My father droned on, oblivious to my horror, about planting "seeds" deep inside my mother.

"*What*," I interrupted, "*does this have to do with Santa!*"

That was as far as he got.

One night when the evening bell called for lights-out, my erection and I turned off the lamp over my bed. By this point, my boner followed me around like Lassie, and I was so used to having one that I didn't even question it. But this particular night Lassie was in a strange mood. I felt an alien sensation when the sheets brushed against my pj's. If I rolled on my side, the feeling increased, and I found that it would build in strength from my slightest movement. And though it was intensely pleasurable, I lay frozen in fear that I might be dying. Before I could cry out for help, I lifted the sheets and pulled down my pj's in time to see what I thought was white blood shooting from my penis. I covered my mouth to suppress not a cry for help but one of ecstasy that would have awakened the whole dorm.

When my heartbeat returned to normal and I realized I was very much alive, I wiped away the mess and lay back in utter satisfaction. I remembered a movie where a couple share a cigarette after lovemaking and understood that moment for the first time. If that was dying, I thought, I couldn't wait to die all over again.

The boys who lived in my alcove in the nineteenth century had only visions of bare ankles under petticoats to beat off to, but I had Raquel Welch, and that poor woman was being defiled in my imagination four times a night. I even found time to knock one off during the day between classes. So committed was I to onanism that I continued my practice over a long weekend in Manhattan while visiting my father. He was producing the movie *The Boys in the Band* and was always on set, so I had the days all to myself. I was an obsessive list maker and plotted my short time in the city down to the minute:

1. Buy bell bottoms at The Different Drummer in the East Village.
2. See "Putney Swope" at the Baronet.
3. Lunch at the coffee shop on Lex.
4. Beat off.
5. Get the new Hendrix from Colony Records.
6. Skate at Rockefeller Center.
7. Beat off.

One day after my round of errands, Dad came home in a foul mood. Seeing the dirty plates and half-drunk cans of soda I'd left scattered around his Beaux Arts sublet, he yanked the needle off the new Hendrix album blaring on the hi-fi and yelled, "Hey, kid, this isn't your own private shithole! I live here, too, you know!"

He stormed into the bathroom, slamming the door behind him while I tidied up. When he emerged, my list of the day's activities was in his hand.

"What the fuck is this?" he asked. "You have to remind yourself to *beat off*?"

Even I couldn't believe I'd added masturbation to my to-do list. Among the piles of clothes I'd left on the floor was a pair of underwear, which he picked up as if holding a dead rat by the tail.

"Clean this place up and take your *beat-off* underwear with you," he said, hurling it at me with such precision that it landed squarely on my head.

Years later, my uncle John wrote a character into his novel *Dutch Shea, Jr.* who was so stupid, he had to write himself reminders to beat off. When I asked John where he got the idea, the memory made him smile.

"Nick told Joan and me about finding your list of 'errands' over dinner at Elaine's. We laughed so hard, we fell out of our chairs."

"Wait . . . Dad thought it was funny?"

"He thought it was *hilarious*. Used to tell that story all the time."

It's a toss-up which of the two continues to irk me more: that Dad shamed me that day and then made a joke of it in public, or that his brother stole my shame and mocked me in a novel. If you grow up around novelists, someday you will be collateral damage for a good story. My aunt Joan had an aphorism that I was to learn the hard way: "A writer is always selling somebody out."

THOUGHTS OF SEX grew as large as hippos on my campus, cockblocking any chance to concentrate in class or even read a book. My preoccupation wasn't only lustful, but also in equal measure romantic. Before considering what girls' breasts looked like under the tank tops, I would fantasize about what it would be like to fall in love with them. I fell in love a lot, always one-sided, and often with fictitious characters. After seeing *The Graduate*, I imagined sitting in the back of the bus with Katharine Ross, still in her wedding gown, wondering what our future might be. We would set up house, where she would make me soup, all before she took off her clothes. My dream life extended to real-life women I imagined delusional relationships with.

I was in love with my math teacher, Mrs. Adams, the only woman on the faculty, because she looked like Marlo Thomas from *That Girl*, who just happened to be another of my fictitious lovers. Mrs. Adams saw how difficult I found math and kept me after class to patiently explain what the other students had no problem understanding. I was aroused by her pity and believed she found my helpless stupidity utterly charming.

DURING ONE OF MY TRIPS home from school, I had made a new friend named Charlie, who lived in a duplex apartment south of Wilshire, an area those living to the north called "the other side of the tracks." Charlie's mother was an attractive divorcée, new to the singles scene, who managed a clothing store during the day and dated prosperous bachelors in the evening.

Both our mothers were divorced, though mine dated infrequently. For a brief time Mom was courted by Daniel Ellsberg, shortly after he released the Pentagon Papers to *The New York*

Times. They had only a couple of dates, but that was enough to warrant a visit from the FBI. Charlie was at the house when I answered the door, and two agents showed me their identification and asked to speak to my mother. I led them to the study, and they introduced themselves after whipping out their IDs again. We both hid within earshot to hear one of the G-men ask, "How well do you know Daniel Ellsberg? Did he ever mention his work at the RAND Corporation or share with you his plans to release secret documents to the media?"

"Not particularly well, why do you ask?" said Mom, as if she hadn't noticed the headlines about him on the front page of every newspaper in the country.

"Mr. Ellsberg is under investigation for violating the Espionage Act, and we are conducting interviews with anyone who has been in contact with him in the past year. Did he ever mention his work at the RAND Corporation or share with you his plans to release secret documents to the press?"

"Well, we met on a blind date, so it really didn't come up."

"And who is it that introduced you?" said the other agent, though they both sounded like they'd watched too many episodes of *The FBI* with Efrem Zimbalist Jr.

"My friend Norma Crane."

Norma was a bawdy broad, and one of Mom's best friends, who was famous for playing Goldie in the movie version of *Fiddler on the Roof*.

"We have already spoken to Miss Crane. Go on."

"Well, there is not much to tell. He took me to dinner—"

"Where?"

"At a place called the Bistro, though I don't see how that matters, and another time at Chasen's. He told me a little about his work, which was way over my head, and I talked about my children. I must have bored him silly because I haven't heard from him since."

The two agents seemed satisfied, though a touch disappointed that they hadn't exposed the next Ethel Rosenberg, and thanked her for her time.

Charlie and I thought her visit from the FBI was the most exciting thing that had ever happened in our lives. Days later, we noticed that every time we picked up the phone, we would hear a click and were convinced Mom's phone was tapped. We took to picking up the receiver at all times of the night and saying to the eavesdropping agent, "While you are listening to a couple of kids, who do you think your wife is fucking right now?" We sent ourselves into hysterics.

Charlie's mother dated most nights of the week, so when I stayed over at his apartment with his sixteen-year-old sister, Debbie, we had a lot of unsupervised time on our hands to do whatever we pleased.

During the spring break of my thirteenth year, Charlie's school was still in session, and while he was in class, I liked to hang out at his apartment with Debbie and her best friend, Naomi. It's bad form to lust after your best friend's sister, but I made an exception for Debbie. Her legs were short but toned and she possessed a devastating figure and an intimidating wit. If Ava Gardner were a child of the sixties who wore tie-dyed tank tops that showed side boob, that would be Debbie. Naomi was a voracious reader and gifted student who had her choice of early acceptances from Ivy League colleges. Her world had recently been rocked by a June Arnold essay that turned her onto feminism, a movement gaining attention in America that she planned to indoctrinate me into, because she thought I had potential to be the "first enlightened male."

The girls found it adorable that I was a virgin and liked to graphically describe giving blow jobs to see if they could make me come in my pants. Naomi was literate-filthy and could quote erotic passages from Sappho to Anaïs Nin, but the conversations always rounded back to the joys of blow jobs.

One day while Charlie and Naomi were at school, Debbie needed my help because she had broken her leg weeks before and couldn't get out of bed. She was in a foul mood and had me running around fluffing pillows, elevating her cast, or changing the music on the stereo, and I wished Naomi were around to mellow her out. I'd just taken up smoking and was still getting the hang of it when Debbie called me to her bedroom to refill her ginger ale. I put my lit cigarette in an ashtray on Charlie's bed, not noticing that when I stood up, it rolled onto the mattress.

I brought her the ginger ale without receiving any thanks, and as I headed back to Charlie's room, she asked me to stay and chat for a bit, which surprised me.

"Oh, Griffin," she sighed. "I'm so sick of this broken leg. I haven't been laid in a month."

"Oh . . . I'm sorry. That must be tough," I replied, not sure if that was the right response.

I was still in the pj's that Charlie had given me when I'd slept over the night before, and was shirtless. She looked at my chest and giggled.

"You're growing little hairs on your chest. That's so cute. Come closer, let me see."

I approached and stood there stupidly as she assessed my bony ribs and skinny arms.

"Ugh, I'm so *bored*," she groaned. "My leg itches so much under the cast."

"That's a bummer. I'm sorry."

"You know what I'd really like to do?"

"No."

"It would be so great if I could just give a blow job to somebody."

Never one to take the hint, I said, "Yeah, that would be great," as if someone would come along for both of us to blow. Then it occurred to me that she might have meant me, and having never been blown, I was very excited at the possibility, but with the ball in my court, I wasn't sure how to make the next move. Debbie looked at me, then at my crotch, and seemed poised to touch me, until she sniffed something in the air.

"Do you smell smoke?"

"Ummm . . ." I looked down the hall to Charlie's room and saw that the mattress was on fire.

"Oh fuck," I whispered.

"What?"

"Nothing. All good. Stay here."

"Is that fire I smell?" she asked, panic rising in her voice.

"Just stay here. I'll be right back."

As I ran to the growing flames, Debbie started to scream, "What do you mean 'stay here'? I can't even move, for fuck's sake. What's happening?"

What was happening was that the mattress was engulfed in flames and my running back and forth from the bathroom with a glass of water was not going to put it out. We had to get out of there. When Debbie overheard me calling the fire department, she started screaming her head off.

"I'm going to burn to death. *Get me out of here!*"

I ran to Debbie's bedroom and put her arms around my neck so I could lift her. She was petite and would have been easy to carry, but the cast, which went up to her hip, made her dead weight. She screamed about not wanting to die and managed to beg God for mercy and call me a stupid asshole in the same breath. When she saw the flames from the bedroom as I lugged her body down the hallway, she became so hysterical I almost punched her in the face to knock her out, before worrying I'd be charged with assault in addition to arson.

I wasn't strong enough to carry her down the stairs, so I just grabbed her arms and dragged her behind me. She had a word for me for every step her cast slammed onto, from the top of the landing to the bottom: "*I. HATE. YOU. SO. FUCK-ING. MUCH.*"

I managed to get her outside and spread her across the lawn just as the fire trucks pulled up. Her teddy was up to her waist, exposing her lady parts as the most handsome men of the LA Fire Department rushed past to soak a smoking mattress after its flames had died out.

"Oh, I want to die," Debbie moaned.

EVEN THOUGH I WAS A VIRGIN, Naomi sought my advice for her stormy relationships with what seemed like several boyfriends. "You're a guy," the questions began. "Do you like it when girls do . . ." one thing or other that I was ill-equipped to answer. I gamely tried anyway to solve her problems with all the authority a thirteen-year-old representative of my gender could muster. Her boyfriends were older and drove Porsches and always seemed to be kicking somebody's ass, so we had little in common, but for reasons unknown, Naomi hung on my every word.

"Well, I think guys like it when girls hold something back, not give themselves over too soon," I'd venture, code for maybe "don't fuck them the first night," advice that was bound to be ignored.

"Oh, that's good, Griffin," Naomi would say. "I can't believe how wise you are for someone so young." She'd gaze at me adoringly, which I found more erotic than the dirty talk, and while I knew I was crazy about her, I started to think that maybe she was falling for me too. When I was back at Walden Drive, she'd taken to calling on the phone and we'd talk for hours. She was nervous we'd lose touch when she started college. Would I write her? she asked. "Every day," I said, and meant it. I cradled the phone to my ear, cozy under the covers in my dark bedroom, tingling all over to the sound of her voice breathlessly describing the plot of Virginia Woolf's *A Room of One's Own*, the best book she'd ever read since her last favorite book from the week before.

"You should read it. You'd love it so much."

"I doubt I will," I said, which made her laugh.

"Then someday," Naomi said, slow and deliberate, "we'll lie in bed, totally naked, and I'll read to you."

WHEN IT HAPPENED, I didn't see it coming, though in all the hours of our conversations, everything was building to this moment. The day before I went back to Fay, Naomi arrived at my house unannounced and asked if there was someplace we could be alone. I led her to our pool house, which no one used and was without furniture, and we sat across from each other on a linoleum floor.

"I want to deflower you," she said with a crooked smile.

I looked to her hands and saw she wasn't holding flowers, and reading my thoughts, Naomi burst out laughing.

"I'm not giving you flowers, silly, I'm going to give you something much better. Actually, I'm going to take something. Your virginity. That's what 'deflower' means."

"Really?" was all that came out, but what I felt was the panic of a little boy who'd been told to kill a lion.

"Would you like that? I think you're ready."

"Yeah, okay, that would be great," I falsely enthused, to keep from saying, "You mean now? Wait a minute, maybe we should—"

"Don't be nervous."

"I'm not," I lied.

"I'm going to do all the work. You just have to lie back and feel pleasure."

She placed her hand on my face and then let it trail to my thumping heart and held it there.

"'Only the united beat of sex and heart together can create ecstasy.' Anaïs Nin said that, which is what we are going to create. Take off your clothes."

I did as I was told and lay back on the cold floor. She disrobed and knelt before me, giving me time to take in the first naked woman I had ever seen. Then Naomi took my hand and placed it against her pubic hair.

"Put your finger inside me and see how wet you make me."

I did as I was told, and she smiled and moaned softly. Naomi looked at my erection, which was doing push-ups on my belly.

"You're going to come really quick, but that's okay because we're going to do it again and again until you're fucking me instead of me fucking you."

She put me inside and I didn't even make it to the second thrust. She laughed but not unkindly, and so did I.

By our third round, I was on top and needed no guidance. When Naomi told me she had an orgasm the same time as mine, I was full blown in love. Worry soon followed about our future: Naomi was older. She had an older boyfriend. I suddenly felt too young to be alive. Reading my thoughts for the second time that night, she said, "Age does not protect you from love. But love protects you from age."

"Anaïs Nin?"

"Yep."

Her letters to me at Fay arrived daily all spring, pages filled with endearments and vivid descriptions of what we planned to do to each other, and, of course, plenty of quotes from Nin and Sappho. Love so distracted me, I'd lost interest in baseball, where I had once been an invaluable shortstop, and now found myself cut from the team. The only times I felt present were at my desk, matching her letter for letter, thinking up amorous expressions that would outdo even hers.

I was in love for the first time and hated every moment. I hated spring with its stupid budding flowers that took forever to bloom, testing my patience for summer when I'd finally see Naomi again. As it turned out, my wait was a waste of longing because by the time I returned home, she'd traded up for a much older boyfriend and I never saw her again.

Eleven

I met the kid who would become a lifelong friend the day we were both picked for the starting lineup of our peewee football team. After the coach made the announcement, he sent us off to run laps around the field, and John Derby caught up with me. We ran side by side in silence until he said without looking in my direction, "Hey, Dunne, I think we are going to be best friends."

Within the week, his thinking was confirmed.

Derby was quarterback and I was his halfback, and we were a formidable duo. He always seemed to know exactly where I would be on the field and could have thrown his passes blindfolded and they still would have found me.

Off the field, we were a couple of Artful Dodgers, making mischief without getting caught by the authorities. The school's motto was "Poteris modo velis," which which is Latin for "You can if you will." I suppose this slogan was intended to encourage us to believe that with a strong will comes greatness, but to me it meant "If you dare to be sneaky enough, you will get away with anything."

In 1967, the rock band Moby Grape released their first album, which got more attention for its cover than its music. Their drummer, Don Stevenson, gave the finger on the album cover and no one noticed till thousands of copies had been sent to record stores all over the country. Kids were being sent to Southeast Asia to die in a war no one wanted, so Stevenson's small act of rebellion resonated with every kid my age.

I was so inspired by his gesture that I decided I would do the same when our football team had our photo taken. John Derby and I lined up next to each other, standing behind the linesmen seated in the row in front of us. As we waited for the photographer to get off a shot, I silently directed John's attention to my hand resting on the back of a linebacker's folding chair and curled all my digits inward, save the middle finger. Click.

The walls of the administration building were lined with framed portraits of Fay's baseball and football teams dating back to nineteenth-century daguerreotypes. They were mounted chronologically, from 1866 to 1968, and stretched up and down the walls of a long hallway. Soon after our team portrait was taken, it joined the other teams' that proudly covered the walls for the past 102 years. Unfortunately for me, the chronology of our team photo placed my middle finger right next to the entrance to the headmaster's office. For the next three years, I felt waves of dread that someone might notice what I had done.

WHEN I HAD EARNED John's trust, he told me about his disturbing family in a matter-of-fact fashion that was devoid of self-pity. Two years earlier, his father had killed himself while in residence at a mental institution. His mother then married a time bomb named Henry, a violent drunk who collected firearms. He'd been married seven times previously (a possible exaggeration on John's part) and, like something out of the movie *Rebecca*, moved his eighth bride into his mansion in Fairfield, Connecticut, where the other wives had lived, divorced, or been murdered. John both despised and feared Henry, whom he called Henry the Eighth, not just for his number of wives, but because he believed that, like the English monarch, he dispatched his spouses when they began to bore him. John had no proof that Henry was a murderer, but his suspicion was real enough for him to always worry for his mother's safety.

Soon after John turned eleven, and only months after his mother's wedding, Henry ordered him banished from the Fairfield mansion and sent to the Fay School.

The first time I was allowed off campus was to spend the weekend with John at the mansion. His mother sent a car for us, and during the hours-long drive, Derby fretted that I might stop being his friend once I saw how he lived. I assured him that would never happen, but secretly I worried about what exactly I was in for.

The driver followed a long driveway past manicured gardens until we reached Henry's enormous French country–style house. At the entrance stood Clara, a Jamaican woman whose easy laughter brought the first smile I'd seen John shine all day. She had been his nanny when he was younger, and his mother wisely kept her on as the only constant in his life after his father's suicide.

John let himself be enveloped in the warmth of Clara's arms, which wiggled like Jell-O when she laughed. From behind her stepped a nervous, birdlike woman looking fearfully at the dying light.

"Hello, John," said his mother. "We must go inside for dinner before it gets dark. Henry will be waiting."

She gave him two quick pecks on the cheek and headed into the house.

Henry wasn't waiting when the three of us sat down to dinner at a refectory table long enough to seat forty. In keeping with the Henry the Eighth theme, the dining room looked like a Tudor banquet hall with high-back chairs that dwarfed John and me. The walls were lined with crossbows and glass cabinets filled with antique shotguns and pistols.

Between our cautious sips of consommé, Henry could be heard in the hallway bumping into walls and cursing at phantoms. Derby's mother refused to meet her son's eyes during the commotion, instead concentrating on a trembling spoonful of broth.

When Henry finally entered the dining room, he took his place at the head of the table so unsteadily, the bourbon in his glass sloshed onto his lap. He didn't acknowledge the homecoming of his stepson or the guest he'd brought from school. Without a word, he handed what was left of the bourbon to John's mother, who hurried to refresh his drink with more ice.

Henry's bloodshot eyes eventually wandered in my direction.

"Who are you?" he demanded.

"He's Griffin," said John. "I told Mom I was bringing a friend from—"

"Not talking to you. I'm asking him if he knows who he is."

Henry smiled at me as if I might be as delighted with his play on words as he was.

I forced myself to look at the broken blood vessels around his nose before answering, "I'm Griffin. I go to school with John. Thank you for having me."

"Wasn't my idea."

He shot a look at his eighth wife, who had rushed back with his drink.

"And where are you from?"

"Los Angeles."

"Where in Los Angeles?"

"Beverly Hills," I said uncertainly.

"Are you Jewish?"

"No."

"A lot of Jews in Beverly Hills."

"Henry, please," John's mother whispered.

Henry challenged her with an unfocused gaze that she avoided by concentrating on the floral pattern that ran along the edges of her Spode china.

Whatever fearsome remark she braced for, Henry instead threw his napkin onto the table and abruptly left the room.

"I hate him so much," John said, once the three of us were alone.

"Honey, let's just get through the weekend."

After dinner I was shown to my room, one of twenty in the house. John's was adjoining, and we changed out of our clothes and into pajamas to get ready for bed. The tension from dinner had since passed, and we even managed to giggle about what a pathetic drunk Henry was.

"Are you a Jew?" John asked me, slurring his words.

Our laughter was brought short when Henry burst into the room waving around a long musket with a bayonet. He smelled of booze and some kind of lubricant he must have used to clean the weapon.

"John, did you break into my gun cabinet?"

"I don't know what you're talking about."

"I keep it locked, and when I just checked, the cabinet was wide-open."

"You probably left it open. I never went anywhere near it."

"You are a sneaky little liar. I *see you*."

"Will you leave so we can go to sleep?"

"I *see you*," he repeated, more to himself than John.

When he turned to leave, a pair of pants that I'd left on the floor got caught around his foot. He kicked them away, then picked them up with the tip of the bayonet.

"Who left clothes on the floor?"

Henry held the offending pants in the air like a sagging flag of surrender. This time he raised his voice.

"I said, *Who left clothes on my floor*?"

"I did," I said, trying to mask the tremble in my voice. "I was going to hang them up before you came in. I'm sorry."

With the pants still hanging on the tip of the bayonet, he flung them off, hitting me in the face.

"This is my *home*. Not some shtetl in Beverly Hills. My *home*! And you will pick up after yourself."

"Yes, sir," I said.

The bedroom door was open, and I willed a sober adult to come rescue us. I wanted to call my mother, which was absurd, because she couldn't do anything, nor did I think she would even believe me. We didn't know people who waved around bayonets and yelled at children. If Henry killed me, I'd be the first person my parents ever knew who'd been murdered.

Suddenly, and without a word, Henry left the room. We dared not move until the sound of his footsteps had faded.

John fell onto my bed and burst into tears.

"I'm so sorry. I'm so sorry," he said over and over, almost choking on snot that ran from his nose. I touched his shoulder to comfort him, saying it was okay and not his fault, but couldn't be heard over his hysteria, so I just let him cry himself out.

When he calmed, I brought him tissues from a quilted box by

the nightstand. He blew his nose at least a half dozen times before finding the exact words he wanted to say:

"Will you help me kill him?"

I knew he meant it and to not take him seriously in that moment would only add to his humiliation, so I matched his grave expression and said, "You bet I will."

We hatched the plot right then and there. I would leave my pants on the floor again and John would lure Henry back into the room. He'd yell at me, and then I would stand up on the bed, further enraging him but out of his reach physically. While I distracted him, John was to take the poker from the fireplace in my room and hit him on the back of the head. Once Henry was down, John planned on smashing his skull with it until he was dead.

In our planning, we acted out the parts where I stood on the bed and taunted Henry while John got the poker. He came up behind the imaginary Henry and mimed bashing him over and over until he'd exhausted himself.

That night I fell asleep elated by our plot and, though not believing it for a moment, for the first time since our arrival, felt some degree of control over the danger in that house.

The next morning, I woke with a bellyache and an urgent need to poop. I'd been seriously constipated for over a week from eating dozens of loaves of Wonder Bread I'd bought in the school canteen. I loved Wonder Bread, and the smell of its loaves brought back Proustian memories of home. The Wonder Bread factory was blocks from our house, and every afternoon, when it fired up its ovens, the smell of fresh bread wafted all over Beverly Hills.

White bread was considered too tacky to find a place in our pantry, though slices of whole wheat and sourdough were there, but with no one to stop me from eating it at school, I'd go through at least three loaves a week. My culinary routine was to bury my hand into the middle of the loaf to extract a clump of soft dough and shape it into a ball to snack on between meals. It turned out one of the drawbacks to my eating ball after ball of Wonder Bread was that it made me constipated, and I'd often go weeks without having a decent poop.

That Saturday morning in Fairfield, my bowels were finally ready to surrender, but not without a fight. In Henry's guest bathroom, I sweated and grunted until finding eventual relief. Before flushing the toilet, I peeked at my work and was stunned by its size. Not that I measured, but it would not be an exaggeration to say I had produced a two-foot turd. If I were to stand it up, it would have reached my knees. I hit the flusher and bid it farewell, only to find the fucker didn't want to leave, or if it did, its size made an exit impossible. I gave another flush, and the turd tried to follow the water circling the drain but was left behind yet again.

Panic-stricken, I woke up John and brought him to the bathroom.

"Jeeeeezus, Dunne! You gave birth to a baby," he said, astonished. "What are you going to name it?"

"Seriously, Derby, what are we going to do? It won't flush, and Henry is going to kill us all."

The thought of Henry killing us before we did the same to him sent my friend into action. He ran down to the kitchen and brought back a plastic garbage bag.

"Put it in the bag and we'll chuck it in the woods," Derby suggested.

I shepherded the massive turd into the baggie like a koi from a fish pond. The only challenge left was to sneak the bag out of the house without being noticed. We went down a back staircase we thought no one used, but before reaching the ground floor, we heard Henry walking up in our direction. He hadn't yet seen us, so John opened the nearest window and motioned for me to chuck the bag outside. When I did, we heard it land with a thud on the roof of the second-floor tier, and then we ran like hell to our rooms.

It was one of the last warm days in September, and the mansion's air-conditioning kept everything cool without being noticeably cold. An otherwise perfect temperature, save for the smell of shit now wafting through all twenty rooms of the estate. The bag I chucked out the window had landed onto the blower of the house's central air-conditioning unit.

We hid in our rooms on the third floor but could still hear Henry raging throughout the house.

"Is that shit?" he bellowed. "Why does my house smell like shit?"

The terrible smell lasted through dinner, which we ate in the kitchen with Clara, who covered her nose with a scarf. She was too disgusted to ask what John and I were giggling about.

After dinner, John entered my room all business and asked where my pants were. I'd changed into pajamas and of course had hung them up, but he went to the closet and threw them on the floor.

"What are you doing?" I asked, though I knew just what he was doing.

"You know what I'm doing. Get ready."

"Wait, wait," I said, panic setting in. "I thought we were kidding."

"Are you going to chicken out on me?"

"No, but let's think about this. Are you actually serious?"

"I told you. I'm going to kill him."

Before I could say another word, he went into the hallway and started yelling, "Henry! Henry the Eighth! Come here!"

"John, stop it!"

"Hennrrryyyyy!"

"Please, John. This is messed up."

Like a dog called to dinner, Henry burst into the room, this time even drunker than the night before.

"What's all this noise," he slurred. "Why aren't you in bed?"

Then he saw my pants on the floor.

When he looked at me, it seemed even more blood vessels had burst on his nose.

"Were you raised in a pigsty?" he said, approaching with clenched fists. To get out of his way, I jumped on the bed, inadvertently starting a plan I didn't want to carry out.

"Get off that bed, you little shit. This isn't your romper room."

Over Henry's shoulder I saw John pick up the poker. *Oh my God*, I thought, *it's really happening.*

"John, don't!" I yelled, but he couldn't hear me over Henry calling me every name in the book while trying to grab me off the bed.

John stood behind Henry, who was oblivious to his stepson being in perfect range to club him to death. I was going to yell one last time for John to abort the mission but saw from his face that I didn't need to. He never raised the poker. He just stood behind the monster, knowing he had the shot but would never take it. John's body caved inward in defeat, and the poker fell from his hand. The sound of it clanging on the wooden floor stopped Henry's rant and he looked behind him. He saw the poker on the ground, the contorted rage on his stepson's face, and even in his drunken state could piece together what had almost happened. Henry backed away and looked at John with sobering horror.

"I hate you," John said, struggling to control the quiver in his voice. "I hate you so much."

Henry digested his stepson's words. The color drained from his face, and giving in to a slight wobble, he seemed to shrink before our eyes. Without another word, he made his way out of the room, even closing the door behind him.

John's mother died of cancer two years later, leaving Henry to take a ninth wife if he so chose. John's much older brother had a family of his own but took John in during the holiday breaks. By then, John and I still didn't know which high schools we should apply to, but decided that no matter where we went, we would go together. Despite our commitment not to part after leaving Fay, we never discussed the night we almost killed Henry.

IN MY LAST TWO WEEKS at Fay, the dread that my Moby Grape homage would be discovered finally paid off when a snitch pointed out my middle finger to Mr. Harlow, our headmaster. When he realized he'd been waltzing past my obscene gesture all that time, he called to order an emergency session of the Student Council Disciplinary Committee. The group was made up of my peers, who voted on how many "swats" should be given based on the crime committed. A swat was a beating on the back of the leg with a long paddle the size of a cricket bat, with holes that had been drilled into the wood so the bat could pick up speed to deliver maximum force. The corporal punishment was dished out by Mr. Harlow, whose tight paunch and horn-rimmed glasses made him look like a preppy bulldog.

The council handed down the maximum sentence of ten

swats. The headmaster ordered me to kneel in front of his leather couch as he shed his coat and rolled up his sleeves, like he was going to arm-wrestle a chimp.

Mr. Harlow flogged me so hard his face boiled in sweat, and on the tenth blow his glasses flew off his nose. I tightly hugged the cushions, never taking my eyes off the members of the student council, who looked on like so many cackling Madame Defarges knitting at the foot of the guillotine. Struggling to stand, I willed myself not to give them the satisfaction of a teary exit.

After I gingerly climbed the steps to my dorm, a bunch of kids followed me into my alcove, whispering, "Let me see, let me see." I pulled down my pants and they gasped at the sight: the welt along the back of my thigh was turning from fire-engine red to dull eggplant right before their eyes, eliciting oohs and aahs, as if they were witnessing a miracle. Where the holes of the paddle hadn't touched, hot-pink circles of flesh dotted the area. When Derby saw I was on the verge of tears, he cleared the room and helped me pull up my pants.

Two weeks later I was on a flight to Los Angeles, using an airline pillow to cushion my still smarting posterior thigh. The skin had turned black, and bits of dead flesh continued to peel, but I considered the wound a Purple Heart for survival in the face of the enemy. John Derby and I would next meet at yet another boys' boarding school in the fall, this time in Colorado. I hoped never to see the autumn foliage of New England ever again.

Twelve

I came home that summer of 1970 deflowered and flogged, and a very different boy from the one who had left for Massachusetts three years earlier.

I noticed that my mother had gone through some changes as well, though not for the better. She had started to drink a bit too much with a new group of friends, a bunch of gay alcoholics. In self-deprecatory jest, she'd started calling herself a "fag hag," a term I'd never heard until then. I'd grown up around gay men and took affection between the same sex for granted, but I despised these new, lonely figures in Mom's life who howled uproariously about nothing and brought out in her the saddest laughter I'd ever heard. The decline in the quality of her companions, who called her "Ducks," made me angry, and I was openly hostile to them.

"Well, *someone's* a little grumpy-poo," they might slur.

One particularly raucous night, I smelled something burning in the living room, where everyone was falling over themselves in laughter—everyone except my mother, who held an unlit cigarette in her mouth and a spent matchstick in her hand.

"What's so funny?" I demanded.

"Your poor mother," one of them said, "set her hair on fire trying to light a Virginia Slim!" This set off another round of hysterics.

A long strand of my mother's beautiful hair had burned up to her scalp, and she slumped her head down, too ashamed to meet my eyes.

"Get the fuck out of our house," I told her friends.

"What? Are you serious? Lenny, Ducks, is he serious?"

"You're being very rude, young man," snapped one of the other drunks. They turned to Mom for backup, and when her eyes came into focus, she seemed to see them for the first time.

"All of you, out! And don't come back."

They stumbled away en masse and out of Mom's life for good. And before I knew it, I became her drinking partner.

In my early teens, I felt terribly grown-up to be allowed a glass of wine—"like kids in Europe," Mom would say—and to be suddenly entrusted with stories of past lovers, adultery, and betrayal. She once reminded me of the time my father took me to Waikiki when I was nine and brought along a friend of his named Don Vachon. I remembered him well: he was younger than Dad and quite fit in Lacoste shirts that I was also made to wear. I was obsessed with the television series *Flipper* and thought he looked like Sandy, the older brother on the show. I had cutout pictures from *Tiger Beat* of Sandy and Flipper the dolphin taped to my walls, so I thought Don was pretty cool.

Dad and I shared a room at the Royal Hawaiian hotel, and Don was in the room next to us. They hung out during the day while I learned to surf. At night we had dinner and laughed our asses off. Don told a story about smoking on the toilet and flicking a hot ash on his dick, which I thought was the funniest thing

I'd ever heard. This was a great trip in my memory, until Mom pointed out that Don was Dad's lover. I don't think I gave more than a "hmmm" in response, but I knew it made perfect sense. Each night during that vacation, Dad would put me to bed and leave until the morning, something I'd never given a thought to until then. Handsome, athletic, funny Don was doing my dad. But more than anything else, my reaction was to feel honored that my mother trusted me with such private information.

If Dad was trying to hide his sexual orientation from me, I can say in retrospect that he did a terrible job. He had, after all, produced *The Boys in the Band*, written by our family friend Mart Crowley, about a party of gay men struggling with shame and self-loathing. He even brought me to see the play when I was twelve, though he waited till the performance began so he could sneak me into the balcony when it was dark. I will never forget the gasps when the audience saw a silhouette of a little boy being led to his seat. I found the play hilarious and tragic, but it also made me think how horrible it must be to be gay, a theme, intentional or not, that was considered heresy by the early LGBT groups that picketed the theater every night.

I noticed how close Dad had become with Frederick Combs, one of the actors in the play, and thought nothing of it; in fact I assumed Frederick was straight and only acted the part of a gay man.

When I moved to New York in 1974, Frederick was one of my first friends, and he looked after me like a big brother. We became close, though platonically, and saw lots of plays, eating afterward at Joe Allen's, an actors' bar, where he later talked Joe into hiring me as a waiter. (Joe Allen personally fired me after two weeks.)

When I asked Frederick what his relationship to my father was, he looked sort of wistful and sighed, "I'm afraid I broke Nick's heart. He was beside himself in love with me but I just didn't feel the same about him. I don't think he ever got over it because we rarely speak anymore. I think it's too painful for him."

I tried to picture Dad crazy in love, pleading on late-night phone calls and then weeping in rejection, expressing all the longings he'd never shown my mother.

"Don't tell your father I told you this," he added.

"I won't," I said, and I never did.

Years later, Frederick moved to Los Angeles to teach acting, and we lost touch until one night he called me in New York to say he was dying of AIDS. I wept uncontrollably. As he consoled me, instead of the other way around, I heard yelling and chaos on his side of the call and asked where he was. Frederick said he was in an AIDS ward of the county hospital as simply as if he were at our old table at Joe Allen's again, probably just to comfort me. His SAG insurance had long run out because he hadn't worked in years, a curse put on many of the actors in *Boys* for playing gay men too convincingly.

When we hung up, I next called the production manager of a movie I was producing called *White Palace*. We were days from shooting in St. Louis, and we hired Frederick (on paper) for a nonexistent part that would work long enough for his SAG insurance to kick in. The next day he was moved into his home in the care of a hospice nurse, who took care of him until he died. I have not forgotten how a five-minute phone call and ten minutes' worth of paperwork can change the remainder of a man's life.

Of the original cast of *The Boys in the Band*, five out of the nine actors died of AIDS-related causes.

WHEN DAD DROPPED by the house unannounced, as he had been asked not to do since the divorce, my mother's anger, which once seemed overblown, now made perfect sense. Since she had taken me into her drunken confidence about Don Vachon, my father looked different in a way I couldn't put my finger on, like someone who'd just had a haircut that takes a moment to register. I didn't feel judgmental, just sad when I imagined the burden of secrets he'd had to carry for so long.

I felt sadder for my mother, whose burden it was to look the other way and pretend she didn't live in a house of lies.

Now that I knew my father's secret, I kept it from him as he did from me, and joined my parents in their subterfuge. The air of secrecy was the oxygen I breathed, and the lies I told in school were fodder for the petty crimes I'd continue to commit.

When Mom stormed off to her bedroom, Dad pretended his ex-wife didn't loathe him, and instead took inventory of the ongoing disrepair in his ex-house: the green satin sofa they bought in New York as newlyweds was stained with red wine, the white drapes hid Bosie's dried turds and smelled of cat piss, and the painted flats of English gardens left over from the Black and White Ball still hung in our picture window, their colors long since washed out by the sun. He looked as sad as a bankrupt earl watching tourists parade through his castle. Clinging to small talk, he asked me how school had been, and I considered telling him how I'd been flogged and fondled, but didn't have the heart. In Dunne family tradition, I kept it pleasant and my secrets close.

Thirteen

I had grown up around celebrities all my life, but until *Slouching Towards Bethlehem* came out, I'd never been related to one. The book was way above my head, but my powers of observation were keen enough to know my aunt was famous when I saw a billboard on the Sunset Strip advertising her book.

John and Joan lived in a large but crumbling Greek-columned house in an area of Hollywood that Joan once described as a "senseless-killing neighborhood." The ceilings were high but the walls peeled paint and the plumbing was moody, though for four hundred dollars a month, there was plenty of room for a literary couple on the rise and their two-year-old daughter, Quintana. Across the street on Franklin Avenue was a mansion that had once been the Japanese consulate until its residents skipped town after Pearl Harbor, leaving it boarded up and abandoned to a turnover of cult leaders who became John and Joan's neighbors.

My parents were no longer married or entertaining, and in a bitter irony that vexed my father, John and Joan became the new "it" couple, hanging with the next generation of film people whose work was more relevant to a younger audience. Dad and the old movie stars who once danced to Peter Duchin in his house, and drank up his liquor, were as baffled as Elvis had been when the Beatles stormed America.

John and Joan gave a lot of parties, but their biggest by far was for Tom Wolfe, who was in town promoting *The Electric Kool-Aid Acid Test*. Joan called my mother to invite her and then added, "Bring Griffin too. Janis Joplin is coming, and I know how much he loves her." I was a precocious kid who always made Joan laugh, so it was not unusual for her and John to include me in their lunches or dinner parties. They knew I could handle myself around their crowd of filmmakers and artists, who would find my curiosity and familiarity with their work as amusing as a parlor trick.

I had been pining for Janis since picking up a copy of *Cheap Thrills* with the R. Crumb artwork. Her raunchy voice and troubled soul called to me, and I imagined (or fantasized) that when we met, she might find me someone she could confide in. I had a worrisome thought—what if, during the party and in the middle of our flirty banter, Janis found out I'd arrived with my mother?

On the ride to the party, I worked up the nerve to ask Mom something that had been on my mind since we'd first been invited. She drove her Chevy Nova in a Pucci dress and smelled of Fracas, a fragrance that still makes me swoon.

"Mom, can you not tell anyone we came together?"

She thought about it for a moment before asking, "You mean pretend we don't know each other?"

"Ummm, yeah."

"So you want people to think you just showed up on your own?"

"Yeah. Is that all right?"

"That's fine, honey, but this is a grown-up affair that is sure to go much later than I plan to stay. So when I say it's time to leave, I don't want to hear any guff."

"Well, if I'm talking to Janis, don't yank me out the door in front of her. And for God's sake don't say 'guff.'"

Mom always got me and took my narcissism in stride.

"No, of course not," she said, suppressing a smile. "We'll have a signal. When it's time to go, I'll give you a wink like I'm just some pretty girl at the party trying to get your attention."

"That's perfect!"

The party was in full swing when we arrived, and my mother peeled off without giving me a second glance.

I explored my surroundings in search of Janis, completely ignored except by some guy who said, loud enough for all to hear, "What kind of parent would bring *a child* to this place? It's shameful."

I whipped around with a dirty look and saw it was only Uncle Earl McGrath, madly giggling at his own prank.

Earl was a family friend I'd met a year earlier at a party we gave on Christmas Day for people who had nowhere to go. He walked up to me and said, "I'm going to be your fake uncle Earl, so open your hand." I did as told, and he dropped a half-smoked joint into it.

"Merry Christmas," he said, laughing at his own joke, a trait of his I would come to know well. And then: "Don't tell your dad."

Earl and John were best friends who constantly feuded, swearing never to speak again and never lasting more than a month before they fell into each other's arms in apologia. I was happy to see him at the party and assumed that they'd patched things up from their last quarrel.

"Where's John?" I asked, yelling over speakers blasting *Sgt. Pepper.*

"Look for the most famous person in the room, and there you will find him, following him around like a drooling puppy."

"I guess you guys are on the outs again."

"No, I don't know why I said that." He seemed genuinely bewildered by his remark. "We just hugged five minutes ago. I love your uncle. I'm stoned, kid, don't listen to me," he said, before wandering to the bar.

The party continued outside, where the backyard sloped to a crumbling tennis court last rolled in 1933. I happened upon my father toking on a joint with Harrison Ford, then a carpenter and unknown actor. When our eyes met, he whipped the joint behind his back, and we pretended not to see each other.

I considered hitting up Earl for some pot but decided against it because I wanted to keep my head clear for Janis, and returned to the house to see if she'd arrived.

Before I could penetrate the mob dancing inside, I was grabbed by an old bald guy who wore a Nehru jacket and spoke in a thick German accent.

"Boy! Sit beside me. *Now!*"

He pulled me onto the chair next to him, holding tightly to my arm. On closer inspection, I recognized him as Colonel Klink from *Hogan's Heroes*, a popular sitcom about Nazis running a POW camp. Colonel Klink seemed far more intense in person and not at all the wacky Fritz he played on TV.

"You must help me," he began, his grip tightening. "I have taken ze acid and am having a bummer. Ze people here are evil, and you are ze only light that is pure. I need you to stay by my side for ze rest of ze night."

In a heartbeat I went from being an awestruck fan of a television star to figuring out how to ditch him. Someone put on

"Get It While You Can," which I took as Janis's entrance, and I tried to stand but the old Nazi held me in place.

"Zat awful music. Pure evil. Ven vill this trip end?" he moaned.

When his attention fixated on the flames inside a hurricane lamp on the windowsill, I yanked my arm free and made a break for it. Running through a cloud of pot smoke and gyrating adults, I heard him screech, "Stop, young man. Come back!" He might also have added, "Halt, or I vill have you shot," but I tend to embellish.

I went from room to room in search of Janis, but still no sighting. Standing by the front door, a woman in a Pucci dress smelling of Fracas pretending not to be my mother gave me a wink, our signal that it was time to leave. I rushed to her in a panic.

"Oh no, come on, Mom! Janis isn't even here yet."

"I know, honey. Joan just told me her show at the Palladium doesn't get out till one a.m., and that's too late for me and way too late for you."

There was no convincing her, and we drove home in silence.

The next day Joan called Mom to rehash the party and then asked her to put me on. In the middle of my telling her about the actor from *Hogan's Heroes*, she stopped me to say, "Wait, hold that thought. *John*, pick up." Whenever something interesting was about to be said, they'd call out for the other to pick up from the extension in their office.

"Okay, start over," Joan said once John was on.

When I told them about Colonel Klink and the bad acid trip, they went into such hysterics I had to let them catch their breath.

"Griffin, that wasn't the guy from *Hogan's Heroes*," John said. "That was the director Otto Preminger."

I had no idea who that was, but the trill in Joan's laugh delighted me. They told me that Preminger was a tyrant film director who came close to actually burning Jean Seberg to death at the stake while filming *Saint Joan* so he could capture the terror in her eyes. I guess I got off easy.

Fourteen

LA is a cruel town for a kid without a driver's license.

When General Motors and Standard Oil killed the streetcar, they didn't consider how difficult they made the lives of kids under sixteen. In 1963, the last trolley was sold for scrap, condemning teens my age to a life of aimless walking or begging their mothers to drop them off at the movies. Bus transportation was an option, but the infrequent stops and byzantine routes that dropped you far from your destination were designed by the auto industry to punish the poor for not buying a car.

Luckily I had parents with more on their minds than to wonder how I spent my days and who were oblivious to the fact that my mode of transportation was to get in the cars of the strangers who picked me up hitchhiking. Before Charles Manson changed the vibe, LA was a friendly place for a trusting kid with a thumb.

I hitched my first ride when I was twelve and got dropped off in front of a head shop called Pandora's Box on the Sunset Strip. I bought a copy of the *Los Angeles Free Press*, Paul Krassner's weekly that was filled with R. Crumb cartoons and gruesome drawings of

American soldiers holding Vietnamese babies at the ends of their bayonets. Pandora's Box was on the site of the once great and now leveled Garden of Allah, where Robert Benchley and Dorothy Parker were known to skinny-dip in the hotel's pool. I became a regular at Pandora's and afterward would cross the street to the Chateau Marmont to visit my fake uncle Earl to try out my new bong.

Earl and his wife, Camilla, a former contessa whose family was related to Pope Leo XIII, lived in suite 64, which had a terrace as big as a tennis court. Earl paid four hundred dollars a month for a two-bedroom, and when he realized they never used the second one, hired his friend Harrison Ford, a struggling actor and full-time carpenter, to close it off with a block of balsa wood. He then called downstairs to the hotel manager to say he didn't need the other bedroom and would now pay only two hundred dollars a month. That there wasn't a door to get into the unused bedroom didn't faze the manager in the least, and he made the adjustment to his rent. That's how it rolled in the sixties at the Chateau Marmont.

When the cops decided to shut down Pandora's, the hippies mobilized to riot, and Earl invited our family to watch the mayhem from the terrace of his penthouse. He passed us firecrackers, which we lit and threw onto the Strip, yelling, "Fuck the pigs!" as kids below had their skulls cracked open by sheriffs' batons.

BEING FOURTEEN AND HORNY is a lethal combination. You're too young to drive a car, and no girl will have anything to do with you until you do. Hitchhiking was fun while it lasted, but it left Charlie and me still reliant on adults to get around and aching to drive. We counted the days till we turned sixteen and could get our licenses, so in the meantime, on the nights we snuck out of my house, we would roam the neighborhood looking for cars with their keys still in the ignition. Sometimes we'd actually find one, and go so far as to sit in it, but chicken out when it came to turning the key.

Charlie was the idea man who thought up schemes I could never have done on my own. It was his idea to spend the entire inheritance I got from my dead aunt Twinkie to make a movie. It was his idea to have a busboy bring a glass of water to Nancy Sinatra with his compliments. (She was charmed.) And it was his idea to take my mother's Mercury Cougar for a little spin at two in the morning.

We gathered as many phone books as we could to prop ourselves up to see over the dashboard, and silently pushed the car down the driveway. As the theft was Charlie's idea, he got to drive first. He turned over the ignition and we looked to my mother's darkened window to see if the noise would wake her up, then tore up Walden.

Staying in one lane was a challenge at first, but we soon became quite cocky. Tiring of the Flats (as the area between Sunset and Santa Monica is called), we were hungry for new terrain and drove up the side streets off Benedict Canyon.

We saw the first cop car as we made a left off Benedict Canyon. Then we saw about twenty others parked right behind it, with their cherry tops swirling red and yellow, maddeningly out of sync. Charlie slowed the car to about two miles an hour, and we looked at each other like terrified characters in a Munch painting. He was bright orange, then yellow, then red.

"Jesus," Charlie said under his breath. "Your mom must want this car back really bad."

"Should we pull over?"

The officers were scurrying about with clipboards, filling out forms. They all looked up at us for a moment and then continued with their work. "Keep going," I said without moving my lips. "They're not here for us. They're here because that's the house . . ."

There was yellow crime scene tape across the driveway of a Mediterranean ranch house on Cielo Drive. Of course. The story had just broken in the afternoon edition of every newspaper in the country. The bodies of Sharon Tate and four of her friends had been found butchered inside that house this very morning. This was not the time to be learning to drive a car.

When we got back to Mom's, we were freaked. Everything that had once been familiar now looked sinister. In the window of our house, I thought I saw a silhouette in the shape of Norman Bates. Even Mom's car looked evil. It wasn't just a Cougar anymore, it was a flesh-eating cat. The telephone books piled in the front seats were damp from our sweat but felt sticky, like blood. There was no way we were going to sleep, so we took a walk. We walked and walked, talking about what must have gone on in that house. It was at least three in the morning when we decided to hit Milton F. Kreis, an all-night coffee shop in the Beverly Wilshire Hotel.

MFK's, as it was known, had once been considered the "soda fountain to the stars." Shirley Temple would come in after school for a banana split. Bogie or Mitchum could be seen sobering up in one of its huge leather booths after a rowdy Hollywood party. By 1969, the booths were patched with gaffer's tape and business was off, way off. But you could still get a pretty decent root beer float, and for five more sawbucks, a pretty decent hooker.

What Jane Goodall was to gorillas, I was to hookers. Not that

I'd ever been with one, they just fascinated me. When I grew up I hoped to marry a hooker like Shirley MacLaine in *Irma la Douce.* I even loved saying the word *hooker. Gimme a hooker and a side of fries. The hills are alive with the sound of hookers.* Or Dian Fossey's famous *Hookers in the Mist.* It was a fun word, and I tried to work it into as many conversations as possible.

The ladies at MFK's looked nothing like Ms. MacLaine, but some were going for Julie Christie in *Darling.* Their madam was named Belle, and she doubled as the coffee shop's hostess. She was a dead ringer for Pat Nixon and had a "den mother" attitude toward her girls that even extended to Charlie and me whenever we wandered in at our usual ungodly hour. We never ordered more than a bottomless cup of coffee, yet Belle always gave us the same ringside booth to best observe her girls hustle sleepless out-of-towners to get in their rooms, or a touring rock band peruse the magazine racks before calling it a night. She didn't find it the least bit odd that we never came in before one or two in the morning and always left at dawn. No "Does your mother know where you are?" shit from her.

A disheveled fellow we knew only as Murray was sitting in the adjacent booth and couldn't help but overhear us talking about Sharon Tate. If Murray was to be believed, he had produced, or "helped set up," *The Fearless Vampire Killers,* which Sharon Tate had starred in back in '67. Did we mind if he joined us? We didn't. He was wearing a tuxedo with a pair of dirty Jack Purcell tennis shoes, and the elbows of his dinner jacket were worn through to the shirt. Murray wore a tuxedo every night, to give the impression he'd just come from someplace incredible. He had a Bentley with a solid-gold grille bought with the profits from *Creature from the Black Lagoon,* which he produced, or at least said he did. Like the booths we were sitting in, Murray's

Bentley was completely beat to shit, and one night, in a vulnerable moment, he confessed that the grille was only gold-plated and that he didn't have the money to fix the dents.

While Charlie and I were telling him about our evening drive past the house on Cielo, Murray's friends joined us. Tor was an actor-wrestler who had made a couple of pictures with Ed Wood. He was bald and so large that he took up two places in the booth. Tor had come "this close" to getting the part of Oddjob in *Goldfinger*, until, as he said without malice, "they decided to go 'Chink' with the role."

The hostess brought over Daisy, one of her ladies who'd been lounging at the soda fountain, eager to join our conversation.

We could always count on Daisy to tell us if she'd blown any of the guests on *The Tonight Show*, which aired only a few hours earlier. She averaged about two guests a week and had no qualms about telling us their names.

The story of our drive past Sharon's was going over very big. Charlie and I told it in relay fashion, a technique I'd perfect in years to come when pitching movies with my producing partner.

The trick is that you never correct the other person, even when the details are exaggerated or outright fabricated. I added the part about running a roadblock, and Charlie told of a brief interrogation by an officer who was just about to order us out of the car when he was called inside to investigate a new clue.

I left out a detail that was true and would have stunned our audience, but even thinking it was too disturbing, and I was far from able to say it out loud. One of the people murdered in the Cielo house was my father's friend and I'd known him most of my life. Jay Sebring cut Dad's hair, as he did the most famous men in Hollywood, and on Saturdays, one of our father-son errands was to stop by Jay's salon at 9000 Sunset so he could take a little off the sides. I'd sit in the adjoining barber chair and listen to them laugh and gossip about the latest celebrity mishap or the weekend grosses. When I was little, he'd wrap me in a barber's cape and pretend to cut my hair in a fashion that "would make the chicks go crazy." I'd giggle and say I didn't like girls and he'd always come back with "You wait and see, stud, that day is going to come."

"You guys actually got in the house?" Murray asked incredulously.

"What?" I said, snapping out of the memory.

"You kids got *in the house*?" he repeated.

Charlie and I looked at each other for the briefest moment. Better not push it.

"Nah, we got the hell out of there."

Something about our experience made everyone reflect on their own lives.

"That could have been me in there," said Daisy sadly.

"How do you figure that, Daze?" asked Murray.

"I used to wear my hair the same way she did in *Valley of the Dolls*."

DAISY MIGHT NOT have known how the earth spins on its axis, but she sure knew how to get around the Beverly Wilshire. She could spot a house dick with his back to her. Hookers weren't allowed in the hotel unless escorted by a guest, and for the first month anyway, that's who security assumed we were. We would escort her to the bank of elevators in the lobby, and she'd manage to stay aloft for hours. Elevators were very lucky for her. "Even the pope doesn't like walking into an empty hotel room," she reasoned. That's when it occurred to us that if she could turn tricks with out-of-towners, why couldn't we work the lobby to meet girls? Everyone likes to meet the local yokels when they're on vacation, to be shown the sights. We could even use the same pickup line Daisy did: "So, where you from?"

The first time we tried it, we couldn't believe our luck. We strolled into the hotel around noon looking pretty spiffy in our Peter Max ties. Within two minutes, an elderly gentleman approached us with a big "How-dy." He called us "boys" and told us he was a grandfather on vacation with his granddaughter and her little friend. He wore a dark suit with cowboy boots, so we pegged him for a Texas oil baron. He had a little proposition for us. If he gave us a hundred dollars, would we mind taking his girls to Disneyland? He'd arrange for a car to take us back and forth.

"Where are they?" Charlie asked suspiciously.

He looked around the lobby.

"I don't see my granddaughter at the moment, but her friend is right over there."

He pointed in the direction of the magazine racks, where a long-legged creature in a miniskirt and tank top was reading *Tiger Beat.* She looked fast and pouty and totally out of our league, and the idea that we would be paid to take this girl to Disneyland was something I would have paid him for. I didn't even need to look at Charlie to know he was thinking the same thing. *She's mine. No, I got her. Screw you, I saw her first. Oh yeah? Well, we'll see about—*

"And by that big ole potted palm sits my darling granddaughter."

She was as beautiful as her friend. It was like having to choose between Betty and Veronica. The only difference between these two was that the granddaughter, the one who was sitting, happened to be sitting in a wheelchair.

Charlie was the first to speak up.

"Do you mind if we talk about this for a second? Just because Mom might need us back at the house for this charity event we're supposed to—"

"Quite all right, boys—take your time."

We pulled each other by the lapels into a huddle. I don't remember who said what, but it doesn't matter—we were equally guilty.

"Shit."

"I know, I know. So what do you want to do?"

"I want to hire a faith healer so the four of us can run off to Disneyland!"

"Well, that's not going to happen, so . . ."

"I know this sounds terrible," one of us began, "but I'm thinking we can do better."

"You mean someone with two hundred dollars is going to come along?"

"This isn't about the money, I'm talking about girls. One for each of us."

"You mean the kind that walk."

"Right."

"Okay, let's get it over with."

We told the guy about some previous engagement and that we must regretfully pass (I don't think we used the word *pass*) on his very generous offer. He was disappointed, but I don't think he suspected what scumbags we were.

"I understand, boys. Tammy, Louisa—shake a leg. I want to hit Disneyland by two."

Tammy put *Tiger Beat* back on the rack and smiled at her poor, tragic, brave but hauntingly beautiful friend Louisa. Louisa put her hands on the arms of her wheelchair, stood up, and walked over to her grandfather. Her gait was as graceful as Grace Kelly's. You could have balanced a goddamn book on her head. We looked at the empty wheelchair. PROPERTY OF THE BEVERLY WILSHIRE was written on the back.

That pretty much killed our morale for the rest of the summer. The only pickup line that felt right was "Hi, we're a couple of heartless little gigolos without a trace of moral fiber. May we show you our fine city?"

They shut down MFK's about a year later and turned it into a Brentano's bookstore. Once I got my driver's license, there was never any reason to go there again.

Fifteen

When my little brother was fourteen, he used the word *love* a lot. Alex loved *Franny and Zooey* because Franny loved *The Way of a Pilgrim*, which he then read and loved. He *loved* Joni Mitchell's *Blue* album, and Joni *loved* Graham Nash.

One night when I was home from my first year at yet another all boys boarding school, this time in Colorado, Alex stood in front of the TV, where my family permanently migrated for dinner, to make an important announcement during the commercial break: "I *love* Carrie Fisher."

"What's she written?" asked Dominique, the only one to bite.

"She's a girl I met today. She's coming over and I want everyone to act normal."

"What do you mean?" I asked.

"Just don't everybody act like it's a big deal that she's here. Don't ask her questions. Just don't . . . tell her I love her."

"Why would we say that?"

"She doesn't know. I want it to be a surprise."

To that I replied, "Well, it *will* be a surprise, Alex, if you just met her today. And not a good one, either, if I can give you a little advice."

"She has got to know how I feel. It's not fair to her."

"I'm not following you, as usual, but you gotta trust me on this. Try to play it a little cool or she will freak." Alex looked at me as if he were finally taking in my brotherly advice, which he wasn't.

"Don't do that thing you do with the girls," he said to me.

"What are you talking about?"

"You know. Your Charles Boyer bullshit." He broke out in a French accent and kissed his own hand over and over while chanting "Ma chérie."

I laughed harder than necessary, while nervously looking around to see if my embarrassment was showing.

"Just don't"—he suddenly reverted to a dead monotone—"trick her into liking you."

Carrie had to let herself in through the kitchen because Alex feared we might come off as "weird" if someone answered a doorbell. She must have followed the noise of *Columbo* to the study, where she found us slack-jawed in the gray glow of the TV. Per Alex's instructions, I ignored her, and Dominique followed suit. My genteel mother, always tirelessly supportive of Alex's passions (once even driving him to the desert to see a performance of *Aida*), couldn't bear having a guest not be properly greeted.

"Carrie, I'm Lenny. Can I get you a soda?"

"Uh, yeah, I guess, why not? Whatever Yeats is having," Carrie said, gesturing toward Alex.

I failed to stifle a snort but refused to look at her in honor of my brother's wishes. And I knew what he meant when he called me on my Charles Boyer bullshit, even if that wasn't how I pictured my burgeoning style with the ladies. Blame it on being denied the human nipple at birth, a desperate reaction to latent homophobia, or simply an out-of-control desire to be desired, but falling for girls was what I did for a living, pro bono. If I was trapped in an elevator with John Lennon, Sandy Koufax, and a girl with body odor and acne, I would strike up a conversation with Lil Ms. Smelly every time.

Carrie was a year younger than me but looked exactly like the teen seductress in *Shampoo* she would soon play, whom Warren Beatty, understandably, can't keep his hands off. I knew I had to get out of the room or I'd break my vow to Alex and to myself.

I gathered up my plate from the TV tray and was about to make my move, when she addressed me. "You're friends with Piper, aren't you?"

I didn't know who Piper was and felt unreasonably ashamed about it. Torn between admitting my ignorance or inquiring about him or her—both of which would have betrayed my brother—I shyly looked down at a few runaway peas rolling around the tray. The effect, though unintentional, made me appear tortured and sullen like James Dean meeting his brother's girlfriend in *East of Eden*.

"Griffin's friends with everybody. I don't even have a name at school. They just call me 'Griffin's brother,'" Alex said cheerfully, if not with downright pride. I was so touched, I wanted to kick his ass for making such a stupid remark in front of the woman he loved.

"Well, at least they don't call you 'Debbie's daughter,'" she said in reference to her mother, Debbie Reynolds.

"Is that tough to live up to?" I asked. *Oh shut up*, I thought to myself.

"It's a burden, but I still get three square meals a day."

"There is that." *Shut up!*

"Always looking on the bright side."

"A glass-half-full kind of broad, are you?" *Oh for God's sake, what is wrong with me?*

"Guilty as charged."

"Who's Debbie?" asked Alex, not keeping up at all.

"*The Singing Nun*. We saw it on *Million Dollar Movie* about five dinners ago," I reminded him, hoping to bring him back into the conversation.

"*Dominique-a, niqua, niqua niqua neek*," Carrie burst out singing, joined by Dominique, who loved the song for obvious reasons and leapt at the chance to wedge her way into the mix. I couldn't look at Alex when it was my turn to improvise a verse of nonsense French lyrics replete with farting sounds—Carrie's contribution to Sœur Sourire's one-hit wonder—but I imagined him looking at the three of us, dancing and singing in perfect Rat Pack pitch, wondering what his absinthe-swilling mother must be doing now.

Carrie later announced that it was a school night and she had to get home or her mother would worry.

"No, I'm kidding, she's asleep for a five a.m. call and has no idea where I am, but I do have to get back. So nice to meet you all. Alex, your family seems incredibly well balanced. You must be very proud."

"Well, how are you getting home?" asked my mother.

"I walked. It's only a few blocks from here."

"Well, Griffin will drive you home," my mother offered.

"No, that's—"

"I insist, end of subject."

I looked to Alex to see if he wanted to join, but to my guilty relief, he remembered he had homework and shyly said good night. I'd finally gotten my driver's license, though I had to drive Mom's very unsexy Chevy Nova station wagon with a MAHLER GROOVES bumper sticker on its fender.

"Who's Mahler?" Carrie asked as I gallantly opened the passenger-side door for her.

"Gustav Mahler is my mother's favorite composer. She goes once a year to a 'Mahler-thon' at a house in Laurel Canyon where they play every one of his symphonies for twenty-four hours."

"She is so cool," Carrie said as she walked around to the driver's side and sat behind the wheel.

"What are you doing?" I asked her.

"Teach me how to drive."

"It's night. I don't know if it's the best time."

Carrie turned over the engine and pulled the gears down the steering wheel as I hopped into the passenger side just before she jerked away from the curb.

"What the fuck!" I cried out.

"It's the *perfect* time to learn."

She drove with both feet, which was the first of my instructions she ignored.

"*Some enchanted evening*," she sang, and then hit the brakes, making us lurch forward, then hit the gas, stopping and starting in time with her singing.

"*You may see a stranger*." She hit the brakes and the gas, the brakes and the gas, as we roared in hysterics. "*Across a crowded roooooom*," she belted, driving onto the sidewalk, and I couldn't tell her to stop because I was laughing so hard. Then she rolled over the front lawn of our neighbor's house and said, as if giving me a tour, "Buddy Hackett lives here."

By the time we got to her house, tears were rolling down our faces, and neither of us could get out of the car.

"You're fucking crazy, Carrie," I said, trying to catch my breath.

"Is that going to be a problem?"

"Not at all," I said.

When we finally collected ourselves, she hopped out and thanked me for an "enchanted evening."

BEST FRIENDS BECOME best friends suddenly, and without knowing that's what's happening until it happens. One insignificant day, only weeks after our Mr. Toad's wild ride, I looked at Carrie and realized she would be in my life for a very long time. Before I failed Spanish, I remember the teacher describing the eve of fluency as when one night you dream in the language and suddenly can speak it the next morning. That is what it felt like when Carrie and I realized we were best friends. To the exclusion of everyone around us, we established our own Sanskrit that baffled the locals and established our reputation alongside the great pairings of all who came before us: Stan and Laurel. Sturm und Drang. Pork and Beans. Griffin and Carrie.

We tried to teach Alex the catchphrases of our shorthand, but he would have none of it. That we were platonic didn't comfort Alex; if anything, it made things worse. Carrie's and my friendship, clearly destined for a long history, meant that my impossibly romantic brother would never have the chance to win his Guinevere, or recite his sonnets, or be knighted for dragons slain to win her love.

Et tu, Carrie? he must have thought when she introduced him only as "Griffin's brother" at a barbecue at her house, and he never set foot there again. I tried to offer a million explanations for our friendship: that she was technically closer to me in age; that our chemistry had just sort of happened; even that he would get her back as soon as I returned to boarding school. But everything managed to sound more pitying than I meant it. Alex and I both knew that something more profound had taken place than just stealing his girl, and that the sweet little kid who used the word *love* in every other sentence would from now on start to use that verb more sparingly.

FIRST OF ALL, let me cut to the chase and say that Carrie *never* became my girlfriend. She knew, long before I did, that being lovers would diminish our possibilities. Carrie was a virgin when we met, and she lived for every lurid detail of my own sexual encounters: from my first kiss to postcoital anxieties I shared with no one but her. Her curiosity was so forensic that I felt like a cadaver undergoing an autopsy. I became her *Farmers' Almanac* to forecast just the right conditions for when she'd be ready to plow ahead into the great outdoors of sexual confusion.

We had both seen *Deep Throat*, and during one such interrogation, she tried to determine how I measured up in relation to the other male members, as it were, of that stellar cast. She floated a theory that the bigger the schlong, the smaller the brain power, an equation that had been percolating since she'd seen a friend's little brother with a traumatic brain injury tie a Batman cape around his enormous boner. "Gotham City will never be the same," she'd said.

"Sometimes I think my brain is damaged," I said. It came out so quietly I hoped the remark might be overlooked.

"Then you must be hung like a yak!"

"I'm not talking about that. I'm serious. There is something wrong with my brain. I can't remember shit that happened two days ago. I forget entire conversations, important directions, car keys, people's names. It takes me all day to read a page from a book. There is something wrong with me. I think I was dropped on my head or something." Oh fuck, I was going to cry. I thought of doing something funny, maybe bursting into an imitation of Charles Laughton as the hunchback of Notre Dame ringing church bells and yelling, "Sanctuary," when Carrie took my hand.

"You're not stupid. You are one of the smartest people I know, which might not set the bar very high, but it doesn't mean there is something wrong with you. I can't believe you would think that."

"Can you keep a secret?" I asked.

"There is a first time for everything," she said, but I knew she would.

"The boarding school my parents sent me to held me back a year. I am a year older than everyone in my class."

"Being a good student is very overrated. Winston Churchill, who I'm sure you are compared to all the time, was held back at Harrow. I just saw that in a documentary. My own mother flunked out of the MGM Little Red Schoolhouse, for God's sake, not that that's very inspiring. Who else? Einstein was academically challenged and a notorious bumblehead, *and* he fucked Marilyn, let's not forget. Here is the problem, Griffin. You are not mentally impaired in any way. You are just very, very distractable. I've seen you get lost driving me four blocks between here and my house. You didn't forget where I live, you just turned up the radio to hear the new Neil Young at the very moment you should have been in the left lane but were too busy expressing your belief that Crazy Horse is better than Buffalo Springfield, which leads to your total recall of every musician, artist, and comic to come out of Canada, which reminds you to again remind me to buy the new George Carlin album because you think he's almost as funny as me, which I did and you're wrong, he's funnier. But usually, you're right about everything else except about being brain-damaged. If I wanted to get home by a direct route, I could just call a cab. Getting lost with you is the smartest fun I've ever had."

WHILE CARRIE WAS A SOPHOMORE at Beverly Hills High, I was in the drama department at Fountain Valley in Colorado Springs, where I had gained a reputation as a "serious actor" after knocking it out of the park as Jerry in Edward Albee's *Zoo Story*. The experience changed me. My grades improved, reading became easier, even enjoyable, and for the first time, I knew what I wanted to do with my life. I couldn't wait to graduate so I could move to New York and *really* become a "serious actor."

The next semester, I noticed during rehearsals for *Othello* that students and faculty would sit in the back of the theater to watch my Iago come to life. Word got back to me that the headmaster had snuck in and described my portrayal as "brilliant."

The night before opening, John Derby came to my room with a huge hash pipe. We had followed through with our pact to stay together after Fay, but as I got more into acting, he got more into drugs. By junior year, his suspicions that we were drifting apart were well founded.

"Come on, man, you're no fun anymore. Just take a hit," he said, pointing his pipe at me.

"My opening night is tomorrow. I have to keep a clear head."

"Yeah, you're Joe Actor, I get it. No time for your old friends."

"Come on, man," I protested.

"Are we even friends anymore? Tell me that and I'll leave you alone."

"Oh, blow it out your ass. Gimme a hit of that."

Hash was filling my lungs when Mr. Severance, our dorm master, walked in my room.

"I'm smelling smoke in the hallway. Is that coming from here?"

"Nope," I said as a silvery plume escaped my lips.

Still a little stoned from my one toke of Afghani Gold, I was summoned to the headmaster's Victorian residence that very night. The atmosphere of gloom in his salon matched the funeral parlor love seat he pointed to for me to sit on. The headmaster regarded me not with disappointment so much as betrayal. His hopes that I might be a mascot for future alumni fundraisers had been dashed. We both knew that the punishment for smoking dope was immediate expulsion, no exception. (Ironic in hindsight, as decades later Colorado became the first state to legalize cannabis.) Still, the headmaster was hoping to cut a deal. If I agreed to say to him, right then and there, that John was the only one smoking dope and not me, I would not be expelled and could perform in *Othello* the next night.

"What about John?" I asked.

"You know the answer to that. It's a miracle he hasn't been kicked out and taken you down with him sooner. You've thrived this year and have an enormous future ahead of you. I can't bear to see you throw it away by having this on your record for the rest of your life. I'm offering you a chance to save yourself."

I didn't say, "So you want me to *lie*? What kind of a lesson is that?" I didn't say, "But what about John's future? He's my best friend." I didn't say anything in his or my defense. I only said, "I can't do that."

The headmaster cajoled, berated, even begged me to change my mind, but I just repeated my mantra: "I can't do that."

"You think you are being noble, but your misguided loyalty will haunt you all of your years."

"I can't do that."

"Then there is nothing more to be said. Let yourself out."

My parents, who were crushed when I called them with the news, booked me a flight to Los Angeles the next day. I took a cab to the airport in Colorado Springs and cashed in the ticket to take a Greyhound instead. I figured as long as I was in this much trouble, I might as well make a holiday of it. At the bus station I purchased a ticket for that night to Raton, New Mexico, which bordered Colorado, and where it was legal to hitchhike. From there, I planned to thumb home to my shell-shocked parents.

Though the drinking age in many states at that time was eighteen, in Colorado it was twenty-one, so as a concession to the younger soldiers at nearby Fort Carson, there were "3.2 bars" that served a beer they called "panther piss" because it had only 3.2 percent alcohol. Sidling up to a barstool of a 3.2 across from the bus station, I downed the first of three pitchers in record time to get my buzz on. I was the only civilian in the joint, which was packed with rowdy soldiers not much older than me, being driven to a frenzy by a stripper, who was forbidden by law to dance topless and had to make the most of it in a bikini. The soldiers didn't seem to care, and were in far better spirits than I was because the Paris Peace Accords had just been signed and the last American troops were finally coming home from Vietnam. Every kid in that room had dodged a bullet.

As Charley Pride rocked out from the jukebox and the fortunate young men begged the stripper to show them her tits, I turned inward, wondering what reason I had to self-destruct after showing such promise to my parents and the faculty. When I tried to say goodbye to Hunter Frost, my drama teacher, whom I admired, he'd looked at me like I was a stillborn of the only son he would ever have. The play, he told me, would go on without me; he would read Iago holding a script, and they would just have to "stumble through."

"You might want to fuck up your life, but *you will not fuck up* Othello!"

Looking at the time, I realized that in thirty minutes I would have been walking onstage to begin poisoning the love Othello had for Desdemona. At the very moment I ordered my third pitcher of panther piss, in a different universe I would be putting on the last touches of makeup and would hear over a speaker backstage, "Half hour, cast members, this is half hour."

I knew deep down that loyalty had nothing to do with why I wouldn't rat out John when we were caught. He was right: I didn't want to be his friend anymore and needed to make new ones who longed to act and write and create art that would enthrall an audience. I had known for some time that should I go to college, John would not be joining, and I'd accepted that he would probably fade to just being a kid I'd gone to school with. In fact, I had that very thought when I reached for his pipe. Guilt pulled the hash into my lungs just as guilt refused to let me sell him out to the headmaster.

And now I was twisting the knife into my parents by not only getting kicked out but hitchhiking home like a Dean Moriarty wannabe. The beer warmed my brain and quickened my heart when I thought of myself as Dean. I was about to go on an adventure just like him in Kerouac's *On the Road*, and I was excited.

I grabbed the Amelia Earhart suitcase my mother used when she was a student at the University of Arizona, one college among many that would now never accept me, and stumbled out of the

3.2 to one of two buses I saw with double vision. I boarded and left Colorado behind.

The driver kicked me off after he pulled out of Raton—the first town past the border of New Mexico and as far as my ticket would take me—when he realized he had one too many passengers on board. I woke up in my seat hungover and squinting from the bus's overhead lights to hear him yelling that whoever was trying to stow away on his vehicle had better own up right now. I looked out the window, and it was snowing sideways. I closed my eyes, hoping not to be noticed, but he pegged me right off and unceremoniously dumped me on Route 64 in the middle of the night, in the middle of a storm.

I put on every piece of clothing I had in the Amelia Earhart suitcase and curled into a ball on the side of the road, praying for a car to pass before I froze to death. Finally, at sunrise, a beat-up pickup weaved from lane to lane in my direction. I flagged it down and squeezed in the cab with three tipsy Navajo men, who dropped me off at a diner miles down the road in Cimarron. My *On the Road* fantasy had begun.

Hitching out of Cimarron, I got a ride from two kids about my age driving a stolen Chrysler New Yorker. They'd just escaped from a reformatory and had a pound of weed in the trunk. There was an orange 76 station ball on the tip of the car's antenna, a brilliant promotional device at the time, and as we approached the Petrified Forest along a flat stretch of Interstate 40, they dared me to climb onto the hood to get it. I rolled down the window and crawled toward it, but as I reached for the ball, the driver floored it and swerved from lane to lane. The juvies inside the car thought my struggle hilarious. I grabbed the windshield wiper with one hand and managed to pull the antenna down so hard it broke off with the little orange ball still at its tip. I held up the antenna to the heavens and cried out in victory like a Viking with the head of a Swede on his pike.

One night, I thumbed a ride from a family headed to Barstow. For some reason the husband had his children sleeping in the front seat and made me sit in the back with his wife. We rode in silence for miles. At some point, the wife put her hand on my crotch and began massaging my expanding cock. Now and then, the husband looked at me in the rearview mirror, clueless, or maybe not, about what his missus was up to. The whole episode was so perverse and erotic that I came in my jeans.

When I got off the 10 in Los Angeles, I used what money I had left to take a cab to Walden Drive. I'd phoned Mom the day of my flight to say I'd decided to take a bus home instead so that I'd have time to think about my future. She didn't ask why I'd arrived four days later than the so-called bus. But she did inquire, "So what did you decide about your future?"

"I want to go to New York and be an actor."

Mom's expression at the end of my declaration was a mask of maternal concern for my future, but behind the mask her eyes almost burned with envy as if to say, "Yes, do what I wish I had done when I had the chance."

BEFORE I PACKED MY BAGS to begin my New York chapter, I got a little distracted and didn't actually get on a plane until a year later. I was in love again. Being of sound mind and reckless heart, I did what any normal seventeen-year-old boy would do: I got married in Tijuana.

The elopement was on me, but I can't help but blame Carrie a little bit for setting the stage of the most ridiculous detour of my life.

While I was away in Colorado, she'd send me letters so packed with gossip and hilarious similes and non sequiturs that the envelopes required extra postage. One such letter also had a picture of a girl so beautiful that when the photo fell from the pages and I picked it up, I looked in her eyes and told her so out loud.

Carrie wrote that she had a new friend named Tanya, and in the course of their conversation had talked me up so highly that her new friend wanted to sleep with me as soon as possible. Tanya was a senior at Beverly Hills High, older than both Carrie and me, whose father was a powerful movie producer. Her lovers were rich and middle-aged, and she'd told Carrie she thought it would be "interesting" to date someone younger. Carrie pitched me for the role and I got the part. Not only did I land the role, but she flew me to LA and put Tanya and me up in a hotel for one night, only if I promised to tell her *everything* that happened. I doubt Debbie Reynolds was aware that her daughter was a pimp or that she spent the whopping allowance her mother earned hoofing six shows a week in Vegas so that Tanya and I could get laid.

I was on a prepaid flight to LA the next weekend and took a cab to the Hyatt House on the Sunset Strip, where Tanya would be waiting in the room Carrie had booked for us. I know the goings-on at the Hyatt that night are now legend from the movie *Almost Famous*, but when I arrived, Led Zeppelin was staying on the same floor, and I had to fight my way through a gaggle of topless groupies shrieking up and down the hallway like they were in the last days of Nero. I didn't see a motorcycle riding down the carpet, but Cameron Crowe got everything else exactly right.

The door to the hotel room was left ajar, and when I entered, everything was dark, save a shaft of light from a billboard on Sunset that broke through mostly closed drapes.

I called out Tanya's name and got no answer. Moving farther into the room, I saw the silhouette of a man about my size move toward me, and cried out in fright. Another cry followed from the bedroom, and a light went on. I realized the man moving toward me was my reflection in a full-length mirror.

"What was that?" were Tanya's first words to me, said in alarm from under the covers, where she was stark naked. I realized my jitters had completely ruined her sexy surprise.

"It was me," I said apologetically. "I thought it was some guy about to jump me, but it was just me in the mirror."

"You screamed at your own reflection?"

"I'm afraid so."

Tanya thought that was hilarious and even better than her sexy surprise and pulled me onto the bed.

CARRIE GOT HER MONEY'S WORTH when I called to tell her about my night at the "Riot House," as the Hyatt was soon to be known. Unbeknownst to either of us, Tanya had had an abortion that week, paid for by her lover, a French restaurateur in his forties who kept an apartment across from Beverly High for their assignations during her lunch hour.

"Yeah, Georges Reno," Carrie said impatiently. "He owns La Petite Coquette and supposedly delivered Marilyn Monroe her last meal. Go on."

I quickly did the math: if Marilyn died in '62 and Georges had the restaurant then, there is no way he was still in his forties.

"No, he's fiftyish for sure," confirmed Carrie. "Kinda gross but get on with it."

"So we go at it the minute I'm in the room."

"Good boy."

"And there is all this crazy noise in the hallway from the groupies, with doors slamming and bottles breaking, and while I'm banging her, she starts yelling at the top of her lungs, *Burst me! Burst me!*"

"What the fuck does that mean?"

"Well, I thought it would be rude to ask in that moment, maybe it's what she says to old guys, but later she told me she just had an abortion and the doctor said not to have sex for at least a week or she might hemorrhage and die."

"You could have killed her."

"Yes, and you paid for it."

"I don't know what I got you into. This could be bad. Maybe you guys should take a break."

"Too late for that. I'm crazy about her!"

BY THE TIME I GOT OFF Interstate 10 after my hitchhike home, Tanya had dumped the French lech and we were now officially a couple. Georges took it well and even made sure we got a prime booth at his La Petite Coquette during my lunch break from Williams-Sonoma, a kitchenware store where I worked as a shipping clerk. An early sign that I was in over my head was when, in the brief time it took to go to the restroom, I returned to our booth to find Jack Nicholson, Roman Polanski, and Warren Beatty seated around my girlfriend like three wolves sniffing a baby lamb. None of the men made room for me, so I had to squeeze a cheek onto the edge of the booth and hold the table to keep from falling off. They first looked at me with a "Can I help you?" expression until Tanya said, "This is *my friend*, Griffin."

Deeming me no threat, they continued with their flirting and, when they finally left, Jack even picked up the check.

"Why did you introduce me as 'your friend'?" I asked on the walk back to Williams-Sonoma.

"Well, if I'm going to be a movie star, it's important that I not seem attached to anyone."

"Why do you always say you want to be a movie star instead of an actress?"

"Anybody can be an actress. Don't you want to be a movie star?"

"No, I want to be an actor and maybe not even do movies. I told you, I want to go to New York and work in the theater."

"That's ridiculous," she said, and we dropped the subject.

At night, I was taking acting classes from Charles Conrad, whom my father suggested because he once hired him years earlier to coach Gardner McKay, the star of *Adventures in Paradise*. Dad had discovered him, literally in a coffee shop, and persuaded him to play the lead even though he had no acting experience or even interest in acting.

Charles Conrad was highly thought of among working actors, though his lack of respect for the written word was suspicious. His technique was to have the students bring in scenes without studying them beforehand, and when performing, look down at the line and "throw it out with whatever you are feeling at the moment." So even though Tennessee Williams wrote that Stanley is crying out to Stella to forgive him, if Brando wasn't feeling it, he might "throw out" the name Stella as if he'd just asked a bartender for a beer.

One night I brought in a scene from *Franny and Zooey* in which Zooey is talking his sister down from a spiritual crisis. I painstakingly typed two copies of the novel and brought it to class, not knowing who my scene partner would be, because according to the Conrad method, finding out whom you will work with at the last second keeps an actor from committing the sin of preparation.

Class started late because a new student would be joining us and Charles wanted to wait until she arrived, which sent titters of anticipation as to who could be so important to our master. I had my money on Jane Fonda, which was far-fetched, but if not her, maybe Ellen Burstyn. The new student finally arrived, and Charles stood to greet her. The woman had frizzy hair and clear aviator glasses and was braless in a fishnet shirt, its stitching so wide a tuna could easily slip through it. *Deep Throat* had been out for a year but was still the talk of the town, and we recognized that our mystery student was the porn star Linda Lovelace. I heard the guy sitting next to me, who had once guest starred in *Little House on the Prairie*, mutter, "What the fuck?" Her presence and our teacher's obsequiousness brought down the class morale in a collective sigh.

After watching a few scenes, Charles looked around the room to choose his next couple. Our eyes met.

"Griffin, how about you and Linda show us what you brought in?"

"Oh, ummm," I hemmed, "I'm not sure—"

"What have you got?"

"*Franny and Zooey*, it's not really a movie or TV show."

"You'll play brother and sister. Perfect."

We got to the stage and sat across from each other at a card table, and I handed her the pages that had taken me so long to type. I looked at Linda's tits and then down at my first line and "threw it out."

We stumbled through the scene, Linda's character wondering

about God's purpose, and me watching my sister's nipples poke through her fishnet shirt. If I had any doubts that my calling was to move to New York to do theater, they were put to rest that night.

When class ended, Linda caught up to thank me for my patience with her inexperience and express how nervous she was.

"I never read the book I was talking about, the *Pilgrim* whatever, so I was just speaking gobbledygook. I never even read *Franny and Zooey.*"

She pronounced it "Zoo-y," but I didn't correct her. In fact, the more we talked, the more she charmed me, and if I didn't think about a cock in her mouth, it was like talking to a kid fresh off the bus from her little farm in the Midwest. She asked me if I would walk her to her car to meet her boyfriend.

A few hundred yards up Ventura Boulevard stood a chauffeur in jodhpurs, high leather boots, and a cap, as if he were waiting to drive Gloria Swanson to the Paramount lot. He stood sentry next to a long black Bentley.

"Hey, Eddie," Linda said sweetly as Eddie opened the Bentley's door with pomp and majesty.

"Sammy," she said to someone sitting in the back seat, "come out. I want you to meet my scene partner."

"I'd love to, baby," I heard from inside the car, and out stepped Sammy Davis Jr.

He gave me a glorious smile and held out his palm, which I knew meant "gimme some skin" instead of a high five.

"Griffin was so sweet to me, and, Sammy, I was just god-awful."

"I find that hard to believe, pumpkin." And then to me: "Thank you for looking after my lady, my young man."

I stopped going to Conrad's class and later heard from the *Little House on the Prairie* guy that Linda never went back either.

One Saturday, Tanya and I got into a fight on the 405 about who loved whom more. We yelled endearments at the top of our lungs proving who was more willing to die for the other, and if someone who didn't speak English had been sitting in the back seat, they would have thought we hated each other.

"If you love me so much, why won't you marry me?" screamed Tanya.

"I didn't know that is something you wanted!"

"You're a coward."

"Fuck you, of course I'll marry you."

"Then drive to Tijuana and we'll do it right now."

I hit the gas.

According to the billboards of marriage brokers that hovered over streets clogged with food carts and mangy-looking dogs, it cost two hundred pesos to get a license. We chose an office at random and gave a guy sitting behind a desk ten American dollars. There was no "do you take this" ceremony, we just signed a piece of paper like we were in a car dealership. The drive home was very lovey-dovey, with lots of promises of what we would do to each other when we got back to LA.

The phone was ringing when I entered the house on Walden, and I got it just in time. It was my father.

"Hey, kiddo," he said. "Just checking in. What's new with you?"

"Oh, not much," I lied.

"Well, I gotta tell you something. I just came back from the most beautiful wedding. The groom was a son of a couple I've known since we lived in New York. It was a class act. Their son was older than you, but when your time comes, that's the kind of wedding I want to give you."

Why is he telling me this? raged in my eardrums as he continued to talk about the flower arrangements and the receiving line to meet the wedding party, and how beautiful the bride was. Tanya and I had sworn on the drive home that we would tell no one, that it would be our sexy secret that would bond us forever, but the karma of him returning from a real wedding was so great that I couldn't stop myself from telling him that I had been married as well, just three hours earlier.

"Well, I'm afraid it's a little late for that now, Dad," I said.

"What do you mean?"

"Tanya and I just got married in Tijuana."

There was the longest pause.

"I can't tell if you are fucking with me or not," he finally said.

"Nope. We just got back."

"I'm coming over. Get your mother."

They were devastated, angry, hurt, confused. Neither landed on the same emotion at the same time, so while Mom cried, Dad yelled, and then they traded passions. By the time I told them that Tanya and I were going to get an apartment together, they were too spent to protest. We found a place off Wilshire Boulevard near the downtown district a couple weeks later.

Tanya cooked our first meal in our new apartment and brought it to a table we made of cardboard packing boxes. It was a frozen London broil Swanson dinner with scalloped potatoes and string beans. As she emptied the foil container onto my paper plate, I cheered her accomplishment as if she'd graduated from Le Cordon Bleu. We were children playing house, living out the lives of families we grew up watching on television, like *Leave It to Beaver* and *Father Knows Best*, who lived in homes that could not have been more different from our own. We'd each grown up too fast, though in our minds not fast enough, and now wanted to put our youth behind us to be the adults our troubled parents pretended to be. Tanya and I were raised in the land of make-believe, so make-believe dinners for a make-believe marriage made all the sense in the world to us.

Maybe because of our similar upbringings and very different personalities, we rarely talked about our parents. I knew very little about her mother other than that she tooled around town in a convertible Mercedes 350SL, the car of choice for hot Beverly Hills housewives, and that her movie mogul father was having an affair with a friend of my mother's, which I wisely never mentioned. Unlike my parents, they had very little reaction when Tanya became a child bride, but if they knew her previous boyfriends were men their age, there wasn't much more their daughter could do that would still surprise them.

I never knew my mother to hate anyone until she met Tanya, but my father, while not supporting the marriage, eventually warmed to my bride and found her thirst for fame both amusing and familiar. Tanya was a salesgirl at a high-end tchotchke store on Rodeo Drive, and when we got off work, we would often stop by Dad's apartment for a drink before heading home.

His front door was always unlocked. One time, we let ourselves in to see a shirtless young man break from a startled embrace with my father and then scurry up the stairs. (Telling Tanya my father was gay was among the many things I failed to mention about my family.)

"Kiddo! Great to see you! Wanna beer?" Dad said with forced joviality in a voice about six octaves higher than usual.

He poured a can of Coors with a trembling hand as Shirtless came downstairs, now fully clothed. Dad introduced Shirtless as his "valet," whom he had just recently hired. Tanya and Shirtless managed to keep straight faces. (Keeping a straight face must be the first thing they teach you in Valet School.) I know Dad didn't have a lot of time to think his story through, but he lost all credibility when he offered his new valet a drink and then poured two stiff ones for each of them.

Tanya and I walked in silence back to my car. Every now and then, I'd sneak a look her way. She seemed deep in thought, though not thinking deep thoughts but something she found amusing.

"What?" I finally said.

"What-what?" she answered in mock innocence, making no effort to hide her grin.

"What is it that is so funny?"

"Oh, I was just thinking about your father and you."

"What about it?" I said to her catbird smile, feeling I was being toyed with.

"Wellllll, if your Dad sucks cock, I just wonder if that means you probably will as well."

"That is such a fucked-up thing to say."

My puny outrage sent her into a fit of giggles. If I let myself get angrier, I might appear defensive and elicit a "methinks thou doth protest too much" comment, not that Tanya went around quoting Shakespeare.

The truth was, for some time I had wondered whether being gay might be hereditary, and even though I was attracted to women and couldn't recall ever being aroused by a man, I worried there might be a dormant "gay gene" that kicks in without warning, and that one morning I'd wake wanting to get it on with dudes.

This might have been the glam seventies, when "Ziggy Stardust" played in rotation on the radio, but I still associated being gay with shame, an outlook I probably *did* inherit from a closeted father who took his son to see *The Boys in the Band.*

What scared me was how afraid I was of being gay. In time, my daughter would have read *I Have Two Mommies, I Have Two Daddies* in nursery school and have friends who loved and supported their trans children, but in those days there was prejudice, especially among casting directors and producers who had control over my nonexistent acting career. If word were to get out, I'd be forever cast as Liza Minnelli's best friend, wearing an ascot and delivering wisecracks holding a martini. They'd probably have me calling her "Ducks!" I'd never even touched a dude and the Gay Inheritance Theory had me terrified.

I've always believed that when something scares me, it's important to confront the fear to find out why. I remembered that, during our awkward drop by, when Dad introduced his valet, he said his name was Torey. He added that he was going out of town for a few days and Torey would be staying in his apartment. Anyone who's seen a Preston Sturges movie knows the valet always travels with his squire, but Torey must have been told to remain housebound to iron Dad's Turnbull & Asser shirts and polish the silver till his master's return.

When I was sure Dad was out of town, and Tanya was in Palm Springs, I took the first step to confronting my fear by knocking on an apartment door that used to be unlocked.

Torey was understandably surprised.

"Hey, Torey," I began my prepared statement, "sorry to bother you, but I think I left a book here last time, and ummm, just want to see if it's here. So I can take it. Home. Where I live."

"Well, come in. What's the name of the book?"

I was ready for this. The book had to land somewhere between Proust and *The Winds of War.*

"*Fear and Loathing in Las Vegas.*"

"Hmmm, I haven't seen it around, but have a look."

He knew I was full of shit, but I went through the charade of looking for it anyway.

"I was just about to make a vodka tonic, have any interest?"

This was the time to get out or stay, and the choice sort of scared me. So bring it on.

"Sure," I said, "why not."

Torey had recently arrived in LA to be an actor. He met my father when he came to see a production of *The Boys in the Band* at a sixty-seat theater in the Valley. Torey played, fittingly enough, a male prostitute hired as a gift for the birthday boy. The cast made a big fuss that the producer of the movie was in the audience and they all got to meet him, but Torey was the only one the producer asked out for coffee.

"And we went to a nearby Denny's, and after a while, he offered me the job."

"What job?" I asked.

"You know, to be his valet."

"Right."

The subtext of mocking our talk of fake jobs and missing books was exhausting, so Torey fixed us another vodka tonic.

He placed the drink on the coffee table and turned to face me, making sure we had eye contact before speaking.

"Griffin, can I ask you something?"

Okay, here it comes. Now he's going to hit on you, so what are you going to do when he does? This is what you came here for, isn't it?

"Yeah, sure," I said.

"You want to drop some acid?"

TOREY FOUND A CANDELABRA and placed it on the coffee table just when the sun was setting and the acid had kicked in. He was surprisingly funny, and when tripping, we were both hilarious. We walked around the block doing a shtick in "Iranian" accents we never knew we had, making flowery pronouncements to a Persian king ("Oh King of Kings, Most Imperial Highness"), and raced back to the apartment when we hallucinated angry mullahs pursuing us. We were new friends, tripping and laughing our asses off, who talked about everything but the pretense that had brought us together.

When the dawn light crept into the living room, Torey blew out the last surviving candle and gave up scraping away mounds of wax that had dripped on the coffee table. No longer tripping, we were silent as he drew the blinds, trashed wine bottles, emptied ashtrays, and did other small tasks until there was nothing left to do but turn in for bed. The subtext was back. Torey stood at the bottom of the stairs, the stairs where I'd first seen him, and said, "I know you are curious who you are, Griffin, and though I might be able to answer that, I doubt you will believe me until you find out for yourself. So I'm going to go upstairs. You want to join, that's great, if not, tonight was really fun, and safe drive home."

I stayed seated in my chair for a good five minutes, though I already knew what I was going to do.

With the solemn dignity of Sydney Carton ascending the guillotine in *A Tale of Two Cities*, I climbed the staircase with purpose, step by step, to sleep with a guy for the first time. *It is a far, far better thing that I do, than I have ever done.*

Torey kicked me out of bed, not unkindly, after I'd let him do stuff to me and I'd done stuff to him, all to no great effect.

"I hate to break this to you, Griffin," Torey said as I put on my pants. "I don't think you've got what it takes to be a homo."

"Well, nobody's perfect," I said, quoting the last line of *Some Like It Hot*, a reference Torey actually got.

Two weeks later, I picked up Dad at his apartment for an early dinner. We hadn't seen each other since Tanya and I walked in on Torey scurrying up the stairs, and this time he seemed relaxed. As he looked for his wallet and keys, I asked, with a frozen pad of butter in my mouth, "Hey, where is that guy, your valet?"

"Oh, you mean Torey? I had to let him go. I can't afford a valet. What was I thinking?"

THIS MAY COME as a huge surprise, but within six months, Tanya and I wanted to divorce. Some nights she wouldn't come home, and once I was so bereft I put my fist through a window. There was blood all over the bed and the floor, but when she came home in the morning, she didn't notice. When she moved out, I got rid of the apartment and returned home.

My parents hired a divorce attorney they got out of the phone book, but Tanya's dad got a guy I would later recognize sitting behind Oliver North at the Iran-Contra hearings.

He told the judge with a straight face that his client was seeking half my yearly salary as a shipping clerk at Williams-Sonoma, which at $2.50 an hour over twelve months came to $2,600.

Tanya was not present, so the judge looked at Iran-Contra, then at me sitting at the table with Yellow Pages, and took his time to collect his thoughts.

"You know," he began, "I've sat on this bench for thirty years, and in all that time, I have never had more ridiculous people in my courtroom. You will not get a penny from this boy. Divorce granted."

IN THE FALL OF 1974, my move to New York was back on track when I was accepted to the Neighborhood Playhouse. Part of their syllabus was to read *The Fervent Years* by Harold Clurman, about the formation of the Group Theatre. The book described the fervent brilliance of artists like Clifford Odets, Elia Kazan, and Sanford Meisner, founder of the playhouse and possibly one of my future teachers. I was in the midst of wondering if I might ever be part of an ensemble of gifted actors and playwrights, when my brother reminded me of our family meeting.

Dominique, Alex, and I sat in the breakfast nook waiting impatiently for our mother to come downstairs. She had summoned us to be at this place, at this time, because she had "something important to share." Mom had pointedly asked us not to have any sleepovers that night, which we took as a bad omen. There was no scenario in our minds in which this news would be good.

Our mother was not one to make pronouncements, and as a single parent, she ran a pretty loose ship. We ate dinner whenever we wanted, usually rice and beans left warm in the oven, on TV trays in front of the latest *Million Dollar Movie.*

Our friends adored Mom and the easygoing vibe in our home, and they came and went at all hours. Charlie had become such a constant fixture that he even lived in my room while I was away at school. He was handy around the house, and Mom made good use of him, fixing her dishwasher or checking out the rattle in the Cougar, now on its last legs.

Dominique's and Alex's besties were Lisa and Melinda Bittan, who'd moved a few years earlier into the Spanish colonial next door. They arrived the day after Mom came home from the hospital, after having a seizure the doctors could never diagnose. She'd experienced problems with her eyesight, loss of feeling in her hands, and numerous other health scares since I'd been born, so a hospital stay was not uncommon. The day she'd been discharged, Dad took us to dinner to let Mom rest, and on our way home, we saw an ambulance with its cherry top spinning in front of our house. Everyone had the same thought, and Dad gunned the Merc down the block. When we arrived, we saw that the ambulance was actually in front of the home of our new next-door neighbors, Lisa and Melinda. It was not our mother in distress, but the mother of the two little girls who had died of a stroke that night. When my father said, "Thank God it wasn't Lenny," we didn't agree out loud but felt shame for even thinking the same thing.

Lisa and Melinda's father was a difficult man whose own grief overwhelmed his household and alienated his daughters. Like Charlie, they adopted my mother as their own and pretty much moved in as siblings in residence.

The first thing we noticed when Mom arrived at the breakfast nook was that she needed a cane to get down the stairs. No one said a word as Alex pulled out her chair so she could join us at the table.

"You're probably wondering what this is about," she said, holding up an oak cane with a pearl handle.

"I've waited to tell you until I had to, and now that I need assistance walking, that time is now. I found out a year ago that I have a disease called multiple sclerosis. It attacks the central nervous system and damages something called the myelin sheath that insulates the nerves and might eventually cause me not to be able to walk. But I'm not saying that will happen, because each case is different and many times the disease goes into remission and won't cause any more problems other than walking with a cane. But I want you kids to know everything I know, so if you have any questions, now is the time to ask."

No one knew where to start. As the self-appointed head of

the household, I put on a brave face and tried to think of something intelligent to ask.

"Is it contagious?" I heard myself say.

"You selfish fucking asshole!" Alex roared. "This isn't about you, it's about Mom."

"No, Alex, that is a fair question. I don't know that it had to be the first one, but since you ask, I'm relieved to say it is most definitely not contagious."

We followed up with worst-case scenarios about how bad it might get, which Mom fielded in calm assurance. I listened for fear in her voice, but there was none. I waited for a complaint, a show of outrage, a fist shake to the heavens, self-pity of *any* kind, but she never strayed from the plot, and described the stages of her possible doom as if she were recalling scenes from a movie—a language we were familiar with from our nights on her bed, watching black-and-white films she'd had seen a million times before.

"You remember that movie we watched, *Suddenly, Last Summer*?" Mom asked in a strange turn of subject.

"The one where Katharine Hepburn's son was eaten by little Mexican boys?" Alex asked, a touch confused.

"The only movie Montgomery Clift sucked in," I offered.

"Everybody was so creepy," said Dominique.

"True," Mom said thoughtfully, "but I liked the line 'There is a word for a widower, but no name for a mother who lost a child.'" Mom went somewhere inside herself for a moment, but soon came back.

"Why are we talking about this stupid movie?" Dominique asked.

"Because tomorrow I'm having a motorized chair installed on the staircase like the one Katharine Hepburn had in the movie."

"Oh, cool," we all said in unison.

"No, not cool. Nothing about my motorized chair is cool, nor is it a toy to be played with. I will need it to get around this house, and I'm telling you kids to *stay off it.*"

We murmured in agreement but managed to break it the first week. The initial transgression might have been my imitation of Robert Redford riding a chairlift in *Downhill Racer*, or Alex pretending he was Dante descending into hell, but Dominique's impression of Katharine Hepburn gliding down the staircase to meet Monty Clift was definitely worth getting yelled at.

A year later, Mom needed a wheelchair, and it became clear that living in a two-story house was impractical, so 714 Walden, with its motorized stairs, was put on the market and quickly sold. Mom bought a bite-size version of our house on Walden, right down to its Georgian style and black shutters.

Dominique was crushed to leave the only home she'd ever known, and she hired a professional photographer to take *House & Garden*–style pictures before the movers could cart her memories away.

Moving is often mentioned as a traumatic event, up there with death and divorce, and I worried what effect the stress of leaving Walden might have on Mom. What I didn't expect was how unhinged it made me feel to see my childhood home when it was left bare by the moving company. The weight of our grand piano, which had been in the living room since the day we moved in, had left grooves in the hardwood floor, evidence that the past had begun. I saw an armoire wrapped in blankets, the last piece to be put in the truck, and opened one of its drawers. Inside was a mound of letters I'd written my mother when I was at Fay. Eager to remember what I was like as a boy, I grabbed the first envelope off the pile and was surprised to see it had not been opened, then downright confounded when it was clear many of the others hadn't been either. I tore into one and was chilled to see that all that I'd written were *x*'s and *y*'s. Every envelope I ripped open were pages with the same letters but no actual words. They looked like ransom notes from an illiterate kidnapper. It took a moment to recall that when I was at Fay, this was how I filled out my mandatory letters to Mom, twice a week for three years. The anger I channeled into a pen that carved all those *x*'s and *y*'s came roaring back, and I wondered why these troubling letters had gone unmentioned. Grabbing as many envelopes as I could hold, I brought them back to the new house on Crescent Drive.

Mom was reclined in a hospital bed smoking a filtered True cigarette from her last carton.

I dropped a handful of the letters on her lap and waited for a reaction.

"What's this?" she asked, her attention torn between me and the local news on television.

"It's a bunch of letters I wrote you when I was at Fay," I said casually. "You want to read one?"

I handed her a page and she looked at it, first perplexed, then amused.

"Oh yes," she said, a smile forming on her face. "You were an odd one."

Not satisfied with her response, I pressed further.

"Well, what did you think when you opened my letters, or stopped opening them? Did you find it at all disturbing?"

Mom thought about it for a while, ignoring the edge in my voice, and replied, "I just thought you didn't have much to say."

Her detachment from my feelings was an early symptom of MS, one that over the coming years would extend to her friends, making communication so impossible they stopped coming by. But at that moment, she at least still had a sense of humor, and even though I was a little hurt, I laughed at her droll comment and never mentioned my letters again.

DOMINIQUE FOLLOWED OUR MOTHER to the new house on Crescent Drive, only eight blocks from Walden, and settled into a guest cottage in the back. One of the first things she did was ask her best friend, an artist named Norman Carby, to paint a mural of Henri Rousseau's *Exotic Landscape* over a blank wall at the rear of the house.

She joined an acting class and started a tradition called the Friday Afternoon Club, or FAC. At the end of every Friday, her friends from class, and of course Lisa, Melinda, and Charlie, would gather in the backyard to drink and party well into the night. George Clooney and Miguel Ferrer, also just breaking into acting, and Tim Hutton, having just won an Oscar for *Ordinary People*, were among the FAC members in good standing. Dominique would wheel Mom out to join the fun until the young people grew too rowdy for her taste, and then return her to bed as everyone wished her good night and thanked her for the wine she'd kicked in for.

They were a good team, Dominique and Mom, and soon life at the little house took on the easygoing vibe of its predecessor on Walden, where friends came and went, and Charlie, Melinda, and Lisa were still always around. Though Mom was now confined to a wheelchair, her spirits were better than ever. It was as if life delivered her a great blast of good fortune right up to the moment when it would all be ripped away.

Sixteen

I can remember now, with a clarity that makes the nerves on the back of my neck constrict, when New York began for me," wrote my aunt Joan in her essay "Goodbye to All That."

New York began for me as an acting student at the Neighborhood Playhouse, and I kicked it off by rewriting my past. Still smarting with the shame of being a high school dropout, I told my classmates I'd gone to Colorado College for three years, and to back up that lie, said I was twenty years old instead of my truthful age of nineteen. At least I came clean about not meeting the Kennedys.

Emotionally, I was still the little con artist I learned to be at Fay, always looking for the angle to do the least amount of work and get away with as much shit as possible. The playhouse was a full-time school with a variety of classes designed to give an actor all the tools needed to perform the classics onstage. Some of the courses interested me more than others: the scene work and improv classes were inspiring, but I thought it was hilarious to wear a ballet belt that made me look like an anorexic sumo wrestler doing Martha Graham. I clowned around so mercilessly that I made the dance teacher, an elderly lady who was actually in Ms. Graham's company, burst into tears and beg me to take my work seriously. There was also something to be learned called the "diphthong technique," where for an hour a day, five days a week, we would curl our tongues to make guttural sounds like inmates in the Marquis de Sade's insane asylum. I eventually deemed both classes unnecessary for my bright future and skipped them altogether.

ONE MORNING, I slipped into an A&P supermarket across the street from the playhouse to find something to snack on. I roamed the aisles of the almost empty market, humming along to a Muzak cover of "Can't Buy Me Love" while toying with the idea of stealing something, only because it looked so easy. I wasn't a kleptomaniac, even though I had fourteen dollars in my wallet, but considered myself more of an Abbie Hoffman acolyte who thought every opportunity to "stick it to the Man" should be acted on. I wore an oversize parka from an army surplus store, with huge pockets that beckoned to be filled with tins of sardines, cocktail olives, and saltines.

A tantalizing little can with a squeeze top labeled CHEEZ WHIZ was my undoing. As I pulled it off the shelf, a security guard rushed toward me, and I tried to make a break for it.

He tackled me before I reached the exit, and we knocked down a display of canned peas stacked like a pyramid. The cashiers shrieked in alarm, and I could not get over my stupidity when the guard yanked my wrists behind my back and slapped me in handcuffs. He then led me to a loading dock at the back of the market, where workers were hauling crates off a truck. He pushed me against a wall and told them to watch me while he called the cops.

When he was gone, one of the workers said, "Make a run for it. We ain't going to stop you. Take this shit with you if you want."

He dropped a huge carton of paper towels at my feet, which got a big laugh, prompting the others to pull boxes off the truck saying, "Take this too. Take all this shit." They doubled over at their own jokes.

The guys wouldn't have lifted a finger if I'd bolted, and I could have figured out how to get the cuffs off later, but the truth was, I wanted to know what it was like to be arrested. Quite possibly I thought the escapade would come in handy someday for an acting role.

As it happened, the police arrived at such breakneck speed that even if I had tried to flee, they would have caught me anyway.

The two officers who took me to the station had parked right in front of the Neighborhood Playhouse. Students who were still filing in, or grabbing a last-minute smoke, gawked in wonder as I was loaded, handcuffed, into the back of the squad car.

"That kid is in my diphthong class," I heard before the door was slammed shut.

After being booked at the Midtown station, I rode in an actual paddy wagon down to the Tombs, the jail where those arrested awaited their arraignment. Once I was processed, my first stop through a catacomb of hallways was a large holding cell with about thirty men either pacing or sprawled out on the few benches provided. An overflowed porcelain toilet, without even a seat, discouraged sphincters and bladders from getting any bright ideas. I was a curiosity in my big parka, which some guy complimented, without a trace of menace, remarking how nice and warm it looked.

I was soon asked, against all con etiquette, what I was in for—which in my world is like asking a lady her age—but as I was clearly a prison outlier, it was a fair question. The cell quieted (a rare moment in this den of noise) when I told them I was an acting student who took a few things from the A&P before my class started.

"Like what?" asked a voice from the back of the cell.

I went through the list, but when I got to Cheez Whiz, the entire cell roared with laughter.

"You should be called the Cheez Whiz Kid," said a guy dressed like Super Fly. An inmate got up from one of the benches and called out, "Hey, Cheez Whiz, rest your feet, you're going to be here awhile."

Over the next ten hours, my nickname followed me from one holding cell to another, each one smaller than the next, drawing me closer to what had now become night court, for my arraignment. Every time I was placed in a new cell, an inmate I'd never seen before would say, "You must be the Cheez Whiz Kid."

It was all fun and games until the hour reached four in the morning and we were told that whomever the judge didn't get to would be transferred to Rikers Island. That place scared the shit out of me, but I was at the last stop, just outside the courtroom, so I prayed His Honor might see me next.

The final holding cell was the smallest yet, boxed on all four sides with wire mesh that made it perfect for cage wrestling. I shared this cramped space with two Black kids who seemed even younger than me. The boys were engrossed in a late edition of the *New York Post*, whose front page they were on for allegedly stabbing a Columbia student earlier in the day. Their disbelief and wonder was the same as anyone's seeing his picture in the paper for the first time.

An Irish cop with an accent as thick as a leprechaun's stood behind the cage and announced, "The judge is turning in for the night and will take only one of you. Whoever is the youngest, up you go. The rest of you, off to Rikers."

The three of us leapt to our feet yelling, "I'm the youngest, I'm the youngest!" The papers identified the kids as a year younger than me, so one of them should rightfully have been chosen. The irony that I made my friends at the playhouse believe I was in my twenties, and now begged to be recognized as a helpless teenager, was not lost on me. To no one's surprise, Lucky Charms chose the white boy in the big parka who hadn't allegedly killed anyone that day. In a way, New York really "began for me" that night, when I realized the color of my skin put me at the front of the line whether I deserved it or not.

The enormous wood-paneled courtroom was empty, save for the judge, the two arresting officers, and a tired A&P security guard who wished he'd never met me and just wanted to go home. I kind of felt sorry for him when the judge refused to press charges and chewed him out for wasting the court's time.

"This city is broke and I barely have enough time to sentence rapists and muggers, and you bring me this shit!" he bellowed.

I was in bed by five a.m. and strapped in my ballet belt at seven thirty, sharing my adventure with a rapt audience who called me the Cheez Whiz Kid for the rest of the year.

THE NEIGHBORHOOD PLAYHOUSE was a two-year course, but the second year was only for students who'd been invited back. My poor attendance to classes I considered unworthy of my time or delusional talent meant there would be no second year for me. I was humiliated and angry at myself for being so arrogant. My behavior toward my dance teacher, the one I had brought to tears, filled me with shame. I had much to learn from a woman who had danced with Martha Graham to original compositions by Aaron Copland, and I blew it.

Years later, I came across a quote of Martha Graham to Agnes de Mille that is still tacked on the corkboard in my office. I read it for inspiration and self-assurance, and as penance should I miss another opportunity to learn from someone:

> There is a vitality, a life force, an energy, a quickening that is translated through you into action, and because there is only one of you in all of time, this expression is unique. And if you block it, it will never exist through any other medium and it will be lost.

I HAD HOPED TO SPEND my second year at the playhouse living off the allowance my mother would give me for rent only if I was still in school. Now that I had been basically expelled from yet another one, I paid my way waiting tables at a restaurant called Beefsteak Charlie's. During the day I was free to go on open casting calls for jobs I never seemed to get. They were often "cold readings," where the actor is handed a script minutes before he has to deliver lines fresh off the page to the director. My dyslexia plagued these auditions, and when I tried to read out loud, the words jumbled before my eyes, throwing off my pace and butchering the writer's prose.

I lived in a studio apartment on East Twelfth, a hooker-infested street in the East Village, though I don't mean "infested" in a bad way, more in a charming Damon Runyon kind of way. As I passed through their parade, I thought of myself as the boxer from the eponymous Simon and Garfunkel song, and when these ladies of the night would ask, "Hey, sugar, wanna party?" I'd hum to myself, *"But I get no offers, just a come-on from the whores on Seventh Avenue."*

One night, in exasperation at being asked the same question from the same hooker every time I came home from work, I said, "Listen, you don't have to keep asking if I want to party, because I'm a broke, out-of-work actor who lives on tips from waiting tables."

She had a sundial of an Afro, which I suspect was a wig, and wore boots that climbed to the cuffs of her hot pants. Even if I could have paid her, my hour would have been spent watching her unlace those boots.

"Okay, kid, then move along. You're holding up my business."

"No, what I'm saying is that even though I can't pay you, you're pretty much my neighbor who you see every night, so instead of asking if I want to party, just say, 'Hey, Griffin, good evening,' or 'How you doing,' or something."

"Who's Griffin?"

"Me, that's my name. What's yours?"

"Why do you want to know if you're not going to pay me?"

"Because it would be really cool if you girls knew my name, and maybe then we'd high-five or something on my way home."

"That's going to cost you."

"Really, jeez, then fuck it. I was just being neighborly," I said as I started to sulk away.

"No, I'm kidding, Griffin. Stupid name by the way. I'm Ramona, heavy on the Moan."

"Nice to meet you."

She lifted her hand in the air and we slapped a high five. I've never felt more Runyonesque.

The next night, I passed Ramona on the street and readied my palm to rise.

"Hey, Ramona," I said.

"Hey, sugar, wanna party?"

AFTER A YEAR OF WAITING TABLES, going to open casting calls, and trying in vain to even meet an agent, I began to worry that I'd never, never get a job in show business. I failed to find it comforting when Evan, a wildly effeminate actor who shared my shift at Beefsteak Charlie's, told me to relax, that he'd been a waiter for five years and so far on the work front, "Not a peep, nada."

Carrie's and my communication had been constant late-night calls to me from Los Angeles and reverse-the-charges calls from me to her. Every sad-sack story I told her about my Manhattan misadventures only made her want to move there more, so she finally relented to her mother's urging to join the chorus of a musical Debbie was starring in on Broadway called *Irene*. They lived in a Midtown hotel with twenty-four-hour room service that sustained me on a daily basis.

At the Minskoff Theatre, I soon became a fixture, or a "stage-door Johnny," as Carrie said. I was always greeted with a hearty whisper of "how they hanging" by stagehands in the rafters above, who held fistfuls of fake snow to float onto the cast below, on my way to the chorus girls' dressing room.

Over the speaker box, Debbie was giving it her all, singing "I'm Always Chasing Rainbows," while I sang along, by then knowing every word, breath, and inflection. The chorus had two more numbers until the finale, so I was free to snoop through the dancers' handbags while they waited in the wings for their cue. I justified this nosiness by telling myself the job of an actor is to be curious about everything. (I obviously hadn't learned a thing from my shoplifting debacle.) The first handbag I rifled through belonged to Gwen, a desperately needy hoofer who had told me in the strictest confidence that she hated Carrie's guts because Carrie never had to work for anything in her life. I came across a pair of rolled-up Danskin tights with a skid mark on them I could have done without seeing, a copy of a Shaw play she'd told me she'd blown an audition for, and an industrial-strength can of spermicide, which I was all too familiar with.

Gwen and I had just had what Carrie referred to as "a fucking accident." That is, when you go to bed with someone against your better judgment, but the combination of liquor and boredom is in such alignment that you slip, fall, and fuck 'em. A fucking accident. Gwen had a drinking problem and was married to a man who secretly liked men, so she checked all the boxes. Just holding the can of spermicide brought on a sense memory of my penis being chemically singed by the wicked stuff the night before.

When I had called Carrie to tell her about my fucking accident, she said Gwen had already spilled the beans and shown her a pair of mittens she was knitting for me. I heaved a mighty sigh.

"By the way," Carrie said, "I think her husband found out about you two, and just so you know, he is kind of a powerful producer."

My gut clenched. "Oh my God" was all I could muster.

"Which is an amazing coincidence because one of his productions is that David Rabe play you want to be in." She listened to my labored breath. Then I heard her smile right through the phone.

"You little twat."

She roared at her own trick, as did I, in sheer relief.

"I could tell you were going to fuck her, though. You had that look."

"What look?"

"You know the one. Two words: Charles Boyer." I laughed, but being reminded of Alex kissing his own hand brought up unsettling feelings.

"And I don't think Gwen's husband is the one you should be worried about," Carrie continued. "She is crazy as a shithouse rat."

"I was starting to notice that."

"How?"

"Let's just say she has anger issues." There was nothing to be gained by describing Gwen toward the tail of the evening, her slurring from tequila and the Quaalude we'd split, oblivious to a cigarette singeing into her nightstand, chronicling in mind-numbing detail every professional slight she'd endured in the school of hard knocks, which Carrie "tragically" never attended, because she had been given a "free pass" all her life.

"Jesus, how pathetic," Carrie said when I told her anyway.

"She suspects you're a virgin."

"So do most people." I heard Carrie light a smoke off the burner of the kitchenette in the hotel suite she shared with Debbie.

"Did you tell her I am? I'll kill you if you did," she demanded.

"Are you crazy?"

Carrie had a boyfriend, a sweet English actor named Donald,

whom she'd been dating for the past few months. He was under the impression that when she was ready to give it up, he would be the one to take it. Donald had stepped into the same black hole as every man who had fallen hard for Carrie, and he did what every man before him had done: appoint me as vizier to advise how he might win her heart. I'd grown accustomed to watching these poor guys be drained of their confidence under her barrage of mixed signals, their late-night calls begging me to translate a cryptic postcard or a parting quip delivered after a furious make-out session. Of all her confused suitors, Donald was the one I liked the most, and I was rooting for him. I thought of myself as Tom Hagen to the Corleones, but in actuality, I was Iago to his Othello (as close as I would ever get to playing that part again, I feared). I couldn't bring myself to tell him that shortly into their courtship, Carrie had bestowed upon me the honor of relieving her of her hymen.

As fucked up as it sounds, there was a certain logic to Carrie's backstreet approach to getting herself deflowered. For years, I'd been walking her through the minutiae of every conceivable sexual act like an ordnance handler telling a housewife how to defuse a bomb. *Yes, it can be really scary but not if you know what you're doing.* Her more recent mentor was the gay choreographer from *Irene*, who'd filled her head with Hogarth visions of urine-soaked bars and collapsed rectums—so yes, sex for the first time might have seemed daunting to her. ("Rectum, damn near killed him!" was an all-purpose phrase she picked up from that conversation.)

Donald was going to be the one, Carrie told me positively, on a night I stayed over at her suite while her mom was out of town. I was half listening to her from the shower, not wanting to kill the buzz from real hot water blasting into my face, a luxury I'd been without since my landlord's battle with ConEd.

"Hey, fuckface!" Carrie yelled, stuffing the dirty clothes I'd brought for a free cleaning into the hotel's laundry bag. "Do you want the shirts on hangers or not? They're going to ask."

"Well, gee, I don't know." I affected a helpless, put-upon voice. "What would Jesus do?" (This was years before that catchphrase caught on, but you'll just have to take my word for it.)

A severed bloody hand, convincingly amputated from the wrist, flew into the shower and landed at my feet. The gruesome rubber prop was promotional swag given to Carrie by the publicist of *The Texas Chainsaw Massacre* and had become the star of an ongoing sight gag between us. I first laid eyes on it under my pillow one night, after Carrie had made my bed with a set of sheets she'd given me that she boasted had an extravagant thread count. I screamed like a little girl, but only for a moment, and then plotted my revenge. Soon after, the hand made its Broadway debut when I snuck into her dressing room and hid it in a Victorian purse she was to open, on cue, to powder her nose in time with the chorus dancing to "The Riviera Rage." Wish I could have asked how the show went, but according to our unspoken rule, we never mentioned the hand. Somehow, Carrie managed to get the bartender at Beefsteak Charlie's to hide it under the romaine at the salad bar during All-You-Can-Drink Sangria Night. I also got wind that she was tracking down any remaining Philip Morris dwarves to deliver it to me during an audition. Carrie now just chucking the hand into the shower was beneath both of us, but I decided to let it pass.

The hotel shower was outfitted with those little shampoo and conditioner bottles, and while I was working up a lather, I felt fingers touch my belly and slowly move down toward my groin.

The soap kept me from opening my eyes, but I was so surprisingly aroused that I'm not sure I would have looked anyway. I wasn't prepared to watch my best friend grope my joint, and was worried that my uninvited hard-on might cross the hazy boundary we maintained toward each other. It took a moment to realize the fingers that were touching me lacked a mobility most digits are known for, which I at first attributed to her understandable tentativeness. But when I finally wiped the soap from my eyes, I saw Carrie holding the amputated rubber hand that cradled my balls.

"You fucking freak!" I screamed as she ran from the bathroom, doubled over in hysterics.

"Griffin got turned on by a dead guy," she sang to the tune of a playground taunt. I looked down at the severed limb at my feet, palm up in mea culpa fashion, as if to say, "Hey, man, she made me do it."

I came out of the bathroom wrapped in a towel, not feeling entirely cleansed. Carrie was on her bed reading Knut Hamsun, and like our roving sight gag, my hard-on in the shower went unmentioned, but there was no denying a change had taken place. She looked different to me, or maybe I was just reminded of my impressions of when we first met. I felt a familiar rumble start to rise again beneath my towel, which I sensed was not going unnoticed. I sat beside her on the bed, took the book from her hands, and kissed her.

It all made sense in the moment, and we both understood that everything we were doing to each other under those covers would not alter our friendship one iota. It was ridiculously fun, and at times even funny, which was a revelation to someone who'd previously taken a more solemn approach to sex. I knew I was only the warm-up for Donald, but didn't mind the role one bit. I liked Donald—difficult though that might have been for him to believe had he seen me fumbling with a second condom—but I loved Carrie more.

Not only did my friendship with Carrie remain unfazed, but so did my relationship with Donald after they finally made love. He remained just as needy and insecure about her feelings toward him, and I never turned down his late-night invitations to watch him cry into his beer. He might not have been the first to pluck Carrie's rose, but he was the first of many of her boyfriends (and girlfriends of mine), to wrongly assume that the rules of a platonic relationship were so black-and-white.

I WAS SUMMONED by Carrie's mother to report to her dressing room at the Minskoff at the end of a Saturday matinee. Carrie wouldn't say what the meeting was about except that I was really "going to like it." For a moment I thought maybe Debbie was going to ask me to join the chorus of *Irene*, but she knew that I neither sang nor danced, and I knew she barely tolerated my impersonation of a musical comedy fan who often greeted her after the show with "Mzzzz Reynolds, you just *slayed* me tonight!"

Debbie came to regard me, if not as her son, then as her daughter's older brother. She was very protective of Carrie and thought nothing of calling to find out whether I thought a particular guy who was sending her flowers to the theater was bad news or not. I would sound concerned or reassuring depending on how I felt, but usually I didn't even know whom she was asking about.

People had been sending Carrie flowers for as long as I'd known her. Debbie would also offer me unsolicited advice about anything, from my career to my personal hygiene, and once gave me an enormous, gift-wrapped crystal from Zitomer's pharmacy. I thought it was a valuable uncut piece of jewelry and planned to fence it, until she explained it was an effective deodorant. She felt I needed it when last she caught a whiff of me after a shift at Beefsteak's.

"Darling, nobody likes BO when they are trying to eat."

"Are you kidding, Mom? People *love* it!" Carrie had said in my defense.

The night of her summons, I pushed my way through Debbie's fans waiting for autographs at the stage door. "She's expecting you," said Edie, the guard who kept the hordes back. I scaled the stairs two at a time, passing Gwen, who gave me a chilly nod. Debbie's wardrobe mistress greeted me with a can of beer as I pulled up a chair next to Debbie at her dressing mirror, where she was sitting in a robe and skullcap taking off her makeup with some kind of cream, presumably from Zitomer's. Carrie stood reading a filthy but funny telegram from Sir John Gielgud, taped to the wall with hundreds of other well-wishes. Debbie got right to it.

"So, Griffin. Carrie tells me you live in a slum."

"I did not put it that way, Mom."

"And that you've been robbed?"

"Only the first few months," I qualified. "It's tapered off now. My place now is really just more of a workshop for thieves learning the ropes."

"Well, that can't be good. Carrie, as you know, is hoping to move into an apartment of her own."

"I can't in good conscience suggest my neighborhood, if that is what you're asking."

"I have found a place, or I should say *we*," she said, nodding toward her daughter, "that is sort of perfect—except for one thing."

"Oh . . ."

"It is a wonderful building with a doorman, just off the park, but the only problem is there are two bedrooms, and Carrie wants to live alone. Which is out of the question." I looked to Carrie for an explanation, but she was engrossed in a telegram from Donald O'Connor as if she'd never seen it before.

"What *we* want to ask you, dear," Debbie continued, "is if you would consider leaving the glamour of your present home and moving in with Carrie."

"Where is it?"

"It's the Hotel des Artistes, on West Sixty-Seventh."

"I couldn't possibly live on the Upper West Side. I'm a Village guy. I'm built to live in a village."

"Told you, Mom. Should have taken the Bing and Bing on Hudson."

"Even if it was in the Village," I interjected, "I don't even have to look at the place to know I couldn't afford it. I can barely make rent right now, and my place is really cheap."

"I would hope so. It doesn't sound like it even has a door. You could pay whatever you are paying now if it makes you feel any better. Look, I know you want to do the whole bongo-playing Marlon Brando thing, but I'll tell you something. Marlon used to have a roommate, a dear man named Wally Cox, and I'll bet if Wally's mother offered to move them to a safer apartment, he would have leapt at the chance."

"We have no way of proving that, of course," offered Carrie. I could see that she was hoping I would go for this and that I wasn't falling in line as quickly as she'd expected. "This place is amazing, which of course you don't feel you deserve—even I don't think you deserve it—but the only way Mom is going to let me move out is if I get a roommate, and there is no one I want that to be more than you. Come on, it'll be fun."

West Sixty-Seventh Street was two blocks from Beefsteak Charlie's and a short walk to the Theater District should an audition ever occur in my lifetime. Plus, I had recently outrun a mugger on Avenue A, an episode I decided not to bring up just then.

"Can I bring my BO crystal?"

Carrie laughed and Debbie didn't pick up on the dig, oblivious that I might still be smarting from her crack about my aroma.

THE DES ARTISTES was a seventeen-story Gothic-style building completed in 1917. It was designed by artists who pooled their money to buy the lot on West Sixty-Seventh to create spaces with enormous windows to catch the southern exposure that would brighten their studios. Well, that was the case for every apartment but ours, which was a two-bedroom on the second floor, where the artists' maids were once housed, all with perfectly normal-size windows. Harry Crosby, a damaged World War I vet and Lost Generation poet, famously (more famous than his poems) carried out a suicide pact with his wife, Josephine, on the twelfth floor in 1929. Rudolph Valentino, Edna Ferber, and Mike Nichols had lived there, as well as the writer Fannie Hurst, who rented the penthouse while being secretly married to a Russian pianist residing in a penthouse across the street. Each would put a potted plant on his or her balcony to signal to the other which apartment they would sleep in that particular night. The artist Howard Chandler Christy, a resident known for his World War I recruitment posters, painted nymphs and satyrs frolicking in a lush forest on the walls of the building's restaurant. One of these fig-leaved satyrs was a then-struggling actor named Johnny Weissmuller, who would later land the role of Tarzan the Ape Man.

At Des Artistes, everyone always knew who Carrie was, but no one was ever quite sure about me, a pattern soon to haunt me throughout the coming years. The building staff called me Mr. Griffin and seemed to assume I was the rightful heir to a vast fortune enjoying my playboy years. Herman, the maître d' at Café des Artistes, always waived the four-month waiting list when I showed up for a table unannounced, not wanting to incur the wrath of my presumed antisemitic, Skull and Bones, dark Masonic family empire should my needs not be met. That might have been his fear at first, but over time he took care of me because I never talked down to him; he appreciated my inquiries about his family and my erudite ability to talk shop regarding table turnover and the pros and cons of pooling tips with the busboys. I can't begin to describe the expression on his face when he brought his family to Beefsteak Charlie's on Surf and Turf Night and I was their waiter. I introduced myself to his wife and told her how great she looked for someone who'd just had a gallstone removed, and congratulated his daughter on getting into Colgate, giving Herman a moment to catch his breath. To his credit, and my amazement, he still gave me a table—with the sly wink of someone who appreciates a good con as much as the next person.

The restaurant also had a bar where a natural phenomenon took place every evening at seven. Before ABC News moved into the building across the street on West Sixty-Seventh, their studio was in what was once an enormous ballroom behind the lobby of the Des Artistes. At six, stagehands pulled thick power cables from a purring generator parked out front and dragged them through the lobby to light up the broadcast of *ABC Evening News* with Harry Reasoner. In those days the network news went on at seven, and every night at six thirty, without fail, Harry Reasoner could be found at his usual stool at the bar at Des Artistes, sipping his first martini. The regulars at the bar knew better than to disturb his peace before he went live to recount global events, and pity the poor tourist who wandered over for an autograph, only to be roughly shooed away by Max, the ham-fisted bartender.

To see Mr. Reasoner order his second martini at six forty-five was a breathtaking exercise in grace and timing, and hands down the best show in town. When a large clock mounted on the wall behind him, which he never once looked at, read six fifty-two, the olives in Mr. Reasoner's second martini were still submerged in gin. Those of us around the bar, all pretending not to notice this choreography, split our looks between the clock, now reading six fifty-four, the martini glass, and the Great Man himself. At six fifty-seven, Mr. Reasoner drained his cocktail, chomped the last olive, got up from the barstool, tucked it back in place, nodded to Max, and gently ambled toward the studio, a mere hundred feet or so away. As soon as he was out of earshot, we all said, "*Max, turn it on*," but he didn't have to be told to fire up the television over the bar. The network logo appeared, and a grave voice announced, "From New York, this is ABC News. Now, Harry Reasoner," and there before our eyes was the same man who'd sat quietly at the end of the bar only minutes prior. We all burst into applause with undying awe, knowing we were probably the only people in America who loudly cheered when the news came on.

OUR APARTMENT TOOK on the appearance of a warehouse for retired artifacts from a turn-of-the-century amusement park. Carrie had an incredible eye for found objects and a hearty allowance from Debbie to support it. I placed my keys on the extended tongue of a demented fun house clown. I hung my coat on a scale that measured whether children were tall enough for a roller coaster (which Carrie also would have bought, if it fit in the apartment). I had to pass through countless crafts and props and paintings by serial killers just to get to my bedroom. There was a vague tension that she was quick to sense if my reaction to an Aunt Jemima cookie jar was anything less than ecstatic.

"It's great. Now the lawn jockey has someone to hang out with."

"What's wrong?" Carrie asked me.

"Nothing, it's just . . . where is my *Blonde on Blonde* poster?"

"I moved it to your bedroom. It looked better there."

"I thought we liked Dylan."

"We do, we just like posters for absinthe more."

"There is nothing of *mine* here anymore."

"I've made your hot plate a mantel for the Fiestaware."

"How camp."

"Come on. No one gets upset about living in a cool apartment. What is really wrong?"

"Every time I come home to this amazing place, I see another amazing arcade machine that costs more than I will make in a year and I feel like a big fat phony. In my time here I haven't even gotten a job as an extra in a soap opera. I can get a table at Des Artistes, but I can't afford the appetizers."

"Then don't eat at Des Artistes."

"I like the food. No, it's not the food. I like taking April there. She likes it."

"Which Rockette is she, again?"

I'd recently started to work as a popcorn concessionaire at Radio City Music Hall. My boss at Beefsteak's had twice warned me to lay off the all-you-can-drink sangria, but I was only a great waiter when I was a little drunk and earned huge tips, so I knew my days there were numbered and decided to find another job.

"April's new. Younger than June."

"But still named after a month."

"Coincidence."

ONE DAY, Carrie said offhandedly that she had landed a job in some science fiction movie shooting in England.

"Is there a part in it for me?" I asked, oblivious to what a normal person would say, like "Congrats" or "That's great!"

"The only one you would have been right for is being played by Mark somebody. It's a really stupid script and you would have turned it down, I promise."

"If I'd known about it," I said suspiciously, as if she and Mark somebody had conspired to keep their movie a secret from me because now he was her best friend. I was dangerously close to being one of those out-of-work actors who grasps at delusional reasons for their continued unemployment. Of course, Carrie picked up on my mood.

"Don't be like that. The other lead is some older guy named Harrison Ford. You wouldn't have heard of him."

In fact, I knew him. He was the carpenter whom my aunt and uncle had hired to build the deck of their beach house up the coast from Malibu when I was seventeen. Like an eager puppy, I'd happily handed him nails to hammer or dug for hardware from the bottom of his worn canvas toolkit. In return, he would slip me one of his Marlboros, the filters of which I clipped off because that's what he did. Harrison cut me off from his endless relay of joints because his stuff was so strong that after one toke I couldn't tell the difference between a saw and a tape measure.

I simply idolized the dude and hated my envy that Carrie would get to spend so much time with him.

"He was the guy I told you about, who built the deck at John and Joan's house."

"You mean the carpenter you worshipped like he was Jesus?"

"Yeah, he's the coolest guy I ever met and is almost as funny as you are. You're going to love him," I whined in despair.

"Well, the good news is, I'm going to be in London for months on end, so you can fuck all the Rockettes you want in my bed. I'll even get you another bottle of Kwell soap before I leave," she said, cruelly reminding me of the weekend she was out of town and I shared her bed with someone who gave us both crabs.

"You being away that long is not good news at all," I said, already starting to miss her. She was gone a week later.

Carrie was correct to notice that many of the Rockettes were named after months of the year. While she was away, I hung out quite a bit with May and April—whom I got to know through June, the aging Rockette I had met the day I applied for a job as an usher at Radio City Music Hall.

I'd become a habitual reader of obituaries in *The New York Times*, and during my morning coffee, while skimming the remembrances of dead Ziegfeld girls or union bosses taken out in mob hits, one particular obit caught my eye, about the first usher to work at Radio City Music Hall in Rockefeller Center.

He was hired when Radio City opened its doors in 1933 to premier *The Bitter Tea of General Yen*, starring Barbara Stanwyck. Roddy, as he was called by his friends, was a gifted singer of scat, once marched on Washington with Paul Robeson, and was the only man John D. Rockefeller allowed to call him "kiddo." All of it was fascinating, but what really struck me was that Radio City might need a new usher.

The trick was not to act like a scavenger in my job interview, though I didn't want to miss the worm in case someone else realized obits were the next wave in help wanted ads. Arriving at Radio City, I reached for the enormous deco doorknob at the same time a woman I could only describe as a real "tall glass of water" was stubbing out an unfiltered Lucky with the end of one of her gams. I held open the door for her with a mock-courtly "after you" gesture.

"Such a gentleman," she said, passing me. "You don't see many of those anymore."

Despite her stunning figure, from the bloodshot eyes, heavily caked makeup, and lipstick on her teeth, I pegged her to be somewhere in her fifties.

"You work here?" she asked.

"I hope to. Actually, I'm applying for a job as an usher." A look of genuine sadness crossed her face.

"Well, you might be in luck, if that is the right word. We just lost one of our own. He was like family.

"I'm sorry, I had no idea."

"How could you? We're going to miss him horribly." I hung my head in respect, desperate to change the subject.

"What do you do here?" I asked.

"I'm a Rockette, can't you tell? Who else would have legs like these?"

"Well, they did catch my eye, to tell you the truth." *Oh, shut up, you're doing it again.* A surge of erotic current flowed from her to me and died on landing.

"Did they now?" she said, delighted with herself. "What's your name?" I told her and she said her name was June. "Though I was born in December, go figure."

"Gosh, I feel terrible. Maybe I should come back when everyone is not in mourning."

"Life is for the living," June said stoically.

"And 'death is for the dead.' Langston Hughes. I love that poem," I said, impressed that a Rockette was so well read.

"What poem? I just made that shit up."

She looked me up and down before saying, "I'm going to introduce you to Mr. Knobler, the general manager. He's one mean turd, but he owes me. I'll tell you why later."

Mr. Knobler was one mean turd. His greeting to me began, "Well, if you think you are starting off as an usher, you're living in a dreamworld, my young friend. Cadets don't begin at West Point as officers, they are plebes until they earn it. Being an usher at Radio City means you have been accepted into a brotherhood of arms, where posture, personal hygiene, and people skills function at the highest levels of gentlemanly conduct. I would put any one of my men against any of those poncy fruits in Buckingham Palace."

"So, I wear a uniform?"

"Obviously not the cap and epaulets of the ushers, but you'll be issued an outfit of sorts. I'm going to take a shot on you, kid."

Of all my "this isn't what I really do for a living" jobs, being a popcorn concessionaire at Radio City Music Hall was, hands down, the best of them all. I was issued the uniform of a paper cadet hat and light blue polyester pants and entrusted with a three-pound set of keys to every door in the catacombs below Rockefeller Center. They turned locks that opened onto Studio 8H, originally built for Arturo Toscanini and where now a new show called *Saturday Night Live* was in rehearsals, and onto the floor of the NBC newsroom that I crashed so often David Brinkley once asked me to get him a cup of coffee. He must have thought my cadet hat tipped smartly to the side was a new outfit for NBC interns. One of my duties was to haul huge bags of pre-popped popcorn from the basement. I always made a point of stopping by a grim, makeshift zoo that housed the camels from the Nativity show to feed them a bag or two, which they loved more than the baby Jesus. There's nothing sadder in the animal kingdom than a grateful camel that has been whisked away from the Gobi to do six shows a day at Radio City Music Hall.

The Rockettes were initially a little snooty to a kid in a paper hat, but they warmed once they heard I was June's nephew, which is how she first introduced me to Mr. Knobler. If her fellow dancers thought it was strange that she asked them to guess the size of her nephew's dick, they didn't let on.

Though June had made it very clear that, like Mr. Knobler, I "owed her one," I managed to parry and thrust around that debt and made sure to chat with all the other girls when hitting the drag bars where they unwound after performing—like the camels—six shows a day. Carrie often joined us when she came back from shooting in London, and they just loved her. She made them laugh until mascara rolled down their cheeks, and one night sang "I'm Always Chasing Rainbows" with a dude dressed as Liza Minnelli, which brought the house down. I think June thought Carrie and I were a couple; she finally stopped hitting on me and started to treat me as if I really was her little nephew.

It was great having Carrie home again, and we fell right back into waking each other up with filthy lyrics from made-up musicals. I'd forgotten how much I missed the phone ringing off the hook and the flower deliveries and unannounced visits from friends at all hours. But now that our old life came roaring back at full pitch, I also kind of missed the quiet routine I'd established in her absence. Not in a bad way—I just needed to oil a few squeaky wheels to get us back in alignment like before. Carrie grew increasingly anxious as the release date for *Star Wars* neared. "You should see what they did to my hair!" she had screamed into the phone when she was on location, usually mornings before going to set for her, four in the morning for me. "I look like I'm wearing two bagels over my ears."

This wasn't the first time I'd heard about the bagels, and I knew she was warming to a repeated monologue that might allow me a moment to drift off until a response was required.

"*And* I'm acting with an eight-foot yeti and a four-foot Brit in a rolling trash can! We shoot at shit we can't see on green screens with ray guns that don't even have a trigger. This movie is going to be a fucking disaster."

"I still don't get the title," I said. "Am I not hearing it right? It sounds like you're saying 'stah-weres.' Is it one word or two?"

"Two words: 'Star' and then 'Wars.' Put 'em together and still doesn't make any sense."

The very first screening of *Star Wars* was at the Ziegfeld Theatre, the largest movie house in Manhattan. It was a sneak preview that attracted a mob of rabid sci-fi fans who lined the block along West Fifty-Fourth as if summoned by signals from a distant galaxy. They clearly knew something about this movie that Carrie did not.

If John and George came back from the dead to play the Garden with Paul and Ringo for one show only, I don't think they could have worked up the crowd the way *Star Wars* did that night at the Ziegfeld. By the last line of the opening crawl, something about "certain doom for the champions of freedom," I knew Carrie's life would never be the same.

Not to put a "certain doom" on it, but neither would our friendship. It was just different for a long while, but never really the same.

I noticed my life had changed as well when shortly after the movie opened, my favorite doorman, Cairn, greeted me with "Good morning, Mr. Fisher."

"Oh, come on, man, you know my name."

Shocked and embarrassed by the faux pas, he corrected himself. "I mean Mr. Dunne."

"Griffin, Cairn. You've always called me Griffin."

Overnight I became "Carrie Fisher's roommate," a delicious karma that Alex might have appreciated, having been called "Griffin's brother" all his life. The off-Broadway actors and chorus girls who dropped by at all hours were soon outnumbered by rock musicians and movie stars I'd grown up idolizing. Glenn Frey of the Eagles wooed Carrie with a stadium-quality sound system he had shipped from the Record Plant in LA.

"Which Eagle is he?" she yelled from the shower when I read her the card.

Coming home after a shift at Radio City, I fought my way through a party of coke dealers and hangers-on to find James Taylor crying in my bedroom to Carrie that Carly Simon didn't love him anymore. The room was very small, so I had to gingerly step around them to put away my paper hat and fold my polyester pants. Richard Dreyfuss could be heard snorting lines off the plaster burger of a Bob's Big Boy statuette while railing about a disastrous review he'd just received for his performance as Iago, the part I would have killed for had I only ratted out John Derby. The fucking ironies just kept coming.

DURING ONE OF MY PARENTS' extravagant parties I got up to pee and caught Judy Garland rifling through the medicine cabinet in my bathroom. Warren Beatty once played the piano in our living room in lieu of joining a drunken game of charades captained by a smashed Ida Lupino. Sean Connery saved me from drowning.

When I moved to New York, I never told my new friends any of this and found my privilege embarrassing and inexplicably shameful. I envied kids who grew up in Kansas and went to real high schools that had proms and who built bonfires before a big football game. The celebrities in our living room were my parents' friends, who lived on a planet I wanted to move far away from, to find a world of my own. And now, with Carrie, I found myself off course, once more the little boy in a matching bathrobe working my way through a room of celebrities it was not my time to meet. This was not my planet, and I knew I would have to move on.

"You've arrived, I haven't even left," I said to Carrie when I broke the news. She took it badly but begrudgingly understood. I found a place back downtown, where I belonged, and hung with people whose struggles more resembled my own. It was always tempting to accept invitations to Carrie's parties or watch her host *Saturday Night Live* from the green room, but I held off until I could tame my insecurities—or at least make enough money from acting to grandly pick up a tab like Carrie had done so many times for me.

In 1982, I thought starring in my first off-Broadway play to good reviews was the straw stuffing I needed to fill the holes to make me feel worthy. I knew acceptance from others was a quick fix—hardly unusual to actors and a flaw I would deal with later—but the minor success nonetheless brought the glow back to my friendship with Carrie. In the years ahead, I was there for her family weddings and she for many of mine. She loved to pretend she couldn't remember which of my exes was which. But of course she knew, and dug for every little nugget about when and where it all went wrong with the same curiosity she'd had about my proclivities when she was a virgin. I wish I could remember our last conversation before she left for London on the trip from which she never came home in 2016. It was probably about Christmas plans or our daughters' shenanigans, but I know, despite not remembering what exactly was said, that we laughed very, very hard.

Seventeen

I made a point of calling (collect) the house on Crescent once a week to check in on my mother and gossip with Dominique.

Over the course of three years, Mom had moved from cane, to walker, to wheelchair, and finally the confinement of her bedroom. She uttered not a word of complaint about the loss of her mobility, nor displayed a trace of fear that one day the disease would deprive her of the pleasure of holding a cigarette, a habit that probably quelled her fears, or reading a novel, robbing her of even the simple pleasure of escaping into someone else's story. Her stoicism was admirable, but sometimes I wished she'd throw a wineglass across the room in a rage, with the little strength she had left.

I could tell just from the sound of her voice accepting the charges that I got her on a good day and she was happy to hear from me.

"So glad you called. Dominique just walked in and is dying to talk to you too. Don't let me forget to put her on."

Mom told me about a book she'd just finished about the black plague in the Middle Ages that she *simply adored* called *A Distant Mirror* by her favorite historian, Barbara Tuchman.

"Did you hear back from Pakula?" I asked. On our last call she'd told me about a thriller she'd recommended to her friend, the director Alan Pakula. When he optioned the book, Mom had been a little miffed that he never thanked her.

"A huge bouquet of roses arrived from him this morning. I was just being a doubting Thomas."

"How are you feeling?" I asked cautiously.

"What do you mean? I'm fine," she said in a tone that warned off any follow-up about her health.

A silence settled between us in which she thought of news to change the subject and I toyed with how to rephrase the same question.

"Dominique wants to talk to you. Can I put her on?"

"Sure. Fine," I sighed, frustrated that it was so awkward to show concern for someone I loved.

"She's going to take it in the other room. I love you. Call me next week. This time is *perfect*."

Dominique picked up from the study and sat, I imagined, on the little settee I'd slept on the only time I'd been in the new house.

"How you doing, kiddo," I asked breezily.

"That's what Dad calls me. It sounds weird coming from you."

Dominique was nineteen but hadn't lost the talent to make me feel just as stupid and intimidated as she had when she was a little girl. She was born knowing who she was and what she wanted, and pity the fool who thought they could change her mind. My father used to call her Little Miss Bossy for the way she would order her older brothers around, demands that Alex and I not only didn't mind but competed over.

"Have you talked to Alex?" Dominique asked me on the phone. "He's sounding a little wiggy."

"Yeah, I noticed."

Alex had moved to Vancouver and started a magazine called *Belles-Lettres*, a gold mine of letters written by artists through the centuries, filled with Mozart's scatological ramblings and cheeky remarks from Joyce to his wife, Nora. When I'd last spoken to him, his excitement about the magazine did little to hide an underlying mania that concerned me.

I told Dominique that he'd gone five straight nights without sleep, and about how he spoke with such despair that the magazine was a failure, that he'd wasted his life publishing something that no one would ever read.

"I told him he couldn't be more wrong, that major universities subscribed to *Belles-Lettres*, but he wasn't having it."

That we were both genuinely worried about him didn't need to be said.

"He's not like us, in a good way. He feels things more than we do," Dominique said.

"Because we're dead inside."

"Exactly," she said, laughing.

Through the phone I heard the sounds of the abandoned dogs and cats Dominique had rescued over the years as they joined her in the study.

"Okay, Ethel, calm down," she said to a balding fat dog with open sores on its back.

"Wash your hands after you touch that thing."

"Oh, don't be mean. Ethel's a good girl."

There was another dog, named Taylor, that she'd picked up off the streets of Boulder, and three black cats who'd shown up at different times on our doorstep on Walden, perhaps hearing a rumor that a young girl inside took in boarders.

I'm not a cat person, but these three creatures were the exception, with distinct talents that would have marveled Steve Irwin.

Panda had adopted my mother from the day she arrived on Walden Drive. She could sense her illness and only left her side to pick her a rose from the garden out front. Panda carried the bud in her mouth and announced her gift to my mother with a high-pitched moan before dropping it on her lap. This happened daily, sometimes three or four times a day, leading to bowls of floating roses throughout the house.

The thorny branches of Mom's rosebushes grew up to five feet, and no one could figure out how Panda pulled a bloom down from such a great height. Nor did we know why, once she snatched the bud, there wasn't a trace of a bite mark on its stem. We never saw how she did it, and if she caught us spying, she'd calmly walk away from the bush.

"How many roses did Panda get for Mom today?" I asked.

"Oh, she was on a tear. Six maybe. Oh, and Brindsley ran away again."

"He'll come back. He always does."

"I know."

Brindsley's front teeth had already been knocked out, and his tongue hung from his mouth like a punch-drunk fighter's. But he was a natural-born killer.

We had an avocado tree in our backyard, whose fruit drew rats from all over the neighborhood. Sometimes they wandered into the house, perhaps looking for vinaigrette, not expecting to run into Brindsley, who was more than delighted to see them. He ate them, fur, bones, and all, except for their little faces, which he licked clean, leaving only a mask of their nose and two holes where their eyes had been. Dominique, Alex, and I collected the little face masks, and when we had a set of five, put them on the tips of our fingers to perform little puppet shows.

"How's Sunijet?" I asked.

"You always ask me about Sunijet. Is she your favorite cat?"

I always asked about Sunijet because I lived in dread of the day Sunijet would tell my sister that I had tried to kill her.

One day while Dominique was at boarding school, I'd been in my room at Walden, talking on the phone with Sunijet asleep on my lap. During my conversation, I was twirling a rubber band between my fingers, talking about something I don't remember, and for reasons unknown, I absentmindedly wrapped it around her paw. By the time the call ended, I'd forgotten all about it.

A couple weeks later, I noticed Brindsley looking intently under a couch and assumed he'd found a rat about to join the Finger-puppet Players. But it was Sunijet, looking sickly and wheezing loudly. She wouldn't come out, so I had to pull the couch from the wall to reach her. Sunijet's front leg was swollen to twice its size and looked as if it were going to burst. Thinking she'd been bitten by one of the avocado rats and might have rabies, I rushed her to the vet.

Dr. Klein had stitched Brindsley up after a fight with a dog, cured Ethel of lice, and put down Bosie and Oscar years earlier, so we had a genuine rapport.

But even he was shocked when he saw the size of Sunijet's paw. Then, on closer examination, he came across something truly alarming.

"Oh my God," he said under his breath.

"What?"

"What kind of monster would do this?"

"What are you talking about?"

He peeled back her fur to reveal a rubber band tightly bound around a swollen limb, just where I'd left it weeks ago. I didn't tell the vet I was the monster, but silently agreed that whoever did this was one sick fucker.

"Is she going to be okay?" I asked, my voice now trembling.

The choices he laid out were that he could snip off the band, but the blood could rush to her heart and lead to cardiac arrest. Or he could leave it on, but more than likely Sunijet would slowly die of gangrene. *Or* he could just amputate it right then and she would be a healthy three-legged cat.

"*Those are the choices?*" I shrieked.

I began hammering the wall with my fist.

"Okay, son, let's bring it down."

I sat on a short stool and found myself eye to eye with Sunijet. She panted through thick white saliva and gave me a look that said, "Make up your fucking mind."

"Cut the band," I told the vet.

"You know what might happen—"

"We've been through this. Let's pray her heart doesn't give out."

"You realize if I just take off her limb, Sunijet will be sure to live. It doesn't have to be a gamble."

The expression I imagined on Dominique's face when she came home to a three-legged cat was not an option.

"Just take it off," I snapped.

"You mean the limb? Wise decision."

"No, for God's sake! The *rubber band*!"

We both held our breath as he gently placed scissors under the band and snipped it as if he were defusing a bomb.

Sunijet didn't go into cardiac arrest and, once free of her constriction, began to lick where the rubber band had been. The vet seemed disappointed, after having given the cat's heart attack such a big buildup.

I know it's illogical, but Dominique was a born animal whisperer, and if anyone could hear Sunijet's accusation, it would be her.

"Enough about the animals," I said on the phone. "Have you gotten a letter from Dad?"

"Yes, like six pages, single-spaced."

"Yeah, me too."

Our father had moved to a cabin in Oregon that didn't have a phone, but he wrote us long letters about his current state of mind almost weekly.

"I know this sounds crazy, but despite everything he's been through, he actually seems happy, if that's the right word," said Dominique.

"Yeah, failure seems to agree with him."

Dominique ripped off a snort and said, "Stop it, Griffin. That's mean."

"I'm just saying, now that Dad's lost his money, possessions, all his friends, and is holed up in a cabin in Oregon, he seems almost . . . enlightened."

Dominique had been on the front line of our father's downfall from the moment it began. His drinking and drug abuse had long been out of hand and known to all, but she was the only one he trusted with his secrets, and the only person who could talk him off the ledge.

In 1972, Dad was shooting *Ash Wednesday* starring Elizabeth Taylor, not knowing it would be the last movie he would ever produce. Toward the end of production he brought Dominique, then thirteen, to the Italian Alps, where the film was on location. In the little village of Cortina, she was witness to Elizabeth Taylor's chronic tardiness, so severe it drove the budget to astronomical sums and took our father's career down with it.

Though he took the fall for the overruns, Dad made Paramount's decision to fire him an easy one.

Dominique was Dad's date on his last night in the movie business. Our father was on a drunken roll, sharing inside gossip with a long table of cast and crew, sending everyone into fits of hysterics. He did an impeccably mean impression of Sue Mengers, then the most powerful agent in Hollywood, whose hefty weight was well-known but never discussed in public. Mengers was also best friends with Bob Evans, head of Paramount and my father's boss. The joke Dad told that night in Cortina was that if they ever made a musical of Sue Mengers's life, it should be called *When the Fat Lady Sings*. I guess you had to be there, and also very drunk. What slipped Dad's mind was that a reporter from *Variety*, invited by the studio to publicize the movie, was seated at the end of the table.

Dominick Dunne's "fat lady" joke was quoted in *Variety* the next morning, Pacific Standard Time, and the vice president of Paramount called Dad's room at the Majestic Hotel to say, "Nick, pack your bags and come home. You're over."

Henry Fonda, Liz Taylor's costar, had given him and the director monogrammed Louis Vuitton suitcases to celebrate the first day of shooting. Dominique helped her father pack his with the clothes he'd brought to Italy.

In pre-internet days, getting blackballed in Hollywood was very difficult to prove because there was built-in deniability. All it took was a phone call from Sue Mengers mentioning to the heads of the six major studios that none of her clients, many of them the most bankable stars in the world, nor any of the talent at her agency, ICM, would ever work on any picture Dominick Dunne produced. Sprinkle that with a little gossip about Dad's drinking problem and incompetence as a producer, and a black ball starts rolling that everyone will deny exists. Calls are not returned, scripts are no longer submitted, and appointments are mysteriously canceled at the last minute.

It was terrifying to me that Dad's career should collapse just as mine was beginning. I watched what people with power could do to a man who loved movies all his life, who had to pinch himself that he was actually making them. Knowing that a dream could be realized and then so casually destroyed scared the hell out of me.

SIX YEARS AFTER THE CATASTROPHE of *Ash Wednesday*, Dad's bank account was down to triple digits and he was being evicted from his apartment on South Spalding Drive. He sold his beloved Mercedes and stooped to driving a used Ford Granada. Before moving out, he held a yard sale, and Dominique helped him put price tags on his Limoges plates, andirons, Persian rugs, even ashtrays from grand hotels, which were sold for a song. People he once entertained, who'd long since dropped him, heard of his misfortune and showed up to haggle and pick through his treasures.

Dominique brought along Norman Carby, the Rousseau muralist, to take over the bargaining, which spared Dad the embarrassment of having to touch the money from his old friends. She noticed a spark between them, and was pleased that her closest friend could make Dad laugh on such a horrible day. Norman was five years older than her, and twenty-five years younger than her father, and she was happy for both of them.

In the last months of my father's life, I found out what Dominque had known until the end of hers: Dad and the man he met at his yard sale would be lovers for over thirty-five years. My little sister sure knew how to keep a secret.

DOMINIQUE AND I ENDED the roundup of our family's woes with our usual dark humor and promised to speak the next week. Through no fault of our own, we had been chosen by divine genetics to be spared sickness and addiction, and nothing in our lives (so far) had troubled us like the misfortunes of our parents or our brother's battle with sanity. Our dumb luck made us partners, with a mission to support them, plotting ways to make their lives easier. It was possible for us to give Mom hope with news of recent advancements to cure MS, or to try to keep Alex relatively earthbound, but our father was on a journey all his own, and with the exception of Dominique paying his last month's rent on South Spalding Drive, even she was powerless to help.

AFTER THE YARD SALE, Dad drove his Granada up the Pacific Coast Highway, with no destination in mind except to head north, with hopes he'd left a town that could no longer kick the shit out of him. But the town had one more indignity in mind before letting him get away.

As soon as he picked up a hitchhiker outside of Malibu, he knew he'd made a terrible mistake. The passenger was "a total crazy person," he wrote to me from Oregon, "with one false eye that stared straight ahead and one crazed eye of a man who would kill."

Dad drove for miles on the empty highway hoping to find safety in a gas station, all the time talking out loud to the hitchhiker about anything he could think of, but inside praying, "God, keep me safe from this man, put a white light around me."

When he finally reached an intersection, Dad pulled the car to the side and told the hitchhiker it was where he was turning off. That's when the guy pulled a knife and told Dad to get out of the car. Everything he owned was in the back seat: Henry Fonda's Louis Vuitton suitcase, some books he'd saved, and a typewriter he'd begun to write a novel on. Dad grabbed the keys out of the ignition and shoved the door open, running down the highway in terror. Realizing my father had outfoxed him, the lunatic chased him down the Pacific Coast Highway, knife in hand.

Cars finally came out of nowhere, and the people who passed him saw a middle-aged man screaming his head off for help. A young man Dad said was about my age was driving in the opposite direction in a camper and pulled him off the road and into his cab to safety.

The highway patrol arrested the hitchhiker, and after questioning my father, told him he was free to go, but to expect to be called back to Ventura County to testify against his attacker. Dad said he'd be happy to, but had no intention of returning and raced to his car to put distance between him and his latest misfortune.

The Granada got a flat tire in a sleepy town in Oregon called

Camp Sherman. Dad had no idea how to change a tire and found a mechanic who could. He was tired from the drive and, intending to stay for the night, asked if there was a hotel nearby. The mechanic suggested a cabin resort called the Twin View. The owners, Joyce and Nick Osika, showed him to a knotty-pine cabin with a single bed and linoleum floors, where he would end up staying for a year.

It was in cabin 5 that he began a novel he'd been miraculously hired to write by Michael Korda, editor in chief of Simon & Schuster. Korda threw him a lifeline and a modest advance when it became clear that Joyce Haber, a gossip columnist who'd written a bestseller about Hollywood called *The Users*, had become a hopeless alcoholic incapable of delivering a sequel. Dad had produced a TV movie based on the book, and Korda, knowing there would be slim pickings among experienced authors eager to write something called *The Winners: Part II of Joyce Haber's "The Users"* and that my father knew a thing or two about avarice in Hollywood, thought him perfect for the job.

Dad understood this was hardly a classy assignment but was grateful for the money and that someone like Korda believed he could be a writer. *Gratitude* was a word he'd come to appreciate since recently becoming sober, and a practice he lived by one day at a time.

He didn't have a phone and, when not writing his book, communicated with single-spaced letters that ran for pages about life in the Northwest, his neighbors, and the characters he met at AA meetings who helped him get sober. The letters read like a writers' workshop, where the author lets himself ramble through incomplete tangents that turned further and further inward, until finally finding the voice that would be his own.

Dad found the meeting in the hamlet of Sisters through an ad in a local weekly paper called *The Nugget*, and despite thirteen miles of winding roads, he went every day.

At the first one he went to, "there were only about eight people," he wrote me. "They just sat around a table and talked. One lady lost her job as a dispatcher at the police station, and when she told her husband, he hit her. They all had bad stories like that. Almost all of them had 'slipped' that week. I felt so at home with these people and when the chairman said to me, 'Dominick, do you have anything you'd like to say?' I started talking and couldn't stop. I suppose in my whole life I never told so much about myself to anyone as I did to that group, two of them were Indians from a reservation. I suppose I figured, what the fuck difference does it make. Griffin, I had them spellbound. I told them all my poor stories that I was too ashamed to tell anyone else, and they were in hysterics, tears rolling down their cheeks. Then I talked about your mother, and the guilt I feel about her. I told them I'm writing a book I hated and I couldn't write it. It was like I needed them and they needed me. When I finished they clapped for me, not just AA polite clap, they really clapped. I can't tell you how lovely it was. Had a good cry too. The next day I started to write."

The man I grew up with based his self-esteem on what table the maître d' at Chasen's chose to place him at. The support he found from battered police dispatchers in a world not his own made me giddy with pride. I laughed out loud when he described the night he watched the Academy Awards with Joyce and Nick Osika, who owned the only television on the premises. All they knew about Dad was that he was a writer counting his pennies, who lived in Los Angeles. When Elizabeth Taylor was presenting Best Actor, Joyce told Nick all the husbands Liz had been married to but got the order wrong. She thought Richard Burton went before Eddie Fisher, and Dad didn't correct her, or mention that he once produced a movie she starred in.

"Who gives a shit," he wrote. "I can't believe I thought all that crap was important."

Eighteen

I moved out of Des Artistes and into another East Village studio I could barely afford on the salary I received from two grand ladies as their personal assistant. They both lived on opposite sides of the Dakota, a creepy Gothic building on West Seventy-Second Street, perfectly cast as where Mia Farrow gave birth to Satan in *Rosemary's Baby*. The Dakota was completed in 1884, before there was an Upper West Side and only grazing cattle surrounded a mammoth apartment building in the middle of farmland. There was very little development above Fourteenth Street in those days, and people said the building was so far away, it might as well have been in the Dakotas.

Both doyennes lived across from each other, separated by a large interior courtyard. One of the ladies, Susan Stein Shiva, was the daughter of Dr. Jules Stein, who founded MCA and owned Universal Studios. On my way to her apartment, I would often share the elevator with John, Yoko, and their toddler, Sean. John always nodded a hello and called me "young man" in a cheeky formal way, as if we were in on his joke together.

I was too shy to tell him that I treasured a photograph of me shaking his hand at a charity event where rich kids had lined up all the way down Benedict Canyon to meet the Beatles. It was during their first American tour, and they sat on stools for hours shaking hands with children as a photographer snapped shots every fifteen seconds so everyone would get a picture.

In mine, Dominique, who was only four, is seen curtsying to Paul, and I am meeting John, who for some reason looks as thrilled to meet me as I him. Alex was before us in line and had just met George, his favorite Beatle, who was spiritual like him, but the picture was taken just moments after and shows a woman steering him from the line. In the way a single image can trump reality, Alex's memory of that day is that the woman who steered him away kept him from meeting any of the Beatles and only Dominique and I were allowed. When my brother would later lose his grip on reality, his rage over the injustice of being denied what Dominique and I experienced grew to epic proportions. It was unfair, because his sister and I got all the breaks. He could rail at me about it, but never Dominique.

I was fortunate to still own an image of my favorite Beatle smiling at me through his Ray-Bans, holding out his hand as if astonished to see me, with an expression that said, "Holy hell, mate, what the fuck are you doing here?"

I never did tell John about that photograph and what it meant to me, but I wish I had. Two years later, I would be in an off-Broadway comedy playing a demented youth who kills a celebrity to become famous. One night after a performance, I biked to a deli on the way home and heard on the radio that John Lennon had just been shot in front of the Dakota. Not believing it could be true, I got back on my bike and madly pedaled, as if under a spell, all the way uptown, until I reached the building. I arrived no more than an hour after the shooting, and a crowd holding candles, drawn by the same calling as me, had gathered outside. It was then that I heard he'd been murdered by a fan who, like the character I'd played earlier that evening, wanted to be famous. The next day I begged the producers to let me out of the play, but they refused. The show went on, but I couldn't reprise the humor I'd once found in the funny little murderer I'd played, and never got a laugh onstage again.

I hadn't known anyone who'd died a sudden and violent death before, and though of course I didn't actually know John, I'd grown up with him, and imagined that he was once happy to see me, and, with countless others, I wept in front of the Dakota until sunrise as if everyone I ever loved had died.

ON THE DAY I met John Lennon for the second time, I also met Susan Stein Shiva, who made me audition for a job she described as her "social secretary." She handed me a thick leather Filofax and told me to call the person at the top of the page and invite them to a party she was to give.

I dialed the number and said to the person who answered, "This is Mrs. Susan Stein Shiva's office calling for Mrs. Onassis. Is she available?"

I waited for the former First Lady to pick up, the same lady I'd once made a paddle for so she could spank her son John-John. I clocked Susan's approving expression out of the corner of my eye. So far, so good.

"Yes, hello, Mrs. Onassis," I said when she came on the line. "I'm calling at the request of Mr. and Mrs. Shiva to invite you to a dinner party on October twelfth at eight o' clock at their home at the Dakota."

WIDOW HEIRESS BRIDE IN DAY

Mrs. Helen P. Griffin, Left $9,000,-000 by Husband, Weds in 24 Hours.

CHICAGO, May 8.—Mrs. Helen Prindiville Griffin Bastedo, who married Lieutenant Commander Paul Henry Bastedo last Tuesday at San Diego, following the death of her first husband, George Griffin, on Monday, in the South, will receive Griffin's $9,000,000 estate by the terms of his will, his attorneys announced today.

Mr. Griffin will be buried at Forest Hills, near Boston, Monday. Mrs. Bastedo's mother will represent the widow-bride at the funeral.

My great aunt's scandalous behavior even made *The New York Times.* She tried to take her new husband to her dead huband's funeral, but the Griffin Wheel Company had Union Pacific derail her private car to Wisconsin, hundreds of miles from where the funeral was taking place.

The first of many matching outfits my father chose for Alex and me. When I look at this young family, newly arrived in Los Angeles, I'm reminded of what Arlene Francis said on *The Today Show* after interviewing my mother as "a typical New York housewife" soon after I was born: "We wish Lenny, Nick, and Griffin all the luck in the world as they begin their bright future."

For years, Dad shot the family Christmas cards on his Rolleiflex, which we posed for as early as summer so hundreds of copies would be ready for mailing to London, New York, and Hollywood. The bamboo chairs, the trellis in the window, and the twin potted plants are what remains from my parents' Black and White Ball the year before.

My sixth-grade class photo from the Fay School. There used to be a picture of me covertly giving the finger in a portrait with my football team, but the obscene gesture was discovered just before I was to graduate, and the headmaster caned me with ten "swats" and destroyed the negative.

Dad and "Little Miss Muffet," as he adoringly called her. Dominique would later be the keeper of his secrets until the end of her life.

The first of Mom's drop-bys on Christmas for friends who had nowhere else to go. This was the day I met my "Fake Uncle Earl" (top row, fifth from the left) who slipped me a half-smoked joint and said, "Don't tell your father." Courtesy of the McGrath estate.

John, Joan, and Dad on the set of *Play It as It Lays*. They had just come from the funeral of my parents' close friend, the actress Diana Lynn, who had been cast in the film but died of a stroke during her costume fitting.

The Dunne Fingerpuppet Players on
Crescent Drive with Brindsley the rat catcher.

I brought Carrie and Mark Hamill to a party at Earl
and Camilla MGrath's the week *Star Wars* opened.
Courtesy of the McGrath estate.

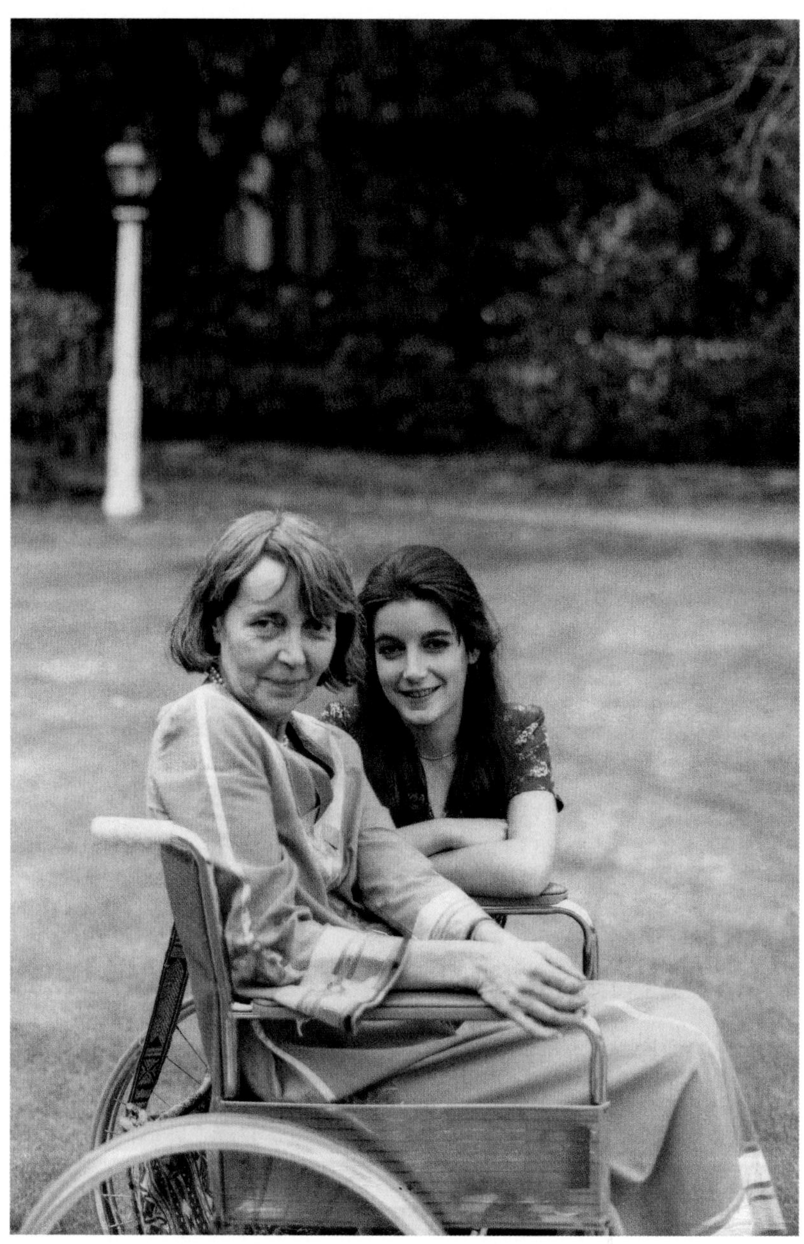

Despite the smiles, this was taken at Robert Wagner's house after the funeral for his wife Natalie Wood, who was one of Mom's closest friends. Less than a year later, Dominque would be buried a few hundred feet from Natalie's grave.

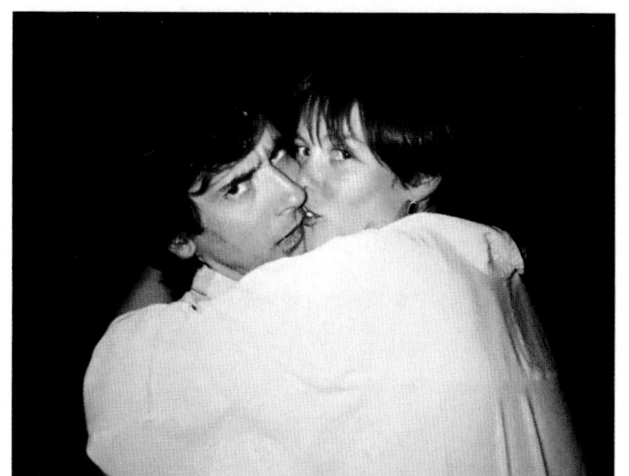

Carey Lowell and me in the throes of early romance.

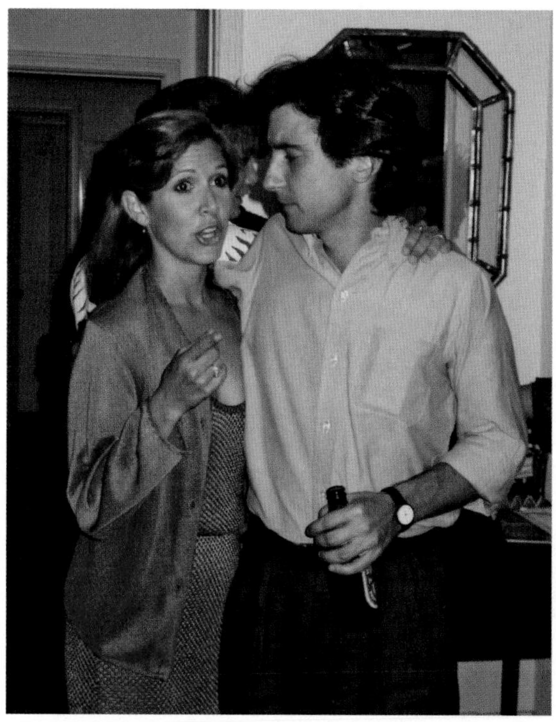

Carrie at a party my mom gave for me on Crescent Drive when *After Hours* was released. Courtesy of Connie Freiberg.

When I'm with my brilliant and hilarious brother, there is never a dull moment. Private collection.

My aunt and me on location while shooting *Joan Didion: The Center Will Not Hold*. Courtesy of Ray Foley.

Mrs. Onassis got a pen and told me about a possible conflict but said she would try to move things around, and as she spoke I responded to her every sentence in a quiet, poncy tone, "Ohhhh-kay . . . oohkay . . . oooookeeeedokey . . . allrightythen," and concluded with, "We will look forward to seeing you then, Mrs. Onassis."

I hung up, terribly pleased with myself, and looked to Susan to see how I did.

She considered me closely before saying, "Lose the 'okeydokey' and you've got the job."

ACROSS THE COURTYARD lived my other paycheck, an aging Southern actress named Ruth Ford, who on December 8, 1980, placed the first call reporting shots fired outside the Dakota. She was once a member of Orson Welles's Mercury Theatre and had been a close friend of William Faulkner's since her college days.

When I worked for Mrs. Ford, she lived in a ten-room apartment with her lover, the writer Dotson Rader, who was thirty-one years her junior, and they hosted dinner parties for a Mount Rushmore of playwrights and artists. Dotson was boyishly handsome and, while a student at Columbia, had made ends meet by cruising Port Authority Bus Terminal as a male hustler, adventures he would later recount in a wonderful book called *Gov't Inspected Meat and Other Fun Summer Things.*

One of my tasks was to ape Ruth's signature on eight-by-ten stills of her in a 1943 movie called *Adventure in Iraq* for the few movie buffs who still remembered the film. If there were fan letters, I would answer them in Ruth's grand Southern tone as if I were thanking Ashley Wilkes for attending my tea dance. My other job was to bartend her dinner parties, which were raucous affairs that required a skill set different from forging the signature of an aging starlet.

One evening Ruth and Dotson hosted a small dinner for their close friend Tennessee Williams. The only others invited were Henry Geldzahler, a powerful art critic, and Truman Capote, the ungrateful guest at my father's Black and White Ball. Ruth bought me a Brooks Brothers shirt and a clip-on bow tie for the occasion. I stood at attention in the dining room in front of a makeshift bar, while a Nepalese butler, who would one day inherit the ten-room apartment from Mrs. Ford, solemnly served a meal left untouched, as the guests preferred booze over food. They drained their glasses faster than I could fill them, and by the time the plates had been taken away, everyone save Ruth Ford was totally bombed. Tennessee had taken to calling me "boy" to get my attention, and soon the others followed suit, running me ragged.

"Boy, another refreshment on the double," and "Boy, a little less ice in the next one ifyouplease," they chimed, finding my struggle to keep up with their orders hilarious.

Truman led the handsy charge when I leaned over to reach his empty glass and he pinched my ass, making me squeal like an Elizabethan barmaid. My yelp really brought down the house, and every drink I delivered after was rewarded with someone grabbing, patting, or fondling any of my body parts below the belt. Ruth was the only one not laughing, nor did she seem to notice the discomfort of her $2.50-an-hour employee. I might have laughed at the first one or two reach-arounds, but soon blamed myself for somehow encouraging their drunken rowdiness.

When Tennessee managed to get a handful of both my balls, Ruth spoke for the first time since dinner had been served.

"You know, Tennessee," she drawled, "this 'boy,' as you call him, happens to be the nephew of Joan Didion, whom I always thought you were rather fond of."

Tennessee's hand snapped away from my crotch as if he'd been bitten by an asp. Embarrassment drained his complexion, and he pushed away a glass of vodka on ice in self-revulsion. After composing himself, he looked me directly in the eye.

"Young man," he began, "though I don't know your aunt well, I adore her words and deeply apologize for my disgraceful behavior. Won't you please sit with us."

He grabbed an empty high-back chair and told Truman to "scoot over." His apology impressed me, and I joined the group with no ill will. I had been groped by men since my earliest teens, and though I realize a younger generation has felt lifelong trauma from similar abuse, I had no such reaction, and accepted my abashment as the price for being young and attractive. I pass no judgment on that generation or my own.

WHEN I CALLED DOMINIQUE the next night, she shrieked, "You met Tennessee Williams!" totally blowing past the ass-pinching part.

"I wish I had your life," she sighed.

A silence followed her kind but disingenuous remark. What wasn't said was that I wished I had her life. My frustration as a mostly out-of-work actor included the added bonus of envying my sister's blossoming career. She had recently gone from job to job, guest starring in television series even I couldn't be snobby about. Mike Nichols hired her to be in *Family*, which he produced, and she'd starred opposite Ed Asner in a *Lou Grant* episode. A prominent talent agency had signed her, though one needn't have been an agent to know she was on the path to stardom. I still lacked representation and relied on a trade paper called *Backstage* for open casting calls to audition for roles that had already been cast. *"Are you crazy?"* I'd yelled at her a year earlier when she called, thrilled with excitement and expecting me to be thrilled that she had decided to become an actress.

"It's a terrible profession. You're just going to get hurt. Every day someone is going to hurt you."

Dominique inherited the family Irish temper and would take on anyone if she felt cornered. Her disappointment in me, and her anger at my reaction, was volcanic, and we yelled back and forth until exhausting ourselves.

"I'm sorry," I finally said. "I'm an asshole. I'm happy for you. You're going to be amazing. But it's going to take a while, so you have to be patient. Look at me, I've been doing this for a few years and have yet to catch a break."

"Maybe we'll be the next Lunts," she said slyly.

"Or Barrymores," I offered.

"The Osmonds," she snorted.

"The Allman Brothers."

"Shaun and David Cassidy!"

We giggled like a couple of dweebs, but our fantasy about someday being a famous brother-and-sister act starring in movies together was no joke, at least to us.

In two years our dream to work together would almost come true when the director Tony Richardson asked if we'd consider playing siblings in *The Hotel New Hampshire*, based on the book by John Irving.

"*Consider?*" we both exclaimed to Tony. "Of course we'll do it."

"Well . . . read the script first," he said mysteriously.

When we did, we understood why he asked us to "consider" playing brother and sister: the roles in Irving's story required that we not only have an incestuous relationship but also fuck countless times on-screen until our attraction for each other runs dry.

Dominique and I could barely look at each other when we'd finished reading the script. The picture of us doing these unspeakable things took days to scrape from our minds, and we called Tony to pass on the first movie either of us had ever been "considered" for.

"Well, I can't say I'm surprised," he said when we told him. "It was just a thought."

One afternoon in 1984, I sat in the back row of a near-empty Rialto Theatre in Times Square to see *The Hotel New Hampshire.* Rob Lowe and Jodie Foster played the incestuous siblings, and they had lots of scenes where they kissed with tongues and fiddled around naked under the sheets. I laughed out loud, alone in the dark, imagining that Dominique was sitting next to me, both of us rolling in the aisles at the sheer ridiculousness of us playing these parts. When I stopped laughing, I got out of my seat and left the theater before I started to bawl.

Nineteen

There was a time when I believed that being able to afford a late-night taxi home was when I'd truly "made it" in showbiz. This might seem a low bar for success, but any New Yorker who's waited on a subway platform at four in the morning in the late seventies knows of what I speak.

In a career detour, the money to hail those late-night taxis wasn't from my work as an actor, but as a movie producer. At the age of twenty-three, I found it easier to produce a motion picture for United Artists than I did to get a role in an off-Broadway play.

The two friends I hung out with most with at that time were Amy Robinson and Mark Metcalf. Amy had starred in Martin Scorsese's *Mean Streets*, but her passion for acting had cooled since then. Before Amy and I would become business partners and lifelong friends, we had been lovers. On the morning after my first night staying at her apartment on Spring Street, we walked to a deli for coffee. In those days, Spring Street east of Thompson was a heavily Italian neighborhood where kids still played stickball with Spaldeens and opened fire hydrants like little ruffians in a Helen Levitt photograph. Every hundred feet or so, someone would yell from a playground or out a window, "Yo, Tereeeesa!" Amy would look in the direction of the caller and give them a shy wave.

"I thought your name was Amy," I said.

"It is, but everybody around here calls me Teresa. The person I played in *Mean Streets*. They think I'm some tough Italian chick from the neighborhood instead of a nice Jewish girl from Trenton, New Jersey, and I don't want to disappoint them."

I met Mark when he was performing in David Rabe's play *Streamers*. His initial interest in me was to date my friend Carrie Fisher, so I didn't count as his friend until he'd struck out.

Amy and Mark were six years older than I was, and they taught me how important it was to never let down my creative guard during our idle hours of unemployment. We looked for plays to perform and settled on Sam Shepard's two-hander, *Cowboy Mouth*, which Mark directed Amy and me in, with hopes it might result in a full-scale production, though it never did.

Amy was an avid reader of *The New Yorker* and an early fan of Ann Beattie, whose short stories first appeared in the magazine. When Ann's debut novel, *Chilly Scenes of Winter*, came out, Amy read it right away and told us to do the same.

"This book would make a great movie," she said, "and we should produce it."

With a little research, we found out that the rights to *Chilly Scenes* were available and that Ann Beattie was teaching at Harvard. Not knowing her address or phone number, the three of us drove a borrowed Volkswagen to Massachusetts, hoping to persuade her to option us the book. When we arrived in Cambridge, we stopped at the first phone booth we saw, found Ann's number in the directory, and cold-called her.

Mark asked if we could meet to talk about her book, and because Ann was bored, or pitied us for making the trip, she invited us to come right over.

When we entered her apartment, Ann said it was as if three of her characters had just walked into her living room. Our rapport was immediate—and fueled by a bottle of vodka we drained that afternoon and well into the evening. Mark was so drunk he made out with her dog. The only thing Ann wanted from us was a walk-on in the movie as a waitress with a beehive hairdo. She called her agent, H. N. Swanson, who had represented F. Scott Fitzgerald, James M. Cain, John O'Hara, and Raymond Chandler, and told him to let us option the book.

"Who are these people?" he demanded. "Have they ever made a movie? I've never heard of them."

"They are very nice," Ann explained, "and they promised me a part in the movie!"

Swanie, as H. N. Swanson was called by his friends, which we certainly were not, charged us two thousand dollars for the option, which gave us one year to find a writer, a director, and a studio that would purchase the book outright. Amy's and my combined savings barely reached a couple thousand dollars, but Mark had just been cast as Neidermeyer in *Animal House* and graciously kicked in his salary to buy the rights.

Our blind luck continued because Hollywood was then going through a period of pretending it wanted to work with women directors, though really the list of acceptable hires was limited to three who were currently in vogue, all coincidentally named Joan: Joan Darling, Joan Tewkesbury, and Joan Micklin Silver.

We had the good timing to get Joan Silver, who had directed an independent gem called *Hester Street*, to write and direct the film. Amy, Mark, and I always saw John Heard in the role of

Charles, one of the few actors who could make his obsession for a married woman seem appealing.

Joan had worked with John and, despite his reputation as a hard-drinking but brilliant actor, thought he was perfect as well. Amy had the inspired idea to suggest Gloria Grahame, whom most people knew as the sweetly promiscuous tart in *It's a Wonderful Life*, to play John's mother. She was fifty-five and still ravishing and, like most women, fell for John, and they had a little May–December romance.

Gloria had also starred in a favorite movie of mine, *In a Lonely Place*, but refused to go down memory lane about her costar Humphrey Bogart or the director Nicholas Ray. She also remained as frustratingly mum about Jimmy Stewart and Frank Capra from *It's a Wonderful Life.*

"I'm not interested in the past," she said to me when I asked what it was like to be directed by Ray, whom she had married but separated from before the start of filming *In a Lonely Place.* The two were so hotheaded, Ray had in his contract that if Gloria dared to disagree with him on set, he could fire her on the spot.

What Gloria also kept to herself was a diagnosis of early stage breast cancer, which would take her life only three years later.

United Artists was founded by D. W. Griffith, Mary Pickford, Charlie Chaplin, and Douglas Fairbanks, with the promise of giving their filmmakers creative control, and our studio executives stuck to tradition, believing in Joan enough to let three unknown actors, without any production experience, oversee a movie with a $3.5 million budget.

We watched dailies at Culver Studios in the same screening room David O. Selznick watched his rushes for *Gone with the Wind.* Our production manager was Howard Hawks's first AD, and he entertained Amy, Mark, and me with stories of adventures on remote locations with the cantankerous director. Our negative cutter was so old she'd worked on *The Birth of a Nation.* We were actors who loved the history of movies, but didn't pretend we knew how to make them, which endeared us to the crew, who were happy to support us and share their years of knowledge. They appreciated that we were unafraid to ask questions, and hated first-time filmmakers who used arrogance to hide their lack of experience.

To our disappointment, United Artists forced us to change the title of *Chilly Scenes of Winter* to the lackluster *Head Over Heels*, because someone in the marketing department thought the words *chilly* and *winter* would turn off an audience. UA did, however, splurge for a first-class premiere at the Baronet on Third Avenue, a prestigious theater for first-run films, followed by a glamorous party that must have cost a fortune, which studios thought nothing of spending at the time.

We were celebrating the movie, but the many actors who were there that night, like William Hurt, Raúl Juliá, and Sigourney Weaver, were also celebrating three actors who made their own work instead of relying on others for employment.

"I want to do what you do," a wobbly Bill Hurt mumbled into my ear, holding on to my collar for balance.

I want to do what you do, I thought, because even though I had produced a movie, I'd yet been able to prove myself as an actor.

Carrie was so proud of me that night, she pulled me into the men's room to make out for old times' sake. She was by then a movie star, and my success aroused us enough to think we were at last, if only for a moment, on equal footing.

The evening was triumphant, but I missed my father. The per diem I'd hoarded from shooting in Los Angeles was more than enough to offer to fly him to the premiere first class from Oregon and put him up in a nice hotel, but he'd turned me down. "I'm so happy for you kiddo," he wrote back. "And that you are making enough dough to treat your old man to an airline ticket fills me with pride to no end. But this is your time to enjoy your much deserved success and this is my time to stay put and face where my life went wrong and figure out how to put it back on track. My plan is to write my way out of this mess and though I wouldn't dare call myself a writer just yet, in time I will be, I just know it. That is who I'm supposed to be, and not the social gadfly who wasted so many years in a drunken fog giving parties for people who were never my friends. I'm coming home, not to Los Angeles, that chapter is over, but New York where I began, and when I do, you will be as proud of me as I am of you right now."

HEAD OVER HEELS was a flop on release (though it would find cult status years later when the film was rereleased as *Chilly Scenes of Winter*). After enjoying so much creative freedom with the production department at United Artists, their marketing team castrated our picture by retitling it and selling it as a wacky rom-com, which it was not, and disappointed anyone hoping to see one. The poster they mocked up was an embarrassment none of us ever kept a copy of.

In taking myself out of the running for any acting parts for two years (not that anyone noticed), I found learning what it takes to make a movie from beginning to end soothed my mind from the relentless grind of auditions and rejections, and brought a feeling of accomplishment that was its own reward. What I didn't expect was that a small part I'd cast myself in would get such huge laughs that casting directors noticed me for the first time. Out of the blue, I found myself working at Joseph Papp's Public Theater, a Lourdes for New York actors, in Wallace Shawn's *Marie and Bruce.*

That part led to a meeting with John Landis, who'd directed Mark in *Animal House* and was now casting a new film he refused to even describe. We talked, or he did, for maybe fifteen minutes, while I waited for him to ambush me with a cold reading I was sure to fuck up. But he only ended the conversation with a polite handshake and sent me on my way.

The phone rang in my apartment as I let myself in. It was Landis.

With a voice that hit high and low notes in the same breath, he said, "A security guard is going to be standing outside your door in about ten minutes. He will hand you a script that you should read with the character of Jack in mind. When you have finished the script, hand it back to the security guard and call me immediately."

I did as told, and loved the script, which was called *An American Werewolf in London*, so much that I had a hard time returning it to the beefy guard in the hallway. I called John back and without hesitation he offered me the part of Jack. To this day, I have no idea why.

A week later I was flown to LA for elaborate makeup and hair tests. It took Rick Baker six hours to apply the prosthetics on my face and arms. His work would later win him the first Academy Award in makeup design.

I was playing a character who'd been killed by a werewolf and haunts his best friend David in three stages of decomposition. The six hours I spent in the makeup chair was for the first stage, which showed the aftermath of the werewolf's attack.

When Rick had painted the final touches of fresh blood to the gaping wounds slashed across my face, I studied my appearance in the mirror and felt something darker than the simple keys of sadness, more an overwhelming grief for someone I didn't know.

The violence of Rick's handiwork was so real, it was as if I were watching my corpse laid out on a coroner's table—details so exact that my severed jugular vein wiggled when I held my breath to keep from crying. It was my first starring role, and I should have been excited, but all I could think of was how horrified my mother would be to see me like this. I worried how the trauma of watching one of her children die such a horrible death would affect her health, and that I would be responsible for her imagining such unthinkable loss filled me with despair. Rick asked me what was wrong, but I didn't have the words to possibly make him understand what I was feeling.

ON THE MOORS OF WALES, moments before the cameras rolled for the first take on the first day of shooting, I had a desperate need to pee. I excused myself and ran to the first camper I saw. I was still midstream when the camper started to move and I splashed all over my wardrobe. After zipping up, I rushed to the forward window to see that the camper was hitched to a pickup truck that, for whatever reason, was leaving the location. I banged and yelled, but it was impossible to get the driver's attention. He drove me for at least an hour until someone from production caught up to block his path and return me to the moors.

"You've been on this picture one day and you've already put us behind schedule!" Landis yelled, though I knew he was kidding.

The crew laughed and patted me on the back, rewarding my mishap with pints of Guinness in a pub that night.

The rest of filming took place in Twickenham Film Studios in London, where the Beatles shot *A Hard Day's Night*, *Help!*, and the documentary *Let It Be.* The commissary had a fully stocked bar, and the stagehands who knocked back rounds of whiskeys over lunch were still able to hang huge tungsten lamps without ever dropping them on the actors below.

My costar, David Naughton, couldn't hold his booze nearly as well, and Landis cut him off when he slurred during a take. We were both hard-partying American boys with fistfuls of per diem, and after night shoots had our driver take us to after-hours clubs, where we drank till sunrise.

London in 1980 was far from the swinging city it was known for in the Carnaby Street days of the sixties. Britain's economy and morale were in a deep depression, and the animus toward Margaret Thatcher fueled race riots in Brixton and nationwide labor strikes. I lived in an apartment in Chelsea, the birthplace of punk, awoken most nights by Mohawked hooligans kicking over trash cans and blasting the Sex Pistols or the Clash from their boom boxes. Across the street from my flat was a travel agency with a faded poster in the window of the most beautiful beach I had ever seen. It read COME TO CEYLON.

Before going to set on the last day of shooting, I crossed the street and told the travel agent I wanted to buy a ticket for the next flight to Ceylon.

He looked confused, so I pointed at the picture of the beautiful beach in the window and said, "There, I want to go there."

"You mean Sri Lanka," he sniffed. "It hasn't been called Ceylon in fifty years."

"Whatever, when is the next flight?"

AFTER A TWELVE-HOUR FLIGHT to Colombo, I bought a chunk of hash at the Pagoda Tea Room and took a train to Negombo to rent a motorcycle and explore the island. The travel agent had neglected to mention that Sri Lanka was on the brink of civil war, and when the Pagoda Tea Room I'd left a week earlier was blown up by a Tamil suicide bomber, I was miles away and oblivious to the tragedy.

Traveling Westerners were a rarity at that time, and whenever I puttered into a village on my Honda 90, I got a glimpse of what the Beatles must have felt when they were mobbed by hysterical fans. Swarms of children surrounded me, grabbing at my skin and pulling on my sari like the little cannibals who devoured Montgomery Clift in *Suddenly, Last Summer.* An outrageously narcissistic thought crossed my mind that within a year I would be premiering in a "major motion picture," and while not expecting a reception like I got from the children in Sri Lanka, I wondered if I was the kind of person who would wilt under the attention of fame, should it come my way.

When not fretting about being a movie star, I spent the majority of my vacation fantasizing that I was with an actress named Brooke Adams. I imagined us riding through jungles that howled with monkeys from the canopies above, her holding me tight on the back of my Honda, or kissing me on a promontory, where I sat overlooking the Indian Ocean.

I'd been in love with Brooke from the moment I'd first seen her in Terrence Malick's masterpiece *Days of Heaven,* which she starred in with Sam Shepard. Though she was a movie star six years my senior and I, a lowly popcorn concessionaire at Radio City Music Hall, there was no doubt in my mind that one day our paths would cross and she would be mine.

Two years later, the night before my flight to London to begin filming *American Werewolf*, Brooke joined an improv group I was in run by Susan Sarandon and her then boyfriend Tom Noonan. We were paired together and given the circumstance of brother and sister sneaking out of the house after curfew. In the scene we became giggly teenagers on the run, and the improv turned oddly incestuous when I took her hand and told her I loved her. The class was a little weirded out by it, and when it was over, we took our seats on opposite sides of the room and never got a chance to say goodbye when the workshop ended.

The night I returned from Sri Lanka, I found two months' worth of messages on my answering machine, but the only one that mattered was the very last. It was from Peter Riegert, who'd costarred in *Chilly Scenes of Winter*:

"Hey, Griffin, Brooke Adams is giving a party tonight, and she asked if I would invite you. Her address is . . ."

It was only nine, and without a moment to lose, not even to shower, I hopped over my unpacked luggage and raced to catch a train uptown.

Brooke was the first person I saw when I entered her crowded apartment. When our eyes met, she motioned me to her and took my hand.

"Don't go anywhere tonight," she whispered in my ear.

We didn't get out of bed for a week, and suddenly, the girl I imagined on the back of my Honda became my girlfriend. Just like I pictured.

Twenty

My mother once told me that people who are both Irish and Mexican are called "happy drunk, sad drunk." The meaning isn't limited to the effects of alcohol, but to the disparity of temperament between the two heritages. Mom is half Mexican, and Dominique and I inherited her easygoing nature that rarely wallows in depression. We were also quite cheerful after a drink or four.

Dad and my brother share the dark side of the Blarney Stone. When Alex lived in Vancouver working on *Belles-Lettres*, he was most certainly bipolar, though the term hadn't yet been coined and the diagnosis in those days was just generically lumped as "acute depression." Dad had long been tormented by a guilt and shame he picked up from an abusive father and the Catholic Church. What Dad and Alex shared most in common, alien to the happy drunk side of the family, were thoughts of suicide.

There was a kitchen knife in Dad's cabin with PROPERTY OF TWIN VIEW RESORT written on its wooden handle, lest anyone get the bright idea to steal it. When despondent with self-loathing, my father held it close to his chest and imagined the blade piercing his heart. All such thoughts came to an abrupt end late one night when Joyce Osika banged on his door to say he had an urgent phone call.

His brother John was on the line with the horrific news that their youngest brother, Stephen, had died by suicide. John described the call in his book *Harp*: "When I told him what had happened, there was a cry of such bleakness that I can remember it still. He pulled himself together and said he had been contemplating suicide himself, perhaps even at the exact same moment as Stephen."

In that "exact same moment," Stephen sat in the family station wagon with rosary beads wrapped around his fingers and let carbon monoxide from the wagon's running engine fill his lungs. The bedroom of his three young boys was directly over the garage, and it was their coughing that woke their mother, who rushed them to safety, but when she dragged Stephen from the car and onto the driveway, he was gone.

There was an underlying tension on their call, despite the gravitas of the occasion, that had festered ever since John and Joan had become highly paid screenwriters and novelists, and was made worse when they lent Dad ten thousand dollars he had no way of repaying. He didn't even have the money to fly east for the funeral, and when he found the gall to ask for his brother's help for the flight, John turned him down, saying he was "tapped out" after recently giving Stephen thirty-five thousand dollars to start his own graphic design firm. He added to Dad's humiliation, intended or not, by telling him he "shouldn't fret" about the funeral, because his nine-year age difference with Stephen meant he "really didn't know him very well."

I had known Stephen, though clearly not well, because his

manner of death shocked me to the core. On city nights when it was too late for him to commute back to New Canaan, Connecticut, he'd take my couch and we'd stay up talking and laughing about everything except what must have really been on his mind.

It was true that while Dad was in boarding school, the army, college, and then Los Angeles, he'd been absent for much of Stephen's life, but to be a no-show at his little brother's funeral was unthinkable. At the last minute, his aunt Harriet rescued him with just enough money to buy a round-trip ticket.

The service was at a Catholic church in New Canaan, where Steve and Laure had chosen to raise their children. Suicide was a mortal sin, and the monsignor at first refused to allow the service on consecrated soil, only relenting after a lot of begging from the family.

Dad sat in a pew behind John, though they barely looked at each other. After warmly greeting my aunt and uncle, I joined my father, taking on the now familiar role of running interference between the three of them. Dad was still irked that I remained so close to John and Joan, but for the occasion, all pettiness was put aside.

My great-aunt Harriet was a devout Catholic, and briefly a nun in the early 1920s, but she left the convent in a cloud of mystery. There was the rumor of a child out of wedlock, though no one ever knew for sure. She was in the pew with Laure and her three boys, Harrison, ten, Justin, eight, and Evan, six, and moaned throughout the service, loud enough for all to hear, "Those poor children. Their father is going to go to hell."

"Shut the fuck up!" John yelled, his profanity echoing off the altar.

The monsignor looked up from his reading of Psalm 23, no doubt regretting that he'd given Stephen's mortal sin a pass.

When the service ended, Dad skipped the reception to head back to the airport for Oregon. We hugged tightly, not sure when we'd see each other again. Walking toward his taxi, he ignored his brother but nodded ever so slightly to Joan.

DAD'S THOUGHTS OF SUICIDE might have been put on hold after Stephen's death, but they were much on Alex's mind.

Not long after the funeral in New Canaan, Alex woke me in the middle of the night with a collect phone call from Abbotsford Airport in British Columbia. He'd escaped from a mental institution in Vancouver, where he'd been committed for attempted suicide.

"*What?*" I shrieked, shooting out of bed.

"I was at the hardware store, and I bought this rubber tube and put one end onto the exhaust pipe of my car and the other through the window. On the drive home I passed out and drove through the front door of my house. I didn't think it would work so fast."

"You were in such a hurry to die that you wanted to kill yourself on the way home?"

"No, no, nothing like that. I just wanted to see if it worked in case I needed it."

"Well, it worked for Uncle Steve! What the fuck, Alex?"

"I'm fine, but listen, I got a ticket to New York, and I want to know if I can stay with you. I got through customs, so the loony bin hasn't put out an APB on me yet, but once I leave Canada, I'll never be allowed back in. I left everything, my apartment, car, *Belles-Lettres*. It's over for me here. Can I stay with you for a while?"

By the time he made his way to the front door of my studio

apartment, the meds the hospital filled him with had worn off and he was in full manic mode. During his stay he never once slept, and sat on the edge of my bed talking nonstop *at* me, not *to* me, oblivious of whether I was awake or not. Alex quoted long passages from the philosopher Teilhard de Chardin and worried that a pop star, whom he imagined he was soon to wed, might be cheating on him. He spoke with a bitterness I'd never heard before, about never being recognized as a chosen son of God whose only mission was to share his love with all sentient beings.

After days of sleepless nights, I had been worn down by Alex's talk of being the Chosen One to where his reasoning began to make sense. He wrote a letter to Stephen Sondheim, Dad's old college chum, politely asking him to admit that the compositions that made him famous would never have been written had they not passed through Alex first. A simple thank-you was all Alex was asking for.

Though I begged him not to send it, I found myself at least open to the possibility that my brother's higher power might have somehow influenced *Sweeney Todd*.

His mania became so infectious that even my skin started to mimic the clammy, itchy texture of his. I sought relief from his contagion by escaping the apartment to buy cigarettes and six-packs of beer to slow my pounding heart, but his madness followed me to the street. I heard my name in the honking from cars on Sixth Avenue, and pedestrians gave me a wide berth as if steering clear of a lunatic.

A WINDOW TO ALEX'S SANITY must have been left open a crack, because two weeks after his arrival, he surrendered to my pleading that he commit himself to a psychiatric hospital. My father had just returned to New York and suggested a mental facility called Silver Hill in New Canaan, despite the unfortunate coincidence that the hospital was a mile from where Stephen had killed himself months earlier. Dad overlooked this grim detail because he'd heard that Truman Capote, Judy Garland, and her daughter Liza had all been patients, but knowing Alex's distaste for name-dropping, he kept this useless information to himself.

I rented a car, and the three of us drove to the hospital's pastoral campus. As we entered the forboding gates of Silver Hill, we passed patients playing softball, their teams divided, Alex later told us, into "the drunks against the loonies." Dad and I somberly watched the admitting staff comb through Alex's personal belongings, squeezing pockets of clothing in search of razor blades, and discard a possibly spiked bottle of mouthwash. Alex regarded his pilferers with dignified tolerance, and I half expected him to bless them each for "they know not what they do."

When it came time for us to part, his holy attitude extended to Dad and me as well. Alex allowed our hugs with a pitying look, and as he was led away by two male orderlies in white uniforms, Dad and I gripped hands, willing ourselves not to change our minds about what we had done.

We were next invited to meet the chief doctor, whom I took an immediate dislike to. When telling him a little about Alex's background, his creativity, his sensitive nature, I found myself choking back tears.

"He's just so filled with love for everyone," I struggled to get out. "He will tell you all he has is love, but that he is not being heard . . . I believe this is somehow destroying him."

The doctor looked at me as if maybe we were committing the wrong brother.

"You sound like you love Alex very much," he said, delighted with himself for having unearthed some hidden perversion of mine.

Dad and I exchanged "what the fuck" looks.

"Yes, I love him very much," I said, tightly deadpanning each word. "Is . . . that . . . a . . . problem?"

"No," he answered, eyeing me curiously, "just pointing it out."

They put Alex on lithium, a now infrequent treatment for bipolar disorder, which I heard progressively deaden his soul during the few phone calls he was allowed to place. He told me that during his first session with the loathsome chief doctor, he handed him piles of notebooks he'd been filling out since childhood.

"I'm not ready to talk about myself yet," he told the doctor, "but everything you need to know about me is written in these books."

Remembering how protective he was over his short stories, I was amazed by not only the trust he placed in this man, but also the bravery it took for him to admit he needed help.

"After a few weeks of sessions with him, group therapy, and baseball with the drunks," he said on our last call from Silver Hill, "I asked him what he learned about me from the notebooks I gave him. He said he hadn't read them, and I asked for them back."

My heart sank, knowing what was coming.

"So he handed them over and I threw every last one in the trash."

"Oh no, Alex. Why?"

"He touched 'em. That's why."

When he checked himself out, no one in the family tried to dissuade him. He stopped taking lithium or any other antidepressant but seemed back to his old self.

He found an apartment in a tenement on Pitt Street in the

Lower East Side, next to an abandoned building where dealers sold heroin through a brick in the wall to junkies lined up around the block. There were surely other apartments just as cheap in less dangerous neighborhoods, but Alex preferred to wear a hair shirt instead of nice cotton. I think he wanted to live with a touch of discomfort because it kept him humble, an ambition foreign to his happy-drunk side of the family. If he still felt he was the Chosen One, he learned to keep it to himself.

DAD KNEW THE OREGON CHAPTER of his life was over when he returned to his cabin after his brother's funeral. He'd finished writing *The Winners: Part II of Joyce Haber's "The Users"* and, while he didn't expect a PEN Award, he was proud of his accomplishment and found no reason to continue hiding from his past.

An unexpected letter arrived from Truman Capote that seemed to read his mind: "That is not where you belong," Truman wrote. "When you get out of it what you went there to get, you have to come back."

He hadn't seen Truman since the Black and White Ball and had no idea how he had gotten his address, but knew if anyone understood what it was like to be banished, it was the man who wrote "La Côte Basque, 1965," which had made Truman a pariah in New York society. Truman's letter affirmed that it was time to move on, and though Dad would never return to Los Angeles, Manhattan was where he'd started out, where anything was possible, and the only place that might let him start over.

HE MOVED TO NEW YORK and set up home in a tiny studio, even smaller than my first apartment in the East Village. But he loved the place. His window was darkened by an airshaft, so he wrote by day with all the lights on. This time he was writing a novel based on his own idea, eventually titled *The Two Mrs. Grenvilles.* What few possessions he still owned from the old days were carefully placed around the studio, giving the impression of an anteroom in Buckingham Palace.

I lived around the corner from him, and we often met for lunch at an outdoor coffee shop on Sheridan Square. Our conversations were constantly interrupted by a series of Bukowski doppelgängers, aging Trotskyites, or drag queens in hairnets who called him "Dom" and paid homage as if he were their local priest. These were the very characters I passed on the street every day, extras in the movie of my life about a kid who left the comforts of Beverly Hills to be among the hardscrabble of New York. But these colorful characters weren't extras to Dad, they were his supporting players.

"How do you know these people?" I asked with pride and a touch of envy.

"The rooms" was all he offered.

He was an overnight sensation and major draw at the AA meetings on Perry Street, sharing the story of his journey to the bottom with a rapt audience who knew a thing or two about failure and redemption. My dad had arrived in New York, and he, more than I, really was "the boxer."

Twenty-One

When *Werewolf* was released in June 1981, Dominique was in the first month of shooting her first movie, *Poltergeist*. Neither of us were big fans of horror films, and we found it pretty funny that our movie debuts were in the same genre.

On a brief trip to Los Angeles to promote my horror movie, I stopped by the set of hers on the MGM lot. Steven Spielberg was the producer, and when he walked toward me, I braced myself to be kicked off his closed set, but instead he told me how funny he thought I was in *Werewolf*. It was one of those moments you dream about, but when it's happening, it feels like it's happening to someone else. I was reminded of a joke that was going around about an actor who'd been told that his agent had just raped his wife, killed his dog, and burned down his house, but the actor only asks in amazement, "My agent knows where I live?" That's what it was like for me to know Steven Spielberg had seen me in a movie.

He next leaned in and said in a hushed tone, so as not to be heard on his deathly quiet set, that my sister was very talented, and he had her in mind for future projects. As Steven spoke, I watched Dominique, at the far end of the stage, whisper something to the actress playing her mother that made her laugh. She looked so at home on the MGM lot, as confident as Clark Gable or Judy Garland, who decades earlier might have kissed or danced only inches from where she stood. As the warning bells rang to start filming and the red lights commanding silence spun in place, I saw Dominique prepare for the scene, a picture of concentration, and thought to myself, *This kid was born to be on a soundstage.*

DOMINIQUE'S AND MY FANTASY about being the next Barrymores or Bridgeses would have been less far-fetched had I not decided to ignore the heat on my acting career after *Werewolf* and chose to work instead behind the camera as a producer with my partner, Amy. It would not be the first time an agent thought I'd lost my mind for halting momentum toward possible stardom. But the majority of offers that came my way were teen sex comedies that hoped to cash in on the box office success of *Porky's*, which I turned down without a moment's thought. The only movie I regret not doing from that time was *The Fly*, which David Cronenberg seemed to want me for, but I gave the brilliant director a feeble excuse that returning to a makeup chair for hours on end was too much to bear.

The truth was that I knew the attention that came with stardom would stir a self-awareness I was ill-equipped to handle, so committing to the next level of success paralyzed me with fear. My personal character was still undercooked, and my ego wasn't strong enough to handle the scrutiny of fame, yet I was just wise enough to know that if I rushed headlong toward it, I'd soon burst into flames and end up a has-been in rehab. Maybe those little cannibals in Sri Lanka really did do a number on me.

The movie I chose to coproduce in lieu of pursuing a future in acting was called *Baby It's You*, directed by John Sayles, based on an episode from Amy's life. The story is about a high school love affair between an upper-middle-class girl, played by Rosanna Arquette, who dreams of being an actress, and a working-class boy who calls himself "the Sheik" and dreams of being the next Frank Sinatra, though he hasn't an ounce of talent. She outgrows the boy when she goes to college at Sarah Lawrence, sending him into a rage that borders on violence.

Dominique was visiting New York when we had a rough-cut screening, and she brought along a towering, heavyset young man she was clearly serious about. His name was John Sweeney and he worked as a sous-chef at Ma Maison, a restaurant so exclusive it had an unlisted number.

I have no memory of Dominique being in love prior to Sweeney. We had actor friends in common who perhaps had dated her, but I never asked, nor did they volunteer. No one wanted to have that conversation. But for Sweeney, she would tell us unabashedly how crazy she was for him, which made us happy for her.

Dominique met Sweeney when John and Joan asked her to join them for lunch at Ma Maison, where they were regulars. They took to my sister in a way they never did Alex, which hurt and confused him, especially when he saw them fold her into their social lives, much like they did to me years earlier.

Before she became an actress, Dominique earned a little pocket money staying over at their house in Brentwood to babysit John and Joan's teenage daughter, Quintana, while they were out of town on business. Q, as her family nicknamed her, was a precocious ninth grader at Westlake School, where Dominique had also gone. Some of the nights my sister babysat, Q gave her a run for her pocket money by sneaking out of the house to hook up with older kids partying in Holmby Hills. Dominique would track her down to whatever *Less Than Zero* bacchanal she found Q in and drag her drunk ass back to Brentwood. Those evenings usually ended with her holding back Q's hair over a toilet bowl while Q puked and begged Dominique not to tell her parents. When John and Joan returned, they'd asked their niece if Q "wasn't too much of a handful," as if knowing she was but feared hearing the details. Dominique once told me that John and Joan's denial about Q's behavior was to cover their desperate worry that they had no clue how to deal with her.

During the lunch when she met Sweeney at Ma Maison, John and Joan got up to table-hop, leaving her alone to notice she was being observed by a large, bearded man she didn't find *un*handsome in his chef's apron. The guy introduced himself and asked how she was enjoying her trout amandine. Dominique declared it delicious, which must have been true, because she was the original foodie and would have had no qualms about telling him his fish sucked ass.

"Well, I cooked it, so that makes me very happy," he said.

That he cooked the amandine was the first of many lies he would tell her. Ma Maison's real chef was Wolfgang Puck, then on the cusp of fame. Sweeney's job as sous-chef was to prepare the food so Wolfgang could work his magic, not to take credit for his dishes.

I was unaware of Sweeney's insecurities before we met at the rough-cut screening of *Baby It's You* in New York, months into his courtship with my sister, but they were glaring from his first words to me after he saw the film.

"Sir, that was me. The Sheik was me," he said, referring to the troubled working-class kid that the ambitious Sarah Lawrence girl outgrows and breaks up with.

I don't know why he addressed me as "sir" since we were about the same age, but what little I did know was that, like the Sheik, Sweeney was from a troubled family and grew up in a coal-mining town in Pennsylvania, so even though his obsequiousness made me cringe, I found his formality oddly touching.

"Sir, you have made a great film. In my estimation, it is worthy of an Academy Award."

At that, he leaned down to hug me, and though I couldn't see his face, I could feel his eyes getting moist.

There is a nonfiction book called *The Gift of Fear*, written by a security specialist named Gavin de Becker, who also happens to be one of my oldest friends. The thesis of his book is that we are all capable of predicting an act of violence or a traumatic event in our future that can be avoided if we listen to the first impression of our instincts. I remember one night in the East Village when I did just the opposite. Walking home on the Bowery, I saw a lunatic raging at an unseen enemy fifty yards in front of me. Every instinct told me to cross the street, which I overrode by thinking it cowardly and paranoid to do so. I was rewarded with a punch in the face so hard I had a black eye for a week.

That Sweeney would one day commit an act of violence that would traumatize my family for the rest of our lives did not occur to me, but my uneasiness when we met was a "gift" I declined to accept. What I listened to was my sister's boyfriend address me with exaggerated respect, but what he was really saying to me that evening was he was just like the Sheik, a character capable of violence and obsessively in love with a girl he did not believe he could keep. Sweeney was telling me that Dominique's privileged upbringing and ambition to be an actress threatened him to the point that he might one day be a threat to her, but I wasn't listening.

"HE'S A PHONY, a star-fucking ass-kisser. What do you possibly see in him?" Alex demanded of Dominique in a West Village Spanish restaurant she'd found in Zagat's. It was her last night in the city, and Dad was taking us all out to dinner. Sweeney had flown back to his job at Ma Maison the day before. Dominique was unfazed by Alex's rant, having long since learned to take his passionate outbursts in stride, so to my discomfort, Dad's and my first opinions carried more weight. With a touch of defiance, she demanded to know what we thought of her boyfriend.

"If he makes you happy, darling, that is all I care about," said Dad, beating me to the line I was going to use.

Dominique dismissed his softball response and set her sights on me. She looked both hungry for my approval and angry with herself for wanting it. I stammered over my first words, amazed that I could still be as frightened of my sister's temper as I had been as a teenager, before finally cobbling together my cowardly opinion:

"I agree with Dad. If he makes you happy, go for it."

"They are both lying," Alex said to Dominique. "They dislike him as much as I do, they just don't have the balls to say so."

Neither Dad nor I made any attempt to disagree. Dominique decided the matter was settled, whether she believed it or not, and changed the subject, for which we were all grateful.

"I'm going to learn how to make paella," she said after a spoonful of hers. "I bet mine will be better than this."

"No doubt, you bet, so much better," chimed three grown men who loved her so much they would have said anything to please her.

Twenty-Two

There was no scenario in 1982 where either Alex, Dominique, or I would have been spared a violent death. At that time and in different ways, the three of us were placed in situations designed to end our lives, though only two of us would survive.

We had wrongly assumed that the demons that haunted Alex had been put to rest when he returned from Silver Hill. He listened to music without demanding credit from the artists and spoke no more of wedding pop stars. But just because he didn't speak of it didn't mean he wasn't thinking it. He had learned that confiding in anyone about his divine powers could send him to a psych ward and had also learned how to live with the burden of his lonely secrets.

Before Alex moved to Pitt Street, he stayed at a rooming house I found for him only a few buildings from mine. One day Dad dropped by unannounced to invite him to lunch. Alex answered the door in a harried state, maybe adjusting to the surprise of his father's sudden appearance.

"Let me get my coat," he said, and then rooted through a cedar closet to find it.

While Alex cursed at the closet for hiding his coat, furiously sliding hangers from side to side, Dad saw a thick rope coiled on a table fit with a hangman's knot. He grabbed it and managed to fit it into his overcoat before Alex turned around.

At lunch, Alex asked Dad how his book was going. The questions were intelligent and showed a real understanding of a writer's process. Dad answered each one with a controlled calm, as if addressing someone strapped to a bomb, and hoped the suppressed panic in his voice would go unnoticed. He thought what a brilliant writer, or maybe an editor to other brilliant writers, Alex could have been if mental illness had not set out to waste his talent.

Dad couldn't bring himself to mention the rope.

"Why?" I asked, when he rushed to my apartment after their lunch to tell me what happened.

"I don't know. I was scared he'd be angry that I invaded his privacy and try to kill himself sooner. When I stole the rope, I thought maybe I'd bought some time. Maybe he'd see the rope was missing and take it as a sign. I don't know, Griffin, I'm so scared. I don't think your mother could take it."

And then all he'd tried so hard to keep pent up during lunch suddenly released in a flood of tears. Great, heaping sobs that must have alarmed my neighbors poured out of him for a long time as I held him, as best I could, until he'd cried himself out.

I didn't bring up the rope to Alex, either, because I was also scared. In fact, so many things scared me: I was scared I would lose him, the thoughts he lived with scared me, the waiting for something awful to happen scared me, and I was scared for my mother if he did such a thing. What Alex might or might not do was out of my control, and that scared me the most.

The Grim Reaper dropped in on me a month later.

It was the first day of rehearsal for a play I'd been cast in called *Hooters*, just like the name of the restaurant chain with the buxom waitresses. It was a coming-of-age comedy written by Ted Tally, the same author who wrote *Coming Attractions*, the play I was starring in when Lennon was assassinated. (Ted went on to write more serious work, even winning an Academy Award for *The Silence of the Lambs*.)

I played an awkward teen who idolizes a tough kid who thinks himself a ladies' man and coaches me on the art of getting laid. Frank Rich would rightly point out in his review for *The New York Times* that I was too old for the role.

After reading through the first act, the cast had broken for lunch, and everyone left feeling certain we had a hit on our hands. I asked the guy playing my idol if he'd like to get a bite, and we decided on a place a block away, on Tenth Avenue, in the heart of Hell's Kitchen.

A beat-up old Chrysler from the seventies rounded the corner where we stood at the curb, and as it slowly passed, the driver hocked an enormous loogie into my costar's face. The phlegm hit him square on the nose and splashed in his eyes. I impulsively managed to get a good, strong kick on the car's taillight. The Chrysler slammed on its brakes, and two of the largest guys I'd ever seen rushed toward me. The guy in the lead wore a Bruce Springsteen T-shirt, and when his fist connected with my face, I swear I was thinking, *I love Bruce Springsteen, he loves Bruce Springsteen, what is the problem?* To my amazement, I didn't go down and instead got him into a headlock that brought us both to the pavement. Then I thought, *Oh shit, now what am I going to do?* My hesitation gave him time to break my headlock, grab my hair, and pound my skull into the pavement, over and over, while punching me in the face between slams. The actor playing the tough kid was nowhere in sight. Finally the guy's friend pulled him off, saying, "Stop it, you're going to kill him."

By now a crowd had gathered, though no one interceded. Despite the blood running from my nose and mouth and my loose teeth, a rush of adrenaline and rage brought me to my feet, and I chased Springsteen, who walked calmly back to his car, and screamed, "C'mere, you motherfucker!"

His friend blocked my path and gripped me by the collar. In a quiet but chilling tone, he leaned his face into mine and said, "You are in real danger here. Stand down." I believed him.

Someone in the crowd yelled, "He's got a gun!" and we both turned around to see that Springsteen had yanked a pistol from the front seat and pointed it toward me.

His friend shielded my body and yelled at him to get back in the car, which he did. They drove off and the crowd went on with their business.

There was no question I would have been shot to death in Hell's Kitchen had that man not saved my life. When shock later took hold, I couldn't get over how stupid I'd been to go back to Springsteen for seconds. I felt not bravado but utter shame for toying with my life and almost causing my mother such grief.

IN THE EARLY MORNING HOURS of October 31, 1982, I was finishing off the remains of a little baggie of coke in the bathroom at Café Central, an actors' hangout on the Upper West Side.

Hooters had opened ten days earlier to tepid reviews, and not a night went by that I didn't drop by after the show to commiserate with colleagues.

While I shuffled, coked to the gills, between the bar and the bathroom, in Pacific Standard Time Dominique was fighting for her life in the front yard of her house at 8723 Rangely Avenue. She was twenty-two days shy of her twenty-third birthday.

A month earlier, to everyone's relief, she had kicked John Sweeney out of her life. Dominique had been confiding in me that their troubles began soon after they moved in together. She was seeing less of her gang from the Friday Afternoon Club because their burgeoning careers made Sweeney feel like a failure for still being a sous-chef at Ma Maison, which he took out on her. He would accuse her of flirting with any man she spoke to and tried to possess every moment of her time.

"Griffin, sometimes I think he loves me *too much*," she said, which I heard, but again, didn't really take in.

What got my full attention was when she told me in a later conversation about his first attempt to strangle her. That attack dispelled the last illusion she had about Sweeney, a point she drove home by leaving his bags on the front lawn and changing the locks to her house.

An argument had escalated the night before, what it was about or how it started I would never know. What is known is that he strangled Dominique to the brink of her blacking out, but somehow she managed to escape through an open window in her house to the safety of her VW Bug. Sweeney was so enraged that he caught up with her in the driveway and climbed on the roof of her car, demanding she get out. Dominique put the Bug in gear and took off, sending him flying to the curb.

She drove to Norman Carby's house and banged on his door

in hysterics. While trying to calm her, he saw dark purple welts around her throat, and as horrified as he was to see his friend so violently abused, Norman knew the attack should be documented and took pictures of her injuries. He wanted to call Dad, with whom he was still close, to tell him what had happened, but even the thought of her father knowing set Dominique back into a state of hysteria, so he held off.

"You want to hear something really fucked up?" she asked Norman later, climbing into the bed he had given her for the night.

"Tomorrow is my first day of shooting an episode of *Hill Street Blues*."

"I think that's great. Work will take your mind off all this."

"Except I'm playing a battered housewife whose husband tried to strangle her."

"Well," Norman said, letting the irony sink in, "at least you won't have to wear makeup."

It was the perfect thing to say, and Dominique belly laughed for the first time since her escape.

Feelings of shame and self-blame, familiar to every victim of domestic violence, began their hateful work on my sister's sense of self. Even though she had taken decisive action by breaking up with Sweeney, doubt still plagued her. Dominique called me a month after their breakup, and the second-guessing in her tone annoyed me. She also caught me as I was halfway out the door to catch a new Woody Allen film called *A Midsummer Night's Sex Comedy*. Dominique didn't exactly say she wanted to get back together with Sweeney, or even that she missed him, but questioned whether she might have been too harsh, and confessed she felt sorry for him. Her sympathy only irritated me further, and I checked my watch to recalculate what time I'd arrive at the

Beekman Theatre if I left right then. I knew I'd miss the trailers but might still make the movie.

In the interest of time, I decided not to tell her that, days earlier, Sweeney had phoned to see if I might help him reconcile with my sister. He was so delusional that he imagined I would actually act as their couples therapist, and then told me I was the only person who really understood him, because I'd produced *Baby It's You*, which he took to be his life story.

"That movie was not about you, and if you watched it carefully, you would have noticed that the Sheik never strangled Rosanna Arquette."

"Griffin, I am so sorry I lost it like that. I never meant—"

"Shut up. Touch my sister again and I will kill you."

"If I ever did, I'd give you the gun to kill me," he said, as if his passionate play on words would win me over.

"Stay the fuck away from her," I said, and hung up on him.

I also did not tell Dominique about that conversation because she might have found romance and genuine remorse in Sweeney's brave gesture of calling her older brother.

I didn't know that the last words I would ever say to my sister would be "Dominique, I'm so sorry, but can I call you tomorrow? I'm running late for a movie." I meant to call the next day but didn't, nor did I the day after that, which was October 30, the date that Sweeney showed up at Rangely Avenue, holding a bag of Halloween cookies he'd just baked. Ten minutes later, his hands were around her throat.

Part Two

Twenty-Three

Dad woke me from my late night at Café Central the second he got off the phone with Mom. He'd spoken to Detective Johnston as well, but didn't know more than that Sweeney had attacked Dominique and she was on life support.

"Griffin, get over here now. I need you."

I raced to his apartment in early morning darkness. While he packed, I made his reservation for the next flight out. The plan was for him to go first and Alex and I would follow. It felt good to be useful, to speak to a ticket agent who didn't know or care about anyone's reason for departure. Her efficiency made my life seem normal, and I wanted to keep her on the line a little longer so it would stay that way.

Dad held up a dark suit and stared at it. "I don't know if it's bad luck to bring it." He looked to me for an answer.

"I don't know either."

He rested the suit on top of the Louis Vuitton suitcase, the one Henry Fonda had given him decades earlier, back when he made movies, when he had money, when his daughter helped him pack on his last day in Cortina.

"I gotta get Alex," I said.

We hugged, neither of us wanting to make a big deal about it, not wanting to give strength to our growing dread. The most Dad could muster was only "Oh, kiddo, what the fuck."

I raced to Pitt Street, cursing my luck to have a brother who refused to own a phone. I climbed his piss-stained stairway and banged on his door for some time before he opened it. He looked startled, then fearful to see me.

"What?" he said, not wanting to know what the what was.

"Alex, something happened to Dominique."

"It's Sweeney, isn't it?"

WE SAT IN THE BACK of a TWA flight that wouldn't arrive in Los Angeles until early evening. We would have caught an earlier flight had we not argued about whether to take a taxi to JFK or a train to the plane, which Alex argued would have been cheaper. I won the battle to get a taxi but lost the war when we couldn't find one and ended up taking the train. Alex and I knew it was ridiculous to fight, but our brotherly bickering felt familiar, and we both leapt at the chance to let off some steam.

We declined the meal from the stewardess, ordering Cokes instead.

"Oh," I said, before she left, "could you bring us some nuts?"

After a brief silence, Alex mumbled something I couldn't make out.

"What?" I asked.

"I said, 'Bring some shit for my fly.'"

"Why does that sound familiar?"

"It's the B. Kliban cartoon that Dominique loved. A guy in a fancy restaurant sits across from a huge fly and orders gazpacho, leeks vinaigrette, a bottle of Côtes du Rhône '59, and then tells the waiter, 'And bring some shit for my fly.'"

The joke didn't make us laugh, but the image of our sister's wicked grin was conjured in the private universe of our separate memories. In mine, I remembered her teasing me for having a crush on one of her friends.

"She wouldn't give you the time of day," she said about a girl who was dating the drummer of Huey Lewis's band.

I held on to her mischievous smile in my mind's eye for as long as I could, but it floated off.

HALLOWEEN WAS IN FULL SWING by the time we landed, and through the cab's windows we watched mobs of trick-or-treaters hustle candy from the wealthy residents of Beverly Hills.

Suddenly an unwanted memory of me as a child, trick-or-treating in a Casper the Friendly Ghost costume, getting fifty-cent pieces in lieu of candy from Frank Sinatra's butler, popped in out of nowhere, and I quietly slandered my ridiculous upbringing.

I saw a little girl's face covered in blood from a hatchet buried in her forehead, while her friend, dressed as a box of cornflakes that read CEREAL KILLER, wielded a knife. I wondered if before that morning I'd ever thought murder was hilarious, and though I probably had, I knew now I would never don a costume for Halloween again. The children covered in blood could laugh at violence and death because it had never touched their lives, and I silently hoped nothing would ever happen to make them lose the same macabre humor I so loved in my sister.

When our taxi reached a stop sign, someone dressed as a

skeleton banged on our window to frighten us, which he did, and Alex went apeshit.

"Fuck off, you motherfucker!"

I took his hand. "Alex, calm down, we're almost home."

Tacked to Mom's front door was a handwritten sign that read WE HAVE NO CANDY. PLEASE DO NOT DISTURB US.

The house was packed with friends of our family and Dominique's friends from high school and acting class, and a lot of people I'd never seen in my life. But Alex and I had eyes only for our mother, and when we found her, we dropped to our knees, carefully taking her in our arms. The chatter around us dropped to a whisper, and Alex began to choke back tears, until Mom said, "Not now, honey. We have to go to the hospital to see her. You've got to be strong. Your sister is waiting."

THERE WERE PHOTOGRAPHERS and news cameras in front of Cedars-Sinai, so someone from the hospital's public relations found another entrance for us to enter.

We announced ourselves to an ICU nurse who explained she couldn't let us in until she saw our identification, because some members of the press had tried to pass themselves off as family to get a picture of Dominique on life support. Detective Johnston was waiting for us, and after gently greeting my mother, introduced himself to Alex, Dad, and me. He seemed genuinely upset, even angered by our circumstance, and we liked him immediately.

Also in the waiting room sat a fraught-looking young man who stared at us so intently that we asked the detective who he was. Johnston said his name was David Packer, and he was with Dominique during the attack. Checking his notes, he continued to say they were both in a television series called *V*, and were running lines for a scene to film the next morning when John Sweeney showed up demanding to be let in. Not wanting to cause a scene in front of a colleague, Dominique excused herself to go outside, and once alone, the actor locked the door behind her. As Dominique was being strangled, Johnston said the actor hid in the bedroom and left a message on his roommate's answering machine that said, "If I get murdered tonight, John Sweeney did it."

Before we could absorb his act of cowardice, the nurse interrupted to say, "You should prepare yourselves," and unlocked the door to the ICU for us to follow her to Dominique's room.

We fell behind the nurse in a formation that would be set in stone in the coming year: Dad pushing Mom, Alex on the right of her wheelchair, and me on the left. Through glass windows on both sides of the hallway, we passed patients and their families on the worst days of their lives. An elegant man, with thick black hair and dark, tanned skin the texture of leather, appeared from one of the rooms to greet my father like a long-lost friend. It was the movie star George Hamilton.

"Dominick!"

"George?"

He pointed to a man dying in the bed behind him.

"My older brother. He hasn't much longer," George said. "What brings you here?"

"Well, umm," Dad stammered, before Mom cut him off.

"Nick, we've got to go."

"Great to see you, Nick."

"You, too, George."

"Well, that was fucking weird," muttered Alex, as we continued on our way.

The three of us slowly entered a room, far from prepared to see a swollen creature connected to a machine that wheezed an accordion-shaped bag up and down in sync with labored breathing.

Dominique's head was shaved, and there were bolts boring into her skull. Her skin was the color of a bruised peach, and her eyeballs bulged like a cartoon character who'd put her finger in a light socket. An air tube, crudely taped into her mouth, was connected to the machine that made the hideous wheezing sound. We stood just inside the room, none of us sure what to do until Mom took control and wheeled over to her bedside. She took her daughter's hand and said, "Darling, it's Mom. I'm here with Dad and your brothers, and we love you."

We joined Mom around the bed, each of us touching a part of Dominique's body, a hand, a leg, stroking her cold skin, each of us overlapping, "We love you, Dominique. We love you so much. We're right here . . ."

WE WENT TO THE HOSPITAL every day. Dominique was unresponsive, but once, when a doctor came to check on her, I felt her grip my hand for just a second.

"I just felt her move," I exclaimed in excitement.

The doctor said it was only an electro-impulse. Her brain still showed no activity.

"If she comes out of it, will there be brain damage?" my father asked.

"Should your daughter recover, I'm afraid the damage would be massive and irreparable."

The subtext was that Dominique would never recover, and at some point she would have to be taken off life support, but no one was ready for that conversation. A worse alternative than death would be for her to live out her life in a vegetative state, and the very thought was so painful I suppressed it as much as possible. Even three days after the attack, I remained somewhat positive, believing in miracles, and that Dominique deserved one because she was too special to be taken from us. My parents and Alex clung to the same hope, and we told Dominique about all the calls, telegrams, and visits from people all over the world who sent their wishes for her recovery, believing we were heard.

"You are so loved, darling," my mother said at the high volume that we'd all adopted when speaking to her.

"Please come back," Dad would say, leaning close to her ear.

Sometimes I had my doubts Dominique would come back, but Alex's faith restored me. At the end of the day, when it came time for us to leave, Alex refused, and stayed all night reading her the poems of Yeats, and W. S. Merwin's "Snowfall" over and over like chants, as if the recitation of high art might somehow awaken her.

This morning
I see that the silent kin I loved as a child
have arrived all together in the night.

Alex also stayed to avoid the steady stream of well-wishers bearing catered meals, booze, and comfort who continued to arrive at the house on Crescent Drive. The most helpful of these visitors was a woman who showed up the first day the news hit the papers. She attended to our every need, bringing Mom a plate of her homemade meat loaf, answering the constantly ringing phone, and making sure all the guests had a fresh drink.

"Does anyone know who that woman is?" Mom asked Dad and me.

"I thought she was with you," he answered.

"I thought she was with you," I said to Dad.

"Never seen her in my life. But she makes a helluva meat loaf," said Mom.

I was happy to see my mother eating, and neither of us had the heart to kick the helpful stranger out.

I watched Ethel, the filthy little dog with bald spots Dominique had rescued years ago, work her way between the guests' legs in search of catered scraps. Every now and then someone would reach down to pet her, realize their mistake, and then try to clean their hands with a cocktail napkin. Ethel had stayed with Mom, but Dominique had taken Taylor, the mutt she'd picked up off the streets of Boulder, to live with her on Rangely. Detective Johnston had one of his officers bring him back to Crescent Drive the morning after the attack.

"Where's Taylor?" I asked Mom.

"He's been lying outside Dominique's pool house since he got here and won't come inside, even to eat. It's like he knows something happened to her."

Dad watched Ethel work the room for several moments before he spoke.

"All of Dominique's animals were strays. She gave them a home. Then one day she brought one back and he tried to kill her."

John and Joan had been at the house every day, and I caught Dad focusing his glare on them across the room. Days before, he had taken them up on their offer to stay at their house in Brentwood on his arrival. John's grief over Dominique was immeasurable, and the two brothers had greeted each other with hugs and gasping tears.

A truce was called, but it didn't last long.

Shortly after Sweeney's arrest, we were shocked to learn from the local news that Ma Maison had hired an attorney to defend their sous-chef. John and Joan were friends of the owner, Patrick Terrail, who knew Dominique as well, and Dad had already been stewing over the fact that Terrail never bothered to reach out to her parents with a word of sympathy.

On a morning when John and Joan were absent, Dad signed for a large orchid that had been delivered to them. To not peek at the card to find out who sent the orchid was simply too much to ask of my father. Dad opened the sealed envelope gently to leave no trace of his trespass. The card read, "My heart breaks for you, Patrick Terrail."

He immediately called me in a rage.

"That fucker lawyered up to protect the killer and then sends John and Joan *flowers*! I bet they're having lunch at Ma Maison right now."

"I doubt that very much," I said, but Dad wasn't buying it.

He couldn't very well admit to reading Terrail's note, but moved out anyway without explanation before John and Joan returned.

John called me soon after his brother's abrupt exit to ask what happened, and I told him about the orchid and that Dad knew who sent it.

"I can't control who sends us flowers, Griffin."

"I know, but I gotta ask. Dad also thinks you still go to Ma Maison. Is that true?"

"Are you crazy?"

"Well, yes, I think we all are."

"We would never set foot in that place and never will."

I chose to believe him, but the unfounded accusation, the orchid, and the note from Terrail sent my brother and Dominique's best friend, Melinda, around the bend. They vowed not to let this treason go unanswered.

On day four of Dominique being on life support, Rupert Allan asked if he could speak to me alone, and I followed him outside. Rupert was a publicist and old family friend whose clients had been Marilyn Monroe, Marlene Dietrich, and Princess Grace of Monaco. He volunteered to field and deny the countless requests from the press to interview the Dunnes. His first order of business was to correct a misconception that was carried in all the papers that only added to my father's anger.

"They all describe Dominique as the niece of John Dunne and Joan Didion," he complained to Mom and her mother, who had just flown in from San Diego.

Mom had stayed close with John and Joan since her divorce from Dad and hadn't the patience for his sibling rivalry. She didn't know about the orchid from Terrail.

"What difference does it make," Mom sighed, irritated to be reminded of superficial concerns that had troubled her ex-husband when they were married.

"Nick's right," said Gammer. "It makes it sound like she doesn't have parents."

Dad knew his mother-in-law could barely tolerate him and was surprised by her sudden support.

"All right," Mom said after mulling it over. "Have Rupert take care of it."

Rupert led me out of earshot from the house and took a long beat before deciding to speak.

"I don't want to bother your parents with this, but when Dominique dies, a statement must be released to the press from the family. I've put something together that is brief and dignified that I wanted you to read before I show it to Nick and Lenny."

I thought maybe I didn't hear him correctly, or maybe misunderstood what he'd said. Or maybe he was the one who was confused.

"But Dominique is not dead. She's still alive."

"No, of course," Rupert admitted, immediately regretting this conversation. But he plugged on.

"I mean, when she dies, a statement must be in place. It's how things are done."

"You mean *if* she dies."

An unexpected assault of tears ambushed me in the driveway. No one until then had ever said that Dominique would die, and I felt like a fool that it was so obvious to everyone but me.

"Oh, son, I'm so sorry to have brought this up. It was a terrible mistake. Please forgive me."

His remorse was genuine, and I knew in that moment that he was just looking out for us, and that, of course, my sister would die.

I went back inside the house, taking in all the people who'd been hugging me for days, telling me to keep strong, that Dominique was a fighter. Everyone looked different than they had only minutes earlier. What I hadn't seen, but which was suddenly clear, was that Alex and I were the last to know that the past four days had been one long wake.

Something shifted within me, and I suddenly felt different as well. My perspective and personality took on a new formation not yet defined. But whoever I'd be in the days ahead would never be the person I was.

ON NOVEMBER 4, 1982, five days after the attack, we went to Cedars-Sinai to give consent for Dominique to be taken off life support and to say our final goodbyes.

By then we'd accepted that there was no chance she'd recover, and though we wished we'd taken her off sooner, it turned out the choice to do so was never just up to us. The reason Dominique had to remain in purgatory would be our initiation to California's judicial system. Detective Johnston had explained that as long as Dominique remained on life support, the charges against Sweeney would remain voluntary manslaughter, but the moment she passed, the indictment would be upped to murder in the first degree. If she had been taken off any sooner, Sweeney's lawyers could argue that the family had acted prematurely.

Detective Johnston met us in the ICU waiting room, and in the presence of two emergency room doctors, formally asked us if we were giving Cedars-Sinai consent to take Dominique Dunne off life support. We nodded the affirmative in his direction, none of us wanting to be the first to speak.

"I'm sorry, Mr. Dunne," apologized the detective, "but I'm afraid you have to tell me."

"Yes, the Dunne family is asking Cedars-Sinai to take my daughter off life support."

"Thank you, sir."

He shook each of our hands and left for LA County lockup, where Sweeney was being held, to charge him with murder.

Mom turned to Dr. Edward Brettholz and Dr. Gray Elrod, who had been by our side since the beginning, and said, "When Dominique dies, we would like her organs donated to the hospital." Dr. Elrod was moved, knowing the request was from a woman with a disease for which there was no cure, and said two patients in the hospital were waiting for kidney transplants. Dominique's heart was sent to San Francisco, where I hope it's still beating. She would have appreciated that, like the Tony Bennett classic, she "left her heart in San Francisco."

By now we knew the way to Dominique's room, and also knew the families who had been bedside with their loved ones as long as we had. George Hamilton's brother had died days earlier, but over hospital coffee, we'd become acquainted with many of the others through sympathetic exchanges about our common misfortunes. They watched us in respectful silence as we passed them down the long hallway, clearly knowing the purpose of our final visit. It reminded me of those prison dramas, where the condemned man passes the inmates on death row on his way to Old Sparky. Only we were the executioners on our way to the condemned.

We gave each other privacy when it was our turn to say goodbye. There were no tears because the reality was too unreal to accept. We talked about this day being "the last time," but it didn't seem possible my sister would have no tomorrow. None of us could hear what the others said, but later, Dad told me he whispered in her ear, "Give me your talent."

MY FAMILY USED TO CALL the Good Shepherd church in Beverly Hills Our Lady of the Cadillacs because of the luxury cars in the parking lot and the hefty sums its well-heeled flock would drop into the collection basket.

"Dean Martin gave *a hundred-dollar bill.* Did you see that?" Dad would ask my mom on the drive home from church.

"The Joker sat right in front of us," Alex once said, meaning Cesar Romero, who played the villain on *Batman*, our favorite TV show.

Dominique had been baptized in Good Shepherd, and the three of us all suffered through Sunday school there to receive our first Communion. When it was my turn, my father's mother,

Gammer Do—a woman so devout she wept looking at the Pietà when it was displayed at the World's Fair—flew in from Hartford for the milestone. During the service, in front of a packed house, the monsignor gave our class a surprise pop quiz to show off how much we'd learned from the Bible.

He picked me out of the crowd and said, "Griffin, what did Moses say to God at the burning bush?"

I had no idea what Moses had said, and while the congregation waited for my answer, I dropped to the floor and hid behind the pew. Monsignor called on me, over and over, before moving on to some kid who'd paid attention in Sunday school. Gammer Do was mortified by my behavior and threatened not to give me the amazing present she'd been planning since hearing of my Communion. I was expecting great sums of money like my Jewish friends got for their bar mitzvahs and was duly unimpressed when she eventually gave me a strand of my very own rosary beads.

After we said goodbye to Dominique that night at the hospital, Dad and I went to see the monsignor—the same monsignor who'd baptized her and given me the Communion pop quiz—to make arrangements for her funeral. He kept us waiting outside his private quarters for a long time. A young priest had come out several times to apologize before we were finally let into his residence. The first thing we noticed was that the monsignor was drunk. Without saying it in so many words, His Holiness made it known that he wasn't crazy about having a funeral for someone who had the poor taste to get herself murdered. He mumbled that he wasn't entirely sure he could accommodate us given the schedule of prior events.

Dad, who under normal circumstances would have called the monsignor a drunk cocksucker, was surprisingly calm. "You know, you baptized my daughter, the person we are here to make arrangements for."

"What was her name?"

"Dominique Dunne."

"I don't recall."

"Her godmother was with us at the baptismal font. Maria Cooper Janis, daughter of Gary Cooper?"

The monsignor's eyes suddenly beamed at us in a bourbon haze. "Ah, Mr. Cooper was a great patron of Good Shepherd. It was my fondest hope Maria would become a nun, but she married a Jewish fella."

The date was set for four days later.

When the funeral cortege pulled up in front of the church, my pal and designated pallbearer Charlie rushed to our limousine before we could exit. "There has been a *huge* fuckup. The funeral is overlapping with a wedding that is just about to end. We have to wait until it's over."

"Oh my God," said Mom.

"That drunk cocksucker," said Dad.

From the limo, we watched a bride and groom descend the steps of the church under fistfuls of rice and suddenly stop, in utter confusion, at the sight of news cameras below, waiting to film the celebrities expected to arrive for the funeral. Once the wedding party and the mourners had passed each other on the steps, we finally made our move to go inside.

"That's the mother! That's the father!" shouted the photographers and cameramen as they swarmed us.

Alex approached the mob, yelling, "Get the fucker out of the—" before Dad ordered him to keep cool and get back in formation.

The rice from the wedding stuck to the wheels of Mom's chair and crunched under our shoes.

"Oh no," said my mother as Miguel Ferrer, Charlie, and a few more of Dominique's friends came down the aisle carrying the casket, draped in pink flowers. "She hated pansies. She hated the color pink." Even the florists, whom Mom had used for years, fucked her over that morning. "That's not what I ordered," she said to no one in particular.

Martin Manulis, Dominique's godfather and the man who brought Dad and his family to Los Angeles twenty-six years earlier to work for him on *Playhouse 90*, gave the eulogy and described her as "an infanta by Goya, only more beautiful."

Alex and I read the Yeats poem "The Song of Wandering Aengus," which was suggested by Joan. In halting voices, we barely managed to get through:

> *I will find out where she has gone,*
> *And kiss her lips and take her hands;*
> *And walk among long dappled grass,*
> *And pluck till time and times are done,*
> *The silver apples of the moon,*
> *The golden apples of the sun.*

The monsignor, presumably sober, never bothered to pronounce Dominique's name correctly, calling her "Dom*inick*," as if he didn't even know the gender of the person he was eulogizing.

Every time he said Dominick, Alex's and my ears burned with rage and we blurted out, "Neeek! Neeek! DomiNEEK!" Heads turned our way but we didn't care, and this time Dad didn't try to halt our outbursts.

We continued for the burial at Westwood Memorial Park, and gathered around a freshly dug plot only yards from where Mom's best friend, Natalie Wood, had been laid to rest a year earlier. As Dominique was being lowered into the ground, a tour bus let out sightseers in front of Marilyn Monroe's crypt. The monsignor approached our family to shake hands, and when he came to me, his arm outstretched, I looked him in the eye and whispered, "You are a piece of shit." He didn't react in the slightest, and moved on to whoever was to my right.

ALEX, DAD, AND I STAYED on in Los Angeles for a couple of weeks after the funeral to keep Mom company, but in the days that followed, she found new company in a group of friends who would comfort and support her to the end of her life.

The day after the disastrous funeral at Our Lady of the Cadillacs, Mom received a phone call from a woman who opened with the line "Mrs. Dunne, I'm afraid you are now a member of a club that no one wants to belong to."

On the other end was Doris Tate, mother of Sharon Tate, calling on behalf of a group called Parents of Murdered Children. Her daughter was eight months pregnant when stabbed to death by Charles Manson's cult members, and she was calling to invite my mother to a meeting of her support group being held that night. Mom asked us if we would like to go, and Dad said he "wasn't ready," followed by a "no fucking way" from Alex, so I took her to the meeting at a church in Brentwood.

I wheeled my mother into a space a parent had made for her in an already formed circle of other parents. Someone brought me a chair to sit next to her, but I felt I didn't belong and was about to leave, when Mom mouthed, "Please stay."

The parents took turns sharing the brutal tragedies they had in common. Some had had children murdered years earlier, others endured fresher wounds, but all seemed grateful to have one day a week to speak to the only people who would understand their loss. My mother was shy even when talking to a group of more than five friends, let alone strangers, but to my amazement, she spoke up without prompting, and described the blow-by-blow events of our family's past seven days. She shed no tears, and seemed almost eager to get if off her chest, but the disbelief in her tone made her story sound as if it had happened to somebody else. Physical affection never came easy to my mother, but when Doris Tate took her hand as she described her daughter on life support, Mom gripped it right back and plowed on.

In the silent anticipation of the next volunteer, a father whose son had been killed by a stray bullet in Compton asked if I'd like to say anything. I wasn't expecting, or even emotionally prepared, to speak, but it felt rude to be the only one not sharing their feelings.

"I know everyone here is a parent, and from listening to all you have been through, I realize that to lose a child is very different than losing a sibling. It's not more or less, it's just different. Or maybe it is more, I don't know."

That's as far as I got before I started to blubber. I felt like an asshole to be the only person in the room who cried, but my tears kept me from expressing an anger I had suppressed throughout the meeting. They seemed to be saying that the grief of someone who raised a child had greater meaning than mine, that of someone who had only lost a sister. I'm sure that was far from their intent, and thankfully, my weeping prevented me from expressing such a self-pitying remark.

On the ride back to Crescent Drive, I felt embarrassed by my display of emotion and hoped it wasn't obvious. At a red light on

Wilshire, Mom turned to me and said, "You were very brave, honey. I know how hard that must have been for you."

"No, Mom," I said. "*You* are very brave."

AFTER NOTICING THAT THE CROWDS at the house had finally thinned but for Mom's most die-hard friends, and knowing that she had made new ones, I felt the time was right to return to my life in New York. There were no understudies for *Hooters*, so the play had closed the day I left, and though I was back to being an unemployed actor, I couldn't imagine ever having to pretend I was a teenager who felt awkward around girls.

Alex, Dad, and I hugged Mom goodbye and she assured us that she would be fine. As we were about to leave, she added, "Well, I guess I'll see you all at the trial."

Yes, the trial. Parents of Murdered Children had already helped her brace for this next chapter in her life, but the three of us were far from ready to even think about what lay ahead.

Twenty-Four

Two days after Dad returned from Los Angeles, he stood at the corner of Seventh Avenue and Eleventh Street in the West Village. It's known to be a confusing intersection because Greenwich Avenue runs through the middle of those two busy streets from different directions, which makes the right of way for pedestrians a free-for-all. Waiting for the light to change, my father saw a truck barrel down Seventh and run over a stroller with a baby inside, not twenty feet away.

"The baby just exploded!" he yelled into the phone when he called me right after. "There were parts of it everywhere. Oh God, oh God," he repeated over and over in horror.

No longer a practicing Catholic but a devotee of Alcoholics Anonymous, my father believed in a higher power and never let a day go by without saying the Serenity Prayer, asking God to keep him sober and "accept the things I cannot change." Through the receiver, I listened to him groan and sob like a dying animal, and thought about what his higher power had done for him lately: strangled his daughter, forced him to take her off life support and arrange a funeral eulogized by a monsignor who couldn't pronounce the name of the girl in the coffin, and then made him an intimate witness to an exploding toddler. It was a miracle he hadn't started drinking again, and I wouldn't have blamed him if he did.

"Well," he said when he was all cried out, "if I haven't started drinking by now, I think I never will."

For a moment, I thought I'd said my thoughts out loud.

THE NIGHT WE'D ARRIVED on Halloween, Alex had moved into the pool house where Dominique had lived until her move to Rangely Avenue. She'd left it looking pretty much the same, not even taking her poster of Henri Rousseau's *Exotic Landscape*, the same painting as Norman Carby's mural on the side of Mom's house. Alex slept in Dominique's bed under a quilt from her childhood, and listened to the music he remembered her loving: James Taylor's cover of "Up on the Roof"; Dan Fogelberg, a holdover from her days in Colorado; and Christopher Cross's "Sailing," which Alex and I had always teased her about, though now the song evoked vividly painful images and memories of her. The song remained on the charts for months and clutched my heart every time I heard it on the radio.

One night in the pool house, Alex had more than just soundtracked images to keep her memory alive. He awoke to see Dominique sitting at the foot of the bed. Alex described her as not ghostly but three-dimensional, and though the bedroom was dark, the moon illuminated her face, hands, and even the buttons on the cotton shirt she wore. He wanted to reach out and touch her, but didn't for fear she would go away.

"Alex," she said to him, "I'm okay, everything is fine with me, but I'm worried about you. I need you to hold it together. I can't move on if you start flipping out and worrying Mom. She needs you to be strong, and so do I."

Alex told me the next morning that he promised her he would, and how they continued talking well into the night. I knew he'd gone to bed sober, and never doubted for a moment that his visitation was real. It was so like Dominique to appear only to Alex, because even though he had been surprisingly strong, she worried he might not hold on much longer and that the only person he'd listen to would be his little sister. And she was right. Alex was far from saddened or disturbed by their conversation; in fact, her visit seemed to bring him peace.

He took a risk in telling me what happened, because I might have thought him crazy, and when I didn't, he decided not to push his luck by telling anyone else. What I didn't tell him was that I felt shamefully envious that Dominique hadn't come to me.

The closest I had to an apparition was a nightmare where she stood before me screaming in terror, the side of her stomach blown away by a shotgun blast. My horrific dream might have been subconsciously planted from a clip of her in *Poltergeist* screaming, "*What's happening?*" that played continuously on the news when I was in Los Angeles. Months later, my nightmare continued to haunt me. The sounds of her screaming and the sight of her gaping wound would ambush me with flashbacks so often and unexpectedly that I decided to see a psychic to find out if I could make contact with her and find the same peace as Alex had.

I had heard of a paranormal reputed to be "the real deal," who saw clients at his apartment in the Ansonia, and made an appointment.

The Ansonia was a Beaux Arts building on the Upper West

Side designed to rival the luxury of the Dakota, which had been built fifteen years earlier. In its prime it was a residential hotel where Babe Ruth and Igor Stravinsky once lived, and even had a small farm on the roof with dairy cows and chickens to supply eggs and fresh milk to the guests below.

By the early 1980s the building was in disrepair, and its grand thirty-room apartments had been sectioned into studios with cheap plaster walls. I had been in the Ansonia once before to see a vocal coach, and again in its basement when Carrie Fisher, Buck Henry, and I witnessed the scene at Plato's Retreat, a sex club so depraved that after stepping over naked bodies on sticky floors, Carrie threw the dress she wore in the trash.

The psychic lived on a high floor, and the sounds of violin lessons and sopranos failing to reach their octaves filled the hallway. The man who answered the door looked like Alec Guinness, if Obi-Wan Kenobi had put on fifty pounds and wore a caftan. He led me to a table through a canyon of old newspapers, proof that my psychic was also a hoarder. When I'd made the appointment I'd told him my name was Tom Griffin, close to the truth but not enough for the psychic to research Dominique or me beforehand.

He faced me across the table and held my hands, then closed his eyes and took a deep breath to let the spirits settle. I was pegged right away as a performer.

"You are in the creative arts, maybe an actor in addition to other prospects, and you will do quite well. That much is clear. But there is something else."

"What is that?" I asked.

"Something dark."

He went further into a trance and muttered, "Oh no, this is bad. This is evil."

"What are you talking about?"

He babbled a lot of mumbo jumbo chants before finally saying, "There is a young girl, alone and frightened. Dom, Dom, Doma-something. She doesn't know where she is and wants to get out. She is terrified. Do you know who it is I'm seeing?"

"I think so, yes," I said, tightening my grip on his hands. Before I could add anything else, he launched into a cascade of words without punctuation.

"There were once two families the Hatfields and the McCoys and they hated each other one act of violence spawned their hate which spawned more violence and on and on it went for generations."

He opened his eyes and yanked his hands from mine with such disgust that I thought he might hit me.

"You possess that hate, and this girl is very angry at you. You have thoughts of revenge, and she wants you to stop whatever you are planning right now!"

"I'm not planning anything!"

"She is in limbo and cannot leave until you rid yourself of hate and vengeance. She is very upset with you. You upset me as well, and I will not have your hate in my home a moment longer. Go immediately."

Obi-Wan got out of his chair and forcibly moved me toward the door.

"Why are you doing this? I don't mean to upset her. Tell her I'm sorry."

"She doesn't want to hear your apology. Out you go."

"Please don't do this. Get her back!"

He shoved me into the hallway and locked the door behind me. I collapsed to my knees and begged him to let me in.

"I'm sorry, Dominique! Tell her I'm sorry!" I yelled, banging on his door.

I carried on like that for some time, drawing "keep it down" from his neighbors, but the heartless bastard was unmoved.

I did have hate in my heart but hadn't been plotting to seek vengeance. That would come later. But even if I had, Sweeney was at that time in jail.

Yet I had no doubt that the anger Dominique felt for me was as real as her visitation to Alex. The psychic either was a sadist or had actually predicted a plot I was a year from contemplating.

IN THE YEAR SINCE Dominique died, Dad couldn't help but notice he'd become a bit of a minor celebrity for all the wrong reasons. At an AA meeting, an acquaintance introduced him to a first-timer to Perry Street. As the two men shook hands, Dad saw out of the corner of his eye that the guy doing the introductions was frantically pointing at him while mouthing to the first-timer, "This is the guy whose daughter was," and then mimed strangling himself.

Society ladies he hadn't spoken to in years were suddenly inviting him to their dinners as the extra man, but Dad knew it was either out of sympathy or to hear the gory details, and turned most of them down.

And yet the day before he returned to Los Angeles for the trial, he reluctantly accepted an invitation to a dinner party that would change the course of his life.

The journalist Marie Brenner was a close and loyal friend he met at his lowest point in Hollywood, who never considered Dad the failure he thought himself. She gently browbeat him to get out of his dark apartment, with the mysterious carrot that she had invited someone important for him to know.

Marie seated him next to Tina Brown, who was in town from London to meet Leo Lerman about reinventing *Vanity Fair.*

During the few social occasions he had attended, Dad never mentioned Dominique, believing it would cheapen her memory to use her death as idle party chatter. But there was something about Tina that compelled him to talk about his daughter's murder, Alex's sensitivity, and the health of his ex-wife, whom he confessed he still loved. He liked the way she listened to him, her eyes that never left his but didn't moisten in sympathy, and her undivided attention that let him feel he was finally being heard. The decibel of conversation around the table lowered as guests tried to eavesdrop, and noticing this, Tina touched Dad's hand to speak more quietly, which only increased their intimacy.

In a hushed tone my father told her the upcoming trial scared him because he knew nothing about court procedure except from movies and the scandalous crimes he followed in the tabloids that always fascinated him, but he never dreamed he'd be called upon to seek justice for the murder of his own daughter. He worried for Lenny, and shared his dread that they both might not be strong enough to survive the span of the trial.

As Tina listened, the idea of a crime story that had never been told before formed in her mind: a man without any legal experience, thrust into a judicial system where a judge and lawyers determine the fate of his daughter's killer, describes the courtroom drama and the effect it has on his family.

Tina leaned in close and said to him, "I don't have the job at *Vanity Fair* yet, but when I do, if you keep a journal every day of the trial, come see me when it's over and I will publish it."

Dad called me when he got home and sounded happier than I'd heard him all year.

"That woman *saw* me, Griffin. Tina knew I was born to be a writer, and she is the only person to seriously believe I am one."

I hung up the phone that day holding two feelings that were—and were to remain—in conflict with one another. I was happy for my father. He had touched bottom and I wanted him to come back as the person he felt he truly was, whoever that turned out to be.

But his enthusiasm and excitement also unnerved me. He seemed all too ready and willing to use Dominique's trial as a springboard for his own midlife metamorphosis. I congratulated him, but only half-heartedly, though I'm not sure he registered my ambivalence.

Twenty-Five

Though now a common but grim duty for a family to attend the trial of a person who murdered their loved one, in the summer of 1983, it was considered most unusual. Parents of Murdered Children told Mom how important it was for the jury to see our family "front row and center" representing her daughter, who could not speak for herself. Mom, Dad, Alex, and I could not have agreed more.

"It will be the second-worst experience of your life," Doris Tate told Mom. "First your daughter is murdered, and they will try to murder her again in the courtroom. The jury will never know who she was unless they see who you are. It's your last order of business in Dominique's life."

When we heard a prosecutor named Steven Barshop had been assigned to the case, we went to the Santa Monica Courthouse to meet him. Mom told us she had left him several messages to make an appointment, and when Barshop finally returned her call, he reluctantly gave us his time.

His office was empty when we showed up at the designated

time, so we made ourselves at home. Manila folders were piled high on his desk, the walls lined with the obligatory law degrees and commendations, and the chairs wobbled as if on their last legs. Maybe ten minutes passed before Barshop dashed in, a man in a hurry.

He was tall as a Laker, early forties, with thick salt-and-pepper hair. He did not sit behind his desk but chose to stand in the middle of his cramped office.

"Sorry to keep you waiting," he began. "I have to warn you, I'm on a short break from court so I don't have much time."

"Well, thank you for seeing us," Mom said tightly, but ever polite.

Dad extended his hand to Barshop and introduced his sons, setting us off on a round of curt handshakes.

"I regret meeting you under these circumstances," Barshop said, his manner softening for the first time. "To be perfectly honest, I was surprised you asked to meet. Not many families do that. The trial process isn't really about the victim's family: it's about getting justice for the victim."

We were momentarily taken aback, until Dad said, "I was under the impression the two were connected."

Barshop studied us like a man comfortable with the tension he thrived on creating in a courtroom.

"So I take it you plan on attending the trial?"

"Is that a problem?" Mom shot back.

"It's your right. It might even be good for the jury to see you. But bear in mind, trials like this one have a way of . . . turning in on themselves."

"What does that mean?" I asked, dreading the direction his answer might take.

"You'd be amazed how quickly blame can shift from the

perpetrator to the victim in a case like this. The defense will say anything they can to discredit her. They'll burrow into her lifestyle. Her past. Her habits. Even her success can be used against her. It's going to feel like *Dominique's* the one up there on trial, not John Sweeney."

"Well then," Alex piped up, "what the hell is it you do?"

"I intend to hold the man who did this fully responsible. It's hard for a layperson to understand, but when all is said and done, the only thing I truly control is the presentation of evidence. And while I appreciate your desire to attend the trial, I won't have any armchair quarterbacks from the bleachers. I work for the state of California, not the Dunne family, and it's my show to run as I see fit."

I couldn't believe we were being scolded for expressing an interest in what he called his "show," but before I could fire back, Mom calmly asked, "Are you saying you don't want to talk to us during the trial? What if we have a question outside of the court hours, may we at least call you?"

"Of course any questions you have I'm happy to answer, and the courthouse switchboard will find me in my office. Now if you will excuse me, I'm needed back in court."

"What an assssshole," Alex bellowed as we fit Mom's wheelchair into the back of the Chevy Nova.

"Maybe it's good he's an asshole," Mom said once we were all back in the car, probably the first time in her life she had ever joined *ass* with *hole*. "Don't we want someone like that fighting for Dominique?"

A COUPLE OF MONTHS before the start of the trial, 20th Century Fox had flown me to Los Angeles for the day to audition for a movie called *Johnny Dangerously*. It was an over-the-top spoof of Warner Bros. gangster movies, starring Michal Keaton and directed by Amy Heckerling. I had one of those rare moments an actor has when he walks into an audition and, before even reading for the part, knows he's got the gig. I was hilarious from the moment I entered the producer's office, and Amy and I clicked right away. One of the upsides of living with grief was that unlike auditions prior to my sister's death, the anxieties about whether I was liked or not now seemed ridiculous in comparison. I simply didn't give a shit either way. I recommend this attitude to all beginning actors, whether someone in your family has been murdered or not.

I accepted the job, because that was my job, but how I would balance my emotional life acting in a slapstick comedy about goofy gangsters who murdered for a living while spending my days off in a murder trial, I would just have to wait and see.

With the per diem I got from *Johnny Dangerously* I was able to rent a hot-shit convertible and a beach house on Leo Carrillo State Park, which was north of Malibu, less than an hour from 20th Century Fox Studios, and a nineteen-minute drive from there to the Santa Monica Courthouse. I found the house in the want ads, and Brooke—who volunteered to come out to LA to support me during the trial—and I fell in love with it at first sight. The house was on stilts, facing a particularly rough ocean that Brooke rarely ventured to, but my greatest pleasure after a day in court or on set was to bodysurf the big waves that slammed me onto the shore. Charlie stayed with us most of the time, as did Alex, and for people who sat through a homicide trial every day, we still managed to have a lot of laughs. Much of our hilarity that summer was bolstered by trips on LSD.

My twenty-eighth birthday fell two weeks before I left for LA, and Carrie had thrown me a birthday party in her penthouse apartment in the El Dorado on the Upper West Side. There was a heat wave, and the elevators were broken, so the guests arrived drenched in sweat after climbing seventeen flights. Seeing Susan Sarandon's glistening body in a tank top was gift enough, but she threw in another present, which was just a piece of paper with rows of red dots on it.

"And this is . . . ?" I asked.

"It's a sheet of acid from Timothy Leary's personal stash. There is a note on the back."

I turned over the page and read what Susan had written: "This is either a brilliant or terrible idea to take during what you will be going through, but I hope it's the former. Happy Birthday Griffin."

And below that, a note from Tim Leary: "This is the finest acid ever produced, and from me, that's saying a lot. Susan told me what lies ahead for you and I hope this might help with your journey."

I have to say it really did. Alex, Charlie, Brooke, and I would moisten those little paper dots on our tongues every weekend, and the trips were amazing. One time the four of us realized we spoke Spanish and launched into an improvisational dance to Bizet's opera *Carmen*, which was playing on the turntable. None of us even knew the plot but, in our transcendental state, followed it faithfully right up to where Alex, as Don José, stabs Carmen, the cunning seductress played by Brooke.

ON THE LAST WEEKEND before the start of jury selection, Dad told me to come into town for a family meeting at Mom's house. She had received a call from the journalist Barry Farrell, who wanted to deliver a message from Sweeney's attorney, Mike Adelson. Barry was my uncle John's best friend, and a crime reporter who was best known for his newsbreaking coverage about the Hillside Strangler. I had known him as far back as the Janis Joplin party and thought him one of the coolest cats in John and Joan's circle. Dad didn't know Barry at all, but the fact that he was best friends with his brother made him suspect and started the meeting off on the wrong foot.

Alex, Dad, and I sat on a couch in the living room, with Mom nearby in her wheelchair, all of us facing Barry in a seat that was too small for him. No one spoke for the longest time.

Barry was so nervous that beads of sweat dotted his forehead, but after fortifying himself with a large glass of scotch served neat by Alex, he got down to the business at hand.

"Please know that I am only here in the capacity of messenger, I have no dog in this fight, but at the request of Mike Adelson, would like to offer a way to spare you a torturous trial, and speaking as a court reporter, I can assure you that is just what you will face."

"Go on," Dad said, and after another large gulp of scotch, Barry continued.

"Mr. Adelson, who is a skilled and respected attorney, has asked me to see if your family will accept a plea bargain to where Sweeney would serve a mandatory seven-and-a-half-year sentence for second-degree murder."

"We've already been down this road," Dad said. "The *respected* Mr. Adelson offered us the same deal months ago through Steven Barshop, the person you should be approaching instead of us, and we readily accepted it, relieved to avoid a trial that would put a strain on my wife's health." (In all the years since their divorce, Dad still called Mom "my wife.") "Two days after we agreed to the plea, your Mr. Adelson reneged without explanation. If he was trying to mind-fuck us, he succeeded, so I take his offer with a grain of salt."

"I can't address that, but even your brother John believes this offer is sincere."

Bringing John into this was the wrong move, and the tension in the room heightened considerably. John had been making it his business to find out what was happening behind the scenes from his contacts in law enforcement. He spoke the shorthand of seasoned cops and DAs who appreciated his dark Irish humor. We had heard he'd dropped in on Barshop unannounced to offer unasked-for advice about how he should strategize his prosecution. The only time we'd heard from Barshop since our first meeting was when he asked us to tell John Dunne to butt out of his business.

Barry registered the scowl on Dad's face at the mention of his brother, and dove into deeper water.

"John and I both know Adelson and consider his tactics to be ruthless. Neither of us believe Barshop is tough enough to handle him. Adelson will try to make Dominique a participant in her own death; he will dig up ugly and irrelevant details that will be difficult for you to hear, even if they're not true. John wants to avoid a trial not just for your sake but because he is certain Adelson will call Quintana to the stand."

"Why would he do that?" my mother asked, mystified.

"To drag down the character of anyone who knew Dominique. John is so worried about Quintana being called that he and Joan are taking her to Paris until the trial is over."

This was the first any of us heard of their skipping town, and we digested the news in a long silence.

Barry drained the remainder of his scotch and stood, eager to make his getaway.

"I'm sorry if my coming here has only added to your troubles, but as I said, I'm only the messenger and I thank you for your time."

Everyone but me remained seated. I liked Barry and was embarrassed by my family's rudeness. I walked him to his battered Karmann Ghia in the driveway.

"Man, that dude really hates my guts," he said, referring to my father. "That was a bitch."

"I know, Barry, we are all—"

"Don't even say it. I get it. I've seen it. You guys are in for hell."

He tried to pull the keys out of his pocket, but they dropped to the pavement.

"Are you cool to drive?" I asked cautiously.

"Fuck yeah. You take care, kid."

He gave me a hug and took off. As I went back in the house, I saw Dad watching me through the window.

ON MONDAY MORNING, the first day of jury selection, we went to Barshop's office before court was in session to tell him about Adelson's intermediated offer.

I pulled Mom's Chevy Nova into a parking space at the courthouse, followed by Dad into a spot next to us in Dominique's electric-blue VW Bug. Not able to afford a rental car for the length of the trial, he requisitioned Dominique's, which had been sitting untouched in Mom's driveway since her murder. In the glove compartment, Dad found the sunglasses he'd given her when she visited him in Italy. From the first day of the trial to the last, they became a talisman he never entered the courtroom without. In the tough days ahead, he would hold them in his coat pocket for strength.

But first we had to pass through a gauntlet of news cameras, supporters from Parents of Murdered Children, Women Against Violence Against Women, and Victims for Victims, which had been founded by the actress Theresa Saldana (Joe Pesci's wife in *Raging Bull*), who had survived ten stab wounds from a stalker. These men and women would attend the trial every day and be a constant source of much-needed comfort in the months ahead. Other diehards who sat with us every day were the friends of Alex, Dominique, and me: Brooke Adams, Bryan Cook, Melinda and Lisa Bittan, Kit McDonough, Erica Elliott, Denise Dennehy, Mark Metcalf, and of course Charlie.

Alex, Dad, Mom, and I entered the courtroom in a formation we set a year earlier when approaching Dominique's room at the ICU. In the months ahead, our formation would never change.

"You didn't accept it, did you?" Barshop asked, infuriated.

"No, we wanted to speak to you first," said Dad. "We trust your judgment and will go along with whatever you decide."

Barshop dropped the tough act, and his attitude toward us softened, even while delivering a sobering reality:

"Well, at this point, the matter is out of your hands. The state wishes to proceed with this trial."

He took out a business card and wrote his home number on the back.

"Feel free to call me at any time, night or day."

From that moment we trusted Steve, and we started calling each other by our first names.

AFTER A FEW DAYS, the jury selection became tedious, and Dad and I would slip away to hang out in the hallway. We noticed that Santa Monica attracted a lot of retired senior citizens who spent their time dropping in on whatever cases were in progress. The bailiffs called them "court groupies" and were on a first-name basis with many of them. As Dad and I were chatting in the hallway, we heard a geriatric couple in matching Hawaiian shirts discussing whether to hit the Sweeney trial.

"Who's Sweeney?" the lady asked.

"Killed some actress," the man answered.

"What's her name?"

"Dom something."

"Never heard of her." And they moved on.

You had to be there, but it made Dad and me giggle. Even Mom and Alex smiled when we told them.

Some days later, when the trial was on a break, Dad looked through the porthole window of the courtroom to find it still empty. A woman about Mom's age was seated alone on a bench outside the entrance.

"Do you know when they're back in?" he asked.

"Not for another ten minutes, I heard."

Alex witnessed the exchange and told Dad that the woman was Sweeney's mother. He said that earlier in the morning he was sitting next to her, unaware of who she was, until he overheard the lawyer for Ma Maison have the regrettable duty of informing her that Sweeney did not wish to see her, despite her having traveled by bus from their hometown of Hazleton, Pennsylvania. Alex said that her eyes welled with tears. We would later learn that she was a battered wife, with five other children, and Sweeney had distanced himself from all of them the moment he left for Los Angeles.

We grew to admire Mrs. Sweeney's dignity as she sat across the aisle from us every day, though we were confounded by her unflagging support for her accused son, who never once agreed to see her during the trial. We took to nodding to each other in greeting every morning as we entered the courtroom.

BARSHOP GAVE US A CRASH COURSE in the art of jury selection: "What I'm looking for are twelve fascists, and Adelson's looking for twelve bleeding-heart liberals or weirdos, and we'll arrive somewhere in between." We ended up with nine men and three women, whose personal lives we knew nothing about except for a baggage handler at LAX and an Irish Catholic widow we heard had six children. My father described Adelson as "mustached and extremely short, his head topped with a full toupee," reminding him of an angry miniature bulldog. Adelson astonished us when he asked a prospective juror, "Suppose you don't like the way I comb my hair. Would that affect the way you listen to the testimony?" We realized that he thought the "quarter pound of hair taped to the top of his head," as Dad called it, was so convincing that everyone must have thought it real. My father would later write that Adelson's question would lead him to "understand the total conviction with which he presented his client's version of the events surrounding the murder, which he knew to be untrue."

Adelson continued his talent for mind-fucking Dad by greeting him repeatedly on the way to court with "Good morning, Mr. Sweeney." Every time Dad corrected him, he'd profusely apologize and then do it again the following day.

The presiding judge was another piece of work. Again, I can't better my father's perfect portrayal of Judge Burton Katz: "In his forties, Judge Katz gives the impression of a man greatly pleased with his good looks. He is expensively barbered, deeply tanned, and noticeably dressed in a manner associated more with Hollywood agents than with Superior Court judges. He has tinted aviator glasses, and on the first day he was wearing designer jeans, glossy white loafers, and no necktie beneath his judicial robes."

For reasons unknown, the judge took an immediate dislike to the Dunne family. Like the monsignor at the Good Shepherd church, he would even mispronounce Dominique's name, calling her "Dominick." He also loathed Steven Barshop as much as he found Mike Adelson endlessly charming. He would amiably tease Adelson about his height, to the delight of the jurors, and overrule the majority of Barshop's objections. One of the few times Katz didn't let Adelson have his way was when, with the jury absent, he denied his request that Mrs. Dunne be barred from the courtroom because her wheelchair was prejudicial enough to elicit the jury's sympathy. Even Katz knew that might be pushing it, and would probably invite advocates for people with disabilities to join the victims' rights groups that were already demonstrating outside the courthouse.

In his opening argument, Barshop told the jury they would hear testimony that would make clear Sweeney's crime was a premeditated murder in the first degree. He alluded to previous attacks on other women who would be called to testify, and that Sweeney's "obsession" with Dominique would lead to her inevitable death at his hands.

Barshop wrapped up his delivery to the jury by saying: "John Sweeney, who claimed to love Dominique, and whose defense will be that this was a momentary crime of passion, a spontaneous act that was not a premeditated murder, but a regretful accident that led to Dominique Dunne's unintentional death—the coroner will testify that it takes between four and six minutes for someone to die by strangulation."

He looked at his wristwatch and then told the jury, "Ladies and gentlemen, I am going to show you how long it took for Dominique Dunne to die."

The courtroom was silent for the next four minutes. Barshop could have chosen the coroner's longer estimate, but the eternity of those four minutes was unbearable enough. Mom, Dad, Alex, and I dared not look at each other and just stared at the clock on the courtroom wall. The time that ticked slowly by was designed to create a silent movie of Dominique's last moments fighting for her life. I saw the dirt from her garden mix with her hair as he held her down, squeezing harder and harder. I saw her fingernails digging into Sweeney's bulging triceps, her arms too short to claw his face. I saw the terror in her eyes, and then the moment they turned vacant with death. At three minutes and forty seconds, my waking nightmare was interrupted by the sound of Sweeney whispering with Adelson. What the fuck could they be talking about? I looked at Judge Katz, glancing at his watch, as if wondering what time he should break for lunch.

Adelson's opening statement was to first describe Sweeney as a "thoughtful young man" who got caught up in a situation that was beyond his control. This case, he told the jury, is not a premeditated murder, but a tragic love story. We listened in disbelief when he quoted from Kahlil Gibran's *The Prophet*:

> *Love has no other desire but to fulfil itself.*
> *But if you love and must needs have desires, let these*
> *be your desires: . . .*
> *To know the pain of too much tenderness.*
> *To be wounded by your own understanding of love;*

And to bleed willingly and joyfully. . . .
And then to sleep with a prayer for the beloved in your heart and a song of praise upon your lips.

"This is how deep John's love for Dominique was," Adelson wrapped up, holding the crowd in his hand, "but her desires were no longer her desires, and he could only sleep with a prayer for his beloved in his heart, and a song of praise that she was no longer interested in hearing."

I read *The Prophet* in high school, even carried a paperback of it in my back pocket to impress girls. I am sure Mr. Gibran would have been as disgusted as we were to hear his words perverted in a courtroom to justify murder.

As Adelson swaggered back to his seat next to Sweeney, it was clear that every awful thing we'd been told to expect during the trial was only just beginning, and that the Dunne family was in for a rough ride.

ONE OF THE THINGS I discovered about myself that summer was that I have a sociopathic gift for compartmentalizing grief and rage.

When not in the courtroom, I worked about two days a week on *Johnny Dangerously*. I considered my days on the set as precious as a prepaid vacation to a tropical island. The film's star, Michael Keaton, became and remains a close friend. We found each other hilarious, which is something to be grateful for if you are in an over-the-top silly comedy. He was the only person I confided in about where I was spending my days off from the movie, but even that knowledge was just an intermission from our constant banter.

Michael was the eponymous gangster of the film's title, and I played Tommy Kelly, his younger brother, a crime-fighting DA, too dim and innocent to know that my brother was Johnny Dangerously, the mob boss I spent most of the movie trying to arrest. I played Tommy with the balls-out energy and enthusiasm of Mickey Rooney in the Andy Hardy movies. The irony of playing a district attorney on the Fox lot and then going to Santa Monica to see a real one was not lost on me, but my exuberance and wide-eyed innocence was so broad that while I was in character, Barshop never crossed mind.

Every now and then there were times when my alternate universe outside our soundstage intruded on the fun I was having inside it.

Keaton and I were shooting a scene with Alan Hale Jr., and both of us could not get over that we were working with the Skipper from *Gilligan's Island.* I told Keaton about crashing the set of *Gilligan's Island* when I was a kid and witnessing Bob Denver, the Skipper's "little buddy," having a meltdown and kicking over a watercooler. This set us off into dueling impressions of Gilligan demanding script changes: "If it was a three-hour cruise, why the hell are we still on this island?" "What's with this stupid red shirt I've worn for three years, and how come I never get to fuck Tina Louise?"

We shared none of this with Mr. Hale, who was having problems of his own. The scene wasn't particularly long, but Alan had aged considerably since his Skipper days and was having difficulty remembering his lines. He played a 1930s police sergeant, and they had him dressed in a thick wool, double-breasted overcoat that made him sweat so heavily he had to be wiped down between takes, only adding to his humiliation. He apologized to Michael and me every time he went up, and we assured him he was doing great and had all the time in the world.

While a makeup team cleaned up Alan, a production assistant approached me to say a guy named David Packer was shooting next door and wanted to stop by to say hi.

Packer was the actor rehearsing with Dominique the night she was murdered. Packer was the guy who locked her out of the house and left the message to his roommate that said, "If I get murdered tonight, John Sweeney did it." Now he was an actor who dropped by because we happened to be shooting on the same lot, when all we really had in common was that I happened to have a sister he watched die.

I yelled toward the stage door on the other side of the set, loud enough for him to hear, "Packer, get the fuck off my set! We got nothing to talk about." The PA rushed off to make sure he had left.

THE NEXT DAY, David Packer was called to the witness stand. I recognized that his wholly inappropriate visit to my set must have had something to do with it.

As he described the events of October 30, he seemed to preen under the attention of the crowd, as if he were on callback for a part in a feature film. But as a fellow actor, I could tell that under his charm Packer was scared—not as terrified as he was of Sweeney that night, but frightened all the same. Dad and Alex were sickened by his performance on the stand, but to my surprise, I felt sorry for him. As Dominique's murder would forever haunt us, her death would trail him as well, but his demons would be his own voice, beginning with "I should have," "I wish I," and "Why didn't I?"

Detective Harold Johnston was called to the stand next and conducted himself with the same quiet dignity we had grown to admire. He frequently called my mother out of the blue, just to say hello and assure her that justice would be served. I've never forgotten his kindness.

Detective Johnston said one startling thing on the stand that day that should have had an enormous outcome on the course of the trial. He quoted the first words out of Sweeney's mouth to Deputy Frank DeMilio, the arresting officer at the scene: "Man, I blew it. I killed her. I didn't think I choked her that hard, but I don't know, I just kept on choking her. I just lost my temper and blew it again."

Again? The revelation murmured through the courtroom, but this information was not news to us. Well before the trial began, Dad was told by Fred Leopold, a family friend who had once been mayor of Beverly Hills, that Sweeney had severely beaten a secretary who worked in his law office. We passed the news to Harold, and he ran with it.

Lillian Pierce was Sweeney's girlfriend before he met Dominique. When Johnston interviewed her, she said he had hospitalized her twice, once for six days, once for four. Sweeney had broken her nose, punctured her eardrum, and collapsed her lung. She had seen him, she said, foam at the mouth when he lost control, and smash furniture and pictures. We later learned that Lillian had stood in front of the Good Shepherd church on the day of Dominique's funeral, but couldn't bring herself to go inside.

She was the next witness to testify after Detective Johnston, and we felt certain that her testimony would establish that Sweeney had a history of violence that could put him away for at least second-degree murder. But, to our horror, Judge Katz granted Adelson's request that the jury be cleared from the courtroom, ruling that Lillian Pierce's testimony might be "prejudicial." This was a word that would come up a lot during the trial and never in our favor.

With the jury absent, Lillian detailed the litany of injuries that Sweeney had inflicted. Dad kept meticulous notes during her testimony and this is his account of what transpired while Lillian was on the stand:

"At that moment—one of the most extraordinary I have ever experienced—we saw an enraged John Sweeney, his prop Bible flying, jump up from his seat at the counsel table and take off for the rear door of the courtroom which leads to the judge's chambers and the holding-cell area. Velma Smith, the court clerk, gave a startled cry. Lillian Pierce, on the stand, did the same. We heard someone shout, 'Get help!' Silent alarms were activated by Judge Katz and Velma Smith. The bailiff, Paul Turner, leapt to his feet in a panther-like movement and made a lunge for Sweeney, grasping him around the chest from behind. Within seconds four armed guards rushed into the courtroom, nearly upsetting Lenny's wheelchair, and surrounded the melee. The bailiff and Sweeney crashed into a file cabinet. 'Don't hurt him!' screamed Adelson. Sweeney was wrestled to the floor and then handcuffed to the arms of his chair, where Adelson whispered frantically to him to get hold of himself.

"Sobbing, Sweeney apologized to the court and said he had not been trying to escape. Judge Katz accepted his apology and explanation. 'We know what a strain you are under, Mr. Sweeney,' he said. I was appalled at the lack of severity of the judge's admonishment. What we had witnessed had nothing to do with escape. It was an explosion of anger. It showed us how little it took to incite John Sweeney to active rage. Like most of the telling moments of the trial, however, it was not witnessed by the jury."

"We know what a strain you are under, Mr. Sweeney." For weeks Alex and I would say that sentence to each other out of the blue, for any reason, or no reason at all. Looking for a parking space: "We know what a strain you are under, Mr. Sweeney." Waiting for an elevator: "We know what a strain you are under, Mr. Sweeney." Watching Luke Skywalker fight Darth Vader in a cinema, I'd mutter to Alex, "We know what a strain you are under, Mr. Sweeney." We couldn't get Katz's ludicrous expression of sympathy for a murderer out of our heads.

THE NEXT DAY, I was back on the set of *Johnny Dangerously*. The next night to be exact, because we were shooting an elaborate song-and-dance number three evenings in a row, which left my days free to attend the trial.

From the beginning of my career, I always loved night shoots. The later the hour, the more a spell of intimacy overcomes the crew. Secret histories and personal details are shared that would never be spoken in daylight. On one movie, a grip with whom I'd had only a nodding acquaintance told me about his wife's infidelity and his fear that he might lose custody of his children. On a different night shoot on another movie, a wardrobe assistant took me behind the Lucy and Desi lavatories to show me how her father used to fondle her. Our perverse but disturbingly erotic encounter was interrupted when I heard over the squawk of a walkie-talkie that I was urgently needed on set.

This being the roaring eighties, I'm sure our overshares on those vampiric nights were fueled by the grams of coke everyone snorted to get through the long hours. But no amount of blow would loosen my tongue on the *Johnny Dangerously* set to talk about where I spent my days.

When I arrived on Stage 10 for the big speakeasy scene, about a hundred extras were already seated at their assigned tables. I had little to do in the sequence and barely a line, but plenty of time to gawk in wide-eyed wonder at Marilu Henner's stunning hourglass figure as she belted a sultry hothouse number. A second AD seated me at a table of four extras with whom I'd be spending the next three nights. The men looked like ex-prizefighters in ill-fitting tuxedos, and their dates were middle-aged broads draped in fake furs and costume jewelry. They were very convincing as patrons of a mob-run speakeasy.

Before I could even put out my hand to them, the second AD said, "This is one of the stars of the film. You are not to address him. He has an important role and needs to stay in character, so please don't distract him with your small talk."

They looked at me like angry peasants forced to bend the knee to the Sheriff of Nottingham. I was mortified.

"I apologize for that man's rudeness, and my feelings would be hurt if you didn't distract me with small talk," I said as soon as the second AD had left. "I'm Griffin."

"Well, hello, Mr. Griffin," the largest of the mobsters said to me. "I guess you aren't the asshole that asshole made you out to be. I'm Leo, and this is Norma, my lovely wife of forty years."

Leo had a head as big as a pumpkin that sat on a tree trunk of a neck. My hand disappeared into his king crab–size fist, and then he made introductions to the couple on his left. The other man's name was Lenny. He looked like Luca Brasi, and opened with "Yeah, I look like Luca Brasi in *The Godfather*, and the funny thing is, the guy who played him was also named Lenny. And this is Ginny, my lovely wife of two weeks. We just got hitched in Vegas."

Ginny looked old enough to be Luca Brasi's mother, but she and Lenny still had the blush of newlyweds.

The two men went "way back," when they did a little "this and that" in Providence, Rhode Island. Now they were retired and shared adjoining condos in Santa Monica, two blocks from the beach, "not that we'd ever set foot in that filthy ocean," Leo added.

I asked if they often worked as extras, or "background performers," as they are now called.

"Hell no," said Leo, "they pay us in peanuts. This is just for fun."

Lenny said they were strolling through the Santa Monica mall when some kid asked them if they wanted to be in a movie shooting on the 20th Century Fox lot.

"I asked what it was about and he said it was a gangster picture and they needed faces in the background that would look realistic. I grabbed him by his little shirt with an alligator on it and said, 'You calling me a criminal? I'm a law-abiding citizen.' Then I straightened out his collar and said, 'I'm just fucking with you, kid. Where do we report?' And here we are."

Before the cameras rolled, a prop guy filled our champagne glasses to the brim and put the bottle in an ice bucket.

"Now this is more like it," Leo said, taking a sip and then spitting it out on the red-checked tablecloth.

"It's fucking *apple cider*! Lenny, we gotta fix this situation."

"I'm on it, Leo."

When we came back from dinner, our five glasses were filled with Cristal champagne and there were two more bottles stashed under the table. We proceeded to get blotto and had to be shushed more than once during Marilu's big number. The men ignored their wives, who were plotting how to steal the furs and fake jewelry when filming was over. Lenny, Leo, and I talked about the pros and cons of *The Godfather* and *The Godfather,*

Part II, but they were unanimous that both films were an accurate depiction of the way things were "back then."

"These days the mob is just rats with weak chins," Lenny said, by now slurring his words. The table made a slight jump when Leo kicked him to shut up.

WITH ONLY AN HOUR of sleep in my dressing room, I went back to the courthouse for my mother's testimony. It seemed the height of cruelty that Barshop would call her to the stand, but he made the case to us that the jury would find her sympathetic, and by then we'd grown to trust his judgment.

Once again, Adelson convinced Judge Katz that the optics of a woman in a wheelchair, whose daughter had been murdered by his client, was too "prejudicial" for a jury to be impartial. So they were dismissed. That dreaded p-word continued to haunt us.

Unlike Dad, Alex, and me, the jury were spared the torturous sight and sound of two grunting bailiffs trying to fit Mom's wheelchair onto a witness stand that had not been designed for accessibility. Once they finally figured it out, one of them placed the microphone inches from her lips, so our shy and reserved mother could be heard by everyone but the jury.

Barshop walked Mom through, step by step, the first time that Sweeney attacked Dominique. I was expecting her to describe the time Dominique escaped the Rangely house and drove to Norman Carby's, but was shocked to learn that incident was not the first, but the *second* attack.

Mom calmly told the room of spectators that at four thirty in the morning, just months after moving in with Sweeney, Dominique burst into her bedroom in hysterics, so scared she got under the covers with her, crying so hard she couldn't even speak.

Mom said that while holding Dominique, she noticed that tufts of hair had been pulled from her head. Soon after, Sweeney was pounding on the front door, demanding to be let in. The two women lay still in bed, hoping he'd go away, but instead he trampled through her rosebushes on the side of the house and banged on the glass of her bedroom window so hard, Mom thought it would break.

"I told him to go away or I would call the police, and he told me to mind my own business and demanded that Dominique go outside," she said. "He only left when he saw me pick up the phone."

"Did you tell anyone about that night?" Barshop asked gently.

She glanced at Dad, Alex, and me for the briefest second before looking down and shaking her head no.

"Could the witness speak into the microphone, please?" said Adelson, seeming to revel in the anguish of the state's star witness.

"Not Dominique's father?" Barshop continued.

"No," she said, and found the courage to lift her head and look each of us in the eye as if asking for forgiveness.

"This will be my final question, Mrs. Dunne, but may I ask why you chose to keep what must have been a terrifying experience to yourself?"

Mom regained what composure she had left before answering.

"Because Dominique begged me not to. She made me promise not to tell anyone and swore to me he would never hurt her again. To agree to what she asked is a regret I will carry all my life."

I found myself actually angry at my sister. I might not have picked up on my "gift of fear" when I met Sweeney, but where was hers after he banged her head into the floor and pulled out her hair? I felt as if she had hidden a defect from me, from her family, and even if it was cloaked in shame and difficult to understand, it bothered me that she kept it to herself. I kept my anger from straying toward my mother, who had more than enough regret and needed all her strength for Adelson's cross-examination.

Approaching her from the defense table, he asked, "Did Miss Dunne tell you what she and Mr. Sweeney argued about that night?"

"No."

"I need you to speak up, Mrs. Dunne."

"No," she said louder. "He hurt my daughter, that was all I needed to know."

"Please keep your answers devoid of commentary. A simple yes or no is all that's required."

I heard Dad mutter "Motherfucker" under his breath and touched his hand to quiet him.

"Are you aware your daughter abused cocaine?"

"No."

"Objection! Irrelevance," barked Barshop, shooting out of his chair.

"Overruled," said Katz predictably. By now there was no doubt that the contempt we suspected he felt for our family was out in the open for everyone to see. Everyone except for the jury.

"Did you know that Sweeney was in great distress over your daughter's habit?"

"I know that a lot of young people experiment with drugs, but Dominique most definitely did not have a habit. I would have known."

"And how would you have known?"

"Because she would have told me. My daughter would tell me everything."

"Well, not everything, and certainly not the reason for their argument. Mr. Sweeney was upset that she continued to use cocaine when she was pregnant."

An audible gasp filled the courtroom, but it might just have been coming from our bench.

"That's a lie," Melinda whispered to Dad, which none of us heard because we were transfixed by the look of utter disbelief on Mom's face.

"When he begged her to stop because it would harm the baby that he hoped to share with her, do you know what your daughter said that left him devastated?"

"No, but I'm sure you will tell me," Mom said, mustering a fury to prepare for the blow Adelson was about to deliver.

"Mrs. Dunne, your daughter said it didn't matter if she took drugs because, behind his back, without even a discussion, she'd had an abortion the day before."

He let that sink in, perhaps curious whether she might die right there on the stand.

"Did you know, a yes or no question, that your daughter, who tells you everything, had an abortion?"

"*Enough!*" snapped Barshop to the judge. "Mr. Adelson's cruelty is despicable. And if you had allowed the jury to see this, they would be as disgusted as me."

Even Katz looked dismayed, and broke the court for lunch.

WE HAD LUNCH every day of the trial near the Santa Monica Courthouse, at a restaurant called the Ivy. Their lovely and sympathetic staff always kept a long table open for our family and a group of friends, who never failed to show in support for us. Oddly, it was also where the jury decided to eat every day, and a table was held for them as well, at the other end of the dining room. We became accustomed to their presence, and our two groups respectfully nodded in one another's direction when taking our places.

When I saw the jury at the Ivy that day, it took every ounce of strength for me not to lunge toward them and scream that they were being kept in the dark about Sweeney's outburst, Lillian Pierce, and the two attacks that put her in the hospital. I believe they would have been appalled by Adelson's treatment of my mother, and the lies he told that virtually any other judge would have ruled inadmissible. Instead, we entered the restaurant in unbroken silence. Charlie, Melinda, Lisa, Brooke, Mark, and the rest of us took our usual seats and stared glumly at menus we now knew by heart. There was nothing to say, and no way to begin. All eyes darted looks of concern toward my mother, which she ignored, having had enough attention for one day.

I got up to pee, or at least that was my excuse for leaving the table, but once in the bathroom, all I did was pace from one end to the other. My hatred for Adelson, the look of shame on my mother's face, her pain at not knowing of her daughter's abortion, true or not, filled me with such rage that I was capable of punching the first person who walked in the bathroom. Instead, I kicked the wall so hard I put a hole in it. I heard some cries of alarm coming from the dining room, but thought nothing of it and drenched my face in cold water.

"You won't believe what just happened," Charlie said when I joined our table. "You know the big outsider art painting that hangs over there"—he was pointing toward the bathroom wall

I'd kicked—"it just flew off the wall and landed inches from where those people are sitting. It could have killed them."

"Lenny," said Melinda, the merry prankster who could always get a laugh out of Mom, "remember when Dominique, Lisa, and I kidnapped Robin Williams from Buddy Hackett's party and brought him up to your bedroom?"

Mom smiled at the memory. Hackett, the cherubic comic, lived at the end our block on Walden. Melinda launched into a story about the night she talked Dominique and Lisa into crashing his party.

"I made out with Buddy's daughter once," mentioned Alex, while piling butter onto a breadstick.

"So, we sneak in through the kitchen," Melinda told us, everyone happy to be distracted, "and we see Don Rickles, Joey Bishop, Henny Youngman, and there, in the middle of all these old comedians, is Robin Williams, looking bored out of his mind."

"*Mork & Mindy* had just come out," added Lisa.

"Then I snuggle up to him and say, 'We are going to kidnap you, is that okay?' And he looks at the three of us and says, 'Where to?' Then we bring him down the block to Lenny's, and when we get in the house he sees—remember that huge life-size teddy bear that was propped up at the piano?"

We all chimed in with "Oh yeah" and "I remember that" and "Where did that bear come from?"

"It doesn't matter," said Melinda. "So anyway—"

"Jimmy Wilson, my cousin from Nogales, sent it to me for my birthday," Mom said.

"Mystery solved," continued Melinda. "So we tell Robin we want him to meet the most amazing lady that ever lived, and he grabs the bear off the piano and follows us upstairs with it."

"But wait," Lisa interjected, "don't you remember? He puts the bear on the motorized chair and does a ventriloquist voice of Katharine Hepburn from . . ."

Alex and I blurted out, "*Suddenly, Last Summer*!"

Now my mom and dad were laughing, all of us caught up in the memory of a story we knew by heart.

"So Robin takes the big life-size bear and follows us into Lenny's room and does a fifteen-minute bit where he becomes Teddy Roosevelt telling the bear to stop calling him Teddy while punching him in the face, and then dances it around the room, singing in a Russian accent, before bending the poor bear over the bed and fucking it in the ass."

Our entire table lost it, and heads turned to see what was so funny. Mom laughed so hard tears rolled down her cheeks, and she looked to Dad, maybe remembering what he'd done to Howdy Doody so many years before. I was aware of our table getting a lot of attention, and while the Robin story was funny, I was also conscious our laughter was a form of release, an expression of defiance, a big, loud "fuck you" to Adelson and Katz and the whole awful morning.

Once the hilarity died down, our appetites were restored, and we looked once again at the menus. I caught sight of the jury, regarding us from their Last Supper table in shock and disgust. I knew what they saw from their perch: privileged, heartless monsters whose daughter dumped a sensitive boy when she became famous, our grief a put-on because it didn't conform to what they thought real pain should look like. The nine men and three women were poorly paid for their civic duty but getting the most for their money by sitting in judgment of us both in and out of the courtroom. I knew in that moment that when the time came for them to deliver a verdict, they would deem Dominique's life to be worth not all that much.

WHEN THAT WORST DAY of the trial (so far) finally came to an end, I went straight to the studio, and with an hour of peace and quiet to kill, grabbed a nap in my trailer. Then I was called to makeup to be dolled up side by side with Keaton, who would pick up our banter from our matching barber chairs, making me grateful to leave all thoughts of Adelson and Katz behind. An hour later, I strolled to set in spats and a tuxedo, my fedora cocked to the side, as *The Love Boat*'s Gavin MacLeod left Stage 19, where they filmed the series. Captain Stubing had docked the SS *Pacific Princess* into port and was wrapped for the day, just as my night was to begin as Tommy Kelly: crime fighter!

I felt both guilty and fortunate to have a job that paid me to be funny on film. It was sinful how happy it made me to be waved onto the lot by a studio guard who knew my name, and to park my car in a space where GRIFFIN DUNNE was painted in bold letters on the curb. My family had no such distractions. They would end their day on Crescent Drive, condemned to gather around Mom's bed to watch a recap of our courtroom travesty on the local news with TV trays on their laps.

A glass of Cristal was poured and ready when I joined the men and their wives at our table. Lenny and Leo greeted me at the speakeasy set with hugs, as if they hadn't seen me in years. During a lighting setup, Leo dropped his usual joviality and whispered in my ear, "When we break for dinner, you and I gotta have a little talk. It's important." I hadn't a clue what it could be about, but the gravity of his tone made me uneasy.

We got our meal from catering, and instead of going into the commissary, I followed Leo to a bench in front of the Darryl Zanuck building. He didn't touch his meal and waited until I'd had a few bites before he spoke.

"Listen, kid, Norma and I don't live in a cave and know what you and your family are going through. How could I not, it's in the papers every day, and we are both sick about it. When I see pictures of your mother, it just breaks my fucking heart. She seems like an amazing woman."

"She is, Leo. I don't know how she does it."

"And that piece of shit who killed your sister, I'd like to kill him with my bare hands."

"Well, I would have no problem with that."

I knew Leo's heart was in the right place, but after my success at putting the trial out of my mind while at work, I was disappointed that this was what he wanted to talk to me about. I tried to think of a way to change the subject, but he wasn't finished with whatever he had to say.

"I just want you to know, Griffin, there is a way to make this trial go away by the end of the week. You and your family would never have to set foot in that courthouse again."

"What do you mean?"

"I think you know what I mean. I got friends who work where Piece of Shit is being held, and they tell me he's got a cell all to himself. It's where they put people who are involved in high-profile cases to protect them from the other prisoners. Some of those guys are my friends too. One of them heard that Sweeney told somebody, 'The rich bitch got what she deserved.' You believe that?"

I believed what Leo was telling me to be accurate. The details sounded real, and if he was saying what I thought he was saying, I believed that to be real as well.

"I will only mention this once, so listen carefully: something could happen in that private cell that could put an end to this and let you and your family go on with your lives."

"I don't know what to say . . ."

"Don't say anything. In fact don't say anything to anybody. Just think about it and let me know by tomorrow. I'll respect whatever you decide."

Irony was fucking with my head once again. I'm on a lunch break from a silly movie about gangsters, sitting on a bench with a real gangster, having a conversation about having someone whacked.

"Maybe I've seen too many movies," I said, "but usually there comes a time to repay the favor, like being forced to rob a bank or something."

That got a laugh out of Leo, which was not my intent.

"You will owe me nothing nor ever hear from me after tomorrow night. I think you are a fine young man who has been wronged, which pisses me off. But I'm really offering this opportunity for your mother. Something about her touches my heart, and I'd like to spare her any further pain."

What do you say when someone offers you an "opportunity" like this? A simple "thank you" seemed trite under the circumstances, but I said it anyway and told him I'd give it some serious thought. Which I did.

I'M NOT SURE EXACTLY WHEN, either after the funeral, waiting for the trial, or during the trial, but at some point everyone in my family had become, each in our own way, totally insane. Not so obvious that it would be noticed by friends, but if our inner lives had been on speakerphone, we would have been cause for serious concern.

My father harbored murderous fantasies, particularly about

Adelson, whom he managed to hate even more than he hated Sweeney. Before the trial even started, a mugger held a knife to Dad's throat on a desolate subway, demanding his money. The guy was twice his size but had the bad luck to choose the wrong guy at the wrong time. My father grabbed the man's wrist and turned the blade back on the mugger, venting his rage so loudly, so insanely, into the man's face that the attacker dropped his knife and ran off.

Mom had periods of strong detachment, and became so unresponsive it was as if she'd lost her hearing. She stopped looking at friends who came calling to her bedroom, choosing instead to stare at the television, whether it was on or not.

Alex always had a unique relationship with reality, but I realized I'd joined his universe when I told him about my conversation with Leo. Even though I'd been told not to discuss his offer with anyone, Alex would never have told our parents and was the only person whose advice I trusted.

I told him how Leo and I met, his affection for Mom, and that he knew people on the inside of the county jail who could kill Sweeney by Friday. The next day was Thursday, so I had to give my answer to Leo on set that night.

"So he'd miss the weekend," Alex said.

"What?"

"Sweeney would miss the weekend," he repeated.

"Yes, that's true. He would totally miss Saturday." Then we burst into maniacal laughter.

Alex then gave the proposal deeper consideration. He had notes, suggestions that might fine-tune the plot.

"What would be cool," he began, "is instead of killing him, is if we have his hands crushed. He murdered Dominique with his hands, right? So what if we asked your friend to have the guy crush his hands so badly he'd never be able to cook another meal? So he wouldn't even be able to hold a fork."

"I love it," I said.

"You know, maybe the guy could sneak a vise into his cell, steal it from a metal shop where they make license plates or something. They must have a vise in there someone could use."

"These are all good ideas, Alex. It also spares us the karma of knowing we killed someone, even if it is Sweeney."

"Yeah, I was thinking the same thing."

"Well, let me run it by Leo and see what he can do."

"ARE YOU OUT of your fucking mind?" Leo said, after I pitched him the idea of the crushed hands, the vise, and the metal shop.

Leo's reasonable question about my sanity was the first time I wondered about it too.

"First of all, kid, you're not ordering a pizza. You don't get to add mushrooms and sausage. There are no special requests in a situation like this. If you tell me yes, it only goes one way. If you say no, it goes the other way, and we forget all about it. Second, you *have* seen too many fucking movies. They don't make license plates in county jails, and the cons don't escape using a nail file smuggled in a cake."

It wasn't until then that I remembered the psychic in the Ansonia accusing me of exacting revenge on Sweeney well before it crossed my mind, and now here I was, contemplating an act of violence that Dominique had begged me not to do from the beyond. Maybe the clairvoyant was the real deal after all.

"Leo," I sighed, "I really appreciate what you are willing to do for me and my family. It's a selfless act of kindness, and at great personal risk to you, and I'll never forget it, but I'm afraid it's something I'm incapable of being responsible for."

"Totally understand, kid, it's not for everybody. You're a good person and a caring son to that beautiful mother of yours, so I thought I'd give it a shot. But as far as you 'never forgetting it,' I want you to start forgetting it right now."

Leo wrapped me in a bear hug and said, "Keep in touch," though we both knew we never would.

NORMAN CARBY WAS NEXT on deck to tell the court about the night Dominique drove to his house after what I thought was the first attack, but was really the second. She hadn't even told Norman that Sweeney had tried to strangle her once before.

Barshop had Norman's pictures of Dominique's black-and-blue bruises blown up and tacked to an easel for the jury and spectators to view. He placed four photographs that showed Sweeney's handiwork from every angle. His fingerprints were still fresh on her throat.

As Norman described my sister's terror, Judge Katz looked bored. He was doodling on a piece of paper, as if playing a game of hangman or tic-tac-toe to pass the time, and I wondered what kind of signal that sent to the jury.

When it was Adelson's turn to cross-examine, he tried as he might to punch holes into Norman's testimony, but every detail in Norman's timeline was bulletproof, and exactly as he first described it to Detective Johnston a year earlier. Adelson's frustration at not being able to crack Norman was obvious.

Finally, he turned to the easel, where the pictures of Dominique took on a life, as if she had been watching Norman's gallant performance as well. Adelson pointed to one photo where she was in profile with a sly grin on her face, and triumphantly announced, "Mr. Carby, if Miss Dunne was as 'terrified' as you told the court, why is she laughing in this picture? What could she have found so funny if she was scared for her life?"

Norman had his answer ready. "Dominique was shooting *Hill Street Blues* the next morning, playing a battered housewife. When I took that picture, I'd just said, 'Well, at least you won't have to go into makeup.'"

The jury smiled at that, and I wondered if for the first time they might have admired my sister's bravery. Norman turned to address them directly, as if to drive the point home.

"Dominique was terrified that night, make no mistake about it, but she also had, like her brothers, a sense of humor for the absurd, and the irony of who she would portray the next morning made her laugh, even when still in pain after her assault. That was Dominique."

His words touched the heart of every juror, and when Adelson saw the Irish Catholic widow stifle a sniffle, he cut his losses.

"No further questions, Your Honor," he said.

Norman joined us for lunch at the Ivy, and we showered him with praise. Mom told him that what he said on the stand gave her the only moment of hope since the trial began.

"I could have kissed you!" I added.

"Well, that wouldn't have been the worst thing."

The table erupted in laughter and I didn't even check to see if the jury across the room was witness to our savoring our tiny victory.

Neither Alex nor I could understand why Dad chose to skip this lunch, of all lunches, and not be with us to thank Norman for his testimony. For all I knew, they hadn't seen each other since he and Dominique helped sell Dad's belongings at his yard sale. But I noticed he kept his distance from Norman when we all gathered in the hallway before entering the courtroom. I'd learn only part of the reason for Dad's odd behavior in the last year of his life, and the rest of the picture would be filled in much later.

IN THE SPRING OF 2008, I flew a Lufthansa red-eye to Munich to see my father, who was at a clinic getting stem cell treatment for a tumor that had slowly spread through his bladder and was now picking up speed. Dad had bought my airline ticket, and there was urgency in his voice when he asked me to come see him. From the airport, I caught a cab for an hour's drive to the tiny hamlet of Übersee, a short distance from Eagle's Nest, Hitler and Eva Braun's holiday retreat.

Stem cell treatment was then a popular but entirely unsuccessful alternative to chemotherapy, and the clinic was at capacity, so Dad had to stay at a hotel across the street, where he got me a room next to his. After dropping off my luggage, I knocked on his door.

A guy a little younger than me opened the door, and it took me a moment to place him as Norman Carby, Dominique's close friend and the impressive witness at her murder trial. I also remembered that he was the artist Dominique had asked to paint *Exotic Landscape* on the back wall of my mother's house.

Dad was in bed, looking grayish and desperately thin when I went to hug him. "You remember Norman," he said, "from the trial?"

"Uh . . . yeah. I do," I said tentatively, trying to piece this puzzle together.

That was Dad's last word on the subject, and he drifted off to sleep.

Norman ordered a bottle of wine from room service, and we polished it off from opposite sides of Dad's king-size bed, speaking softly so as not to wake him. We talked about Hawaii, where he now lived, and his paintings and my career, until I finally cut to the chase.

"So, I gather you and Dad kept in touch after the trial."

"Well, we had met years earlier when I helped Dominique sell all his stuff."

"Oh, I didn't know you guys knew each other beyond then."

"I know you didn't," he said, betraying a slight bitterness in his tone. "We met at a terrible time for him, and I kind of helped him get through it. We've been a big part of each other's lives ever since. Not that he'd have told anybody."

"Did Dominique know that you and Dad . . ."

"Yes. She thought it was hilarious that she was the matchmaker."

That was so Dominique, to be entrusted with a secret and not even share it with her brothers. Though I admired her discretion, I was a little hurt, and thought Alex would have been as well, but not entirely surprised, because we both knew our sister would never betray the confidence of anyone she loved.

"From then on, I looked after him when he was down and out, but just as your dad started to make money, I suddenly became quite ill and was hospitalized without any insurance, and it became his turn to look after me. He paid for my entire stay, every doctor visit, and continues to pay for the meds I still need to take. He even sends checks when I can't make ends meet from my gardenia paintings, which are brilliant but no one wants to buy. We've been celibate for a long time, but he's never stopped caring for me."

Norman gave me time to digest this onslaught of new information. After uncorking a second bottle of wine, he decided I was ready to hear more.

"I was with your father when you called to say you were kicked out of school. I was the first person he called when he found out Lenny had MS. I don't know why I call her Lenny; we only met a few times when I painted the mural on her house. But your father never let me get near you boys. He told me everything you and Alex were up to, and he'd call me most nights in Oahu to report on whatever party he'd just returned from. I flew back when Dominique died, and he wept in my arms. But I was never allowed further into his life than that. It makes perfect sense that you know nothing about me and I know everything about you."

Norman's tone approached the edge of anger, which I feared might wake Dad, but he was still out of it.

I asked, "Were you there when Dad sold his dog?"

Norman smiled. "I haven't thought about that little Scottie in years."

"Alfie." His name just popped into my mind.

"He really loved Alfie, but he needed money. The lady he sold him to was some socialite—"

"Connie Wald."

"Yes, she was the one who bought him, and they were friends, but I remember how much it hurt him when he heard she was telling people, 'Dominick Dunne is the kind of man who would sell his own dog.'"

We mulled that over for a bit until I added out of the blue,

"My parents once got me a cat when I was in the first grade, even though I really wanted a dog." I hadn't thought about Charlie in years.

"He was an incredible cat," I continued, no idea why. "When the bus dropped me home from school, Charlie waited for me on the front lawn every day. I loved that fucking cat. One day, he just disappeared. I got off the bus, he wasn't there, and I never saw him again."

"That must have been awful for you," Norman sighed in sympathy.

Suddenly the dying man between us, whom we'd both forgotten about, blurted out as if talking in his sleep, "I took him to the top of Mulholland and let him go."

"What?" Norman and I said in unison. Dad opened his eyes and looked at me, the skin on his face sagging over his cheekbones.

"You were allergic to him. Don't you remember? You had ringworm all over your body. We tried to get you to give him up, but you became hysterical whenever I tried to talk to you about it."

I did remember the ringworm. It was so bad I still have a few scars on my legs as a reminder.

"Why didn't you take him to an animal shelter for someone to adopt?" I asked.

"They didn't have stuff like that in those days, and none of our friends wanted to take him." And then he slipped back to sleep.

I was taken aback by a flash of anger about a cat he ditched almost fifty years ago, but let it go, because what I really heard was part of a deathbed confession. Dad's cancer brought back memories filled with regret for his behavior from long ago, and now, with so little time left, he wanted to come clean about as much as he could remember. My flying to Germany wasn't just to look after him in his frail health, as I expected to do, but was really to meet his lifelong companion and hear him rid himself of the last of his secrets.

BEING AN OPENLY GAY MAN living in a cosmopolitan city in 1983 was a lot easier than it had been for previous generations of gay men. When my father moved to New York in the 1950s and then Los Angeles in the early '60s, you could be rounded up by the police for being in a gay bar. If your employers discovered your sexual orientation, you could lose your job, and if you happened to be at the wrong place at the wrong time, you could get killed.

In 1983, gay people weren't being murdered for being out in the open. What was killing them was AIDS and the Reagan administration's indifference. My father was fifty-seven during the trial, and this rampant disease killing so many young men was a far bigger social stigma than just being considered gay. People in cosmopolitan cities didn't care about whom you slept with but about their friends who were dying in great numbers, in most cases because of whom they had slept with.

Dad's fear of being outed was anachronistic and posed no threat to working in entertainment, as it once had in the early years of television. Why he still kept it a secret was as baffling as why he thought anyone would care. But it explains the distance he put between himself and Norman Carby on the day of Norman's testimony.

What I found out years after Dad died was that his anxiety that day was about more than simply the threat that Mom and her boys might discover that he and Norman were lovers.

Four years after my father died, I went to Austin, Texas, to visit the Briscoe Center for American History, where his papers were archived. I missed him and wanted to wade through the stacks of his Smythson notebooks, filled with handwritten reflections, and read early drafts of his articles and novels containing details that never made it to print, because I wanted to hear his voice.

I came across a notebook that must have been the diary Tina Brown asked him to keep during the trial. The date August 23 contained an entry that explained what was really going through his mind on the day of Norman's testimony.

> Adelson is a dangerous and wicked man who hates me as much as I hate him. I believe his hatred has led him to hire a detective to dig into my background and that my relationship with Norman has been discovered. Katz has allowed him to pursue irrelevant lines of questioning for the purpose of destroying Dominique's character and I believe he will do the same to me when Norman takes the stand in the morning. This loathsome and cruel man will expose our relationship to discredit his testimony and my character. "You have carried on a secret affair with the father of your close friend all these years? What kind of a friend does that make you? What kind of a father has an affair with the friend of one of his children? What is the age difference between you and Mr. Dunne, who I believe qualifies as a senior citizen?" The chances there is not at least one homophobic juror are slim, and I can already imagine the disgust the baggage handler will feel toward me. If Adelson uses my relationship with Norman to affect the verdict in Sweeney's favor, I will kill myself. I will not be able to live with the disappointment Lenny and the boys will rightly feel toward me. This time I will really do it. I have no one to talk to about this so I beg you, my Higher Power, to watch over me, whether I deserve it or not.

The torture my father felt every minute Norman was on the stand was unimaginable. Brief flashes of his face that day came to me as I reread the passage in the Briscoe Center. It was contorted, and he emitted little groans I hadn't remembered hearing until now. It turned out Adelson didn't play that card in what must have been the longest day of my father's life. If I went through his archives because I missed him, my trip to Austin only made me miss him more. I would have done anything to be able to hug him and say how sorry I was that he had to go through all that alone.

BROOKE HAD TO RETURN to New York to start a movie, and I was sad to see her go. She could not have been a more supportive partner during the trial, but we had drifted apart. I had not kept my word to ease up on the drinking, and she must have tired of me getting into bed every night slurring my words. She never scolded me for it because she knew the stress I was under, but even drunk, I could feel her disappointment and her love slipping away. When she left, we knew without saying that while our romance might have ended, our friendship never would.

Charlie and Alex moved into the Leo Carrillo beach house pretty soon after to keep me company. We still had half a page of Timothy Leary's acid left, but by then we'd grown tired of hallucinating. We'd drive to Oxnard for Mexican food, or Neptune's Net for lobster, and Charlie bought an inflatable Zodiac in which we risked our lives getting over the enormous waves in front of the house to go fishing. The peace I found living on the beach was intermittently shattered every time I heard "Every Breath You Take" by the Police, which topped the charts that summer and was impossible to escape. It was a sinister song about a man obsessed with a woman he would never let out of his sight. I heard a threat of violence in the lyrics, should the woman get the idea to leave him.

Every move you make
And every vow you break
Every smile you fake
Every claim you stake
I'll be watching you

It pained me when some of my intelligent women friends would embrace "Every Breath" as a "love song." They thought to have a man so obsessed with a woman was sexy and romantic, where I found the character Sting portrayed to be a sick fuck who would eventually kill the woman he's singing to and every one of them if he had a chance.

The popularity of "Every Breath You Take," and its misinterpretation, reminded me how much domestic violence had changed my life, and how alone and misunderstood I felt by everyone but my family.

A SCRIPT ARRIVED in the mail from Amy Robinson, one that so excited her she had express mailed it to me right away from the Sundance Lab in Utah, where she was mentoring. We had projects in development but nothing near ready to shoot, and Amy's note clipped to the script read, "This is the one. Also, the part seems written for you."

The title we'd later settle on would be *After Hours*, but at the time, it was called *Surrender Dorothy*, written by Joe Minion, a graduate student at Columbia's film school. I sat in my favorite chair on the deck facing the ocean and started reading. By the tenth page the terrible things happening to the hero of the story made me so anxious I couldn't read sitting down, so I put the script on the floor and finished it standing up, turning the pages with my big toe. I was perfect for the role. The misadventures of Paul Hackett, the main character, could only have happened to me.

I was about to call Amy, when I noticed a bewildered elderly couple standing in my living room.

"Umm, may I help you?" I asked cautiously.

"You can start by telling me why you are in our house," said the wife, who seemed the tougher of the two.

"I rented it for the summer. From the owner. So who are you?"

"This has been our house for twenty years, and I can prove it."

She showed me the deed that was in her name and I showed her the ad I answered, which was not. The lady didn't recognize the name of the person who'd placed it, but immediately figured out who had conned me. They employed a part-time worker who ran errands for them ever since they'd felt unsafe driving on the Pacific Coast Highway at their age. Her name was Madalyn, she was kind of a hippie, but on second thought, they now doubted that was even her name. Madalyn was aware they were leaving town for three months to see their grandchildren and had seemed overly interested in whether they wanted to sublet the house while they were gone.

"I told her certainly not, and that we couldn't imagine having *strangers* in our house," the lady said to me quite pointedly. "We did ask if she could check in on the place and water the flowers when needed."

"I can tell you she was never here, but I always watered the flowers."

"I see that. Thank you. Well, I guess we've both been duped."

I called the number on the ad but the phone had been disconnected. I realized I had no way to get ahold of Madalyn or whoever the fuck she was. With the couple still standing in their own living room, I next called Detective Harold Johnston and explained the situation.

"I don't know where she is, or what her name is, all I know is that I gave her three months' rent and a deposit in advance."

"In a check?"

"No, a money order, and like an idiot I mailed it to a post office box. I don't even know what she looks like."

"Why don't you put the owner of the house on and I'll see what I can do."

The lady's husband had yet to say a word, so I explained to her who Detective Johnston was, which required me to explain that I rented the house so I could attend the trial of my sister's killer, and that he would like to speak to her.

"That's your sister? I'm so sorry. We've been reading about it in the papers."

"Thank you," I said, and made a motion toward the phone, where Johnston waited on the other end.

The lady and Johnston spoke for about a half hour, and he managed to drain every detail out of her he could get about Madalyn. Then he asked her to put me on.

"I've got a lot to go on and should have her tracked down in a day or two," he said. "Hang tight and we'll get her. Give my best to your lovely mother."

"Harold, I can't thank you enough."

"This is the last thing you need, and it will be my pleasure to scare the living shit out of her." Then he hung up. Man, I loved that guy.

Johnston called two days later at my new digs, a borrowed house where I was dog-sitting Harry, the greatest canine I'd ever come across. Harry was a huge mutt who was born with a boneless front leg so that when he ran, it just flopped around from side to side.

"Well, that was easy," Harold said. "It turns out the woman who robbed you did a little time. Her probation officer told me she works at the See's Candies factory on La Cienega. I thought I'd pay her a little visit, if you'd like to come along."

"I'd love to. Plus I've always wanted to see the inside of the See's factory."

"Yeah, me too. I'll pick you up in an hour."

Harold flashed his badge at the front desk and asked where he could find Linda Templeton, an awfully grand name for a con artist. We followed the factory foreman, passing vats of fudge and toffee being softened up to make See's famous lollypops.

"I like the caramel ones the best," Harold told me.

"But the chocolate ones aren't bad either."

"I'll give you guys an assortment on your way out," the foreman said.

He pointed out Linda, a woman in her midthirties in a paper hairnet. Harold asked the foreman if there was somewhere private we could talk, and the foreman called Linda from her workstation and led the three of us to a back office.

Once we were seated, Harold showed his badge and introduced himself, then pointed to me.

"Do you know who this young man is?"

"Haven't the slightest. Should I?" Her tough act was betrayed by the fear in her voice.

"You rented him a house that wasn't yours on Leo Carrillo Beach for three thousand dollars."

"I don't know what you're talking about."

"I thought you might say that, so I came prepared to offer you two options: we can go to your bank, or look under your mattress, wherever you keep your cash, and you will pay Mr. Dunne every cent you stole from him."

"But I'm telling you—"

"Option number two," Harold interrupted. "Or I can book you right now, and with your priors, you'd be back with the gals in Chino pretty soon. Personally, I like option one because Mr. Dunne gets back his money, and if it's two, he might never see it, and you'd just be doing more time. It's just a lose-lose, Linda, but your choice."

By now Linda was ashen with fear but still sticking to her story.

"I'm telling you you have the wrong person. I don't even know what you're talking about."

"Fair enough," Johnston said, getting to his feet. "Stand up and put your hands behind your back."

"Wait. I don't know if I even have that much in the bank."

Linda looked at me in desperation and said, "What if I pay you back in installments, like once a month."

"I don't think Mr. Dunne is interested in a long-term relationship, Linda. It's all or nothing. Either way, you're getting in my car, and where we go is up to you."

The three of us got in Johnston's Dodge Dart and drove to the nearest Wells Fargo, where Linda had an account. She sat glumly in the back, and I rode shotgun.

We stood behind her at the teller as she withdrew what she said was "every cent I have," which neither of us cared about or believed.

After handing me a thick envelope, Linda followed us back to the car, and as she reached for the back door, Harold said, "Where do you think you're going?"

"Aren't you going to drive me back to work?"

"Nah, it's rush hour, and I gotta get this man to Malibu. Take a bus."

Once we were on the road, I cracked open the See's assortment the foreman had given us. Harold had chocolate and I had caramel.

WHEN IT WAS SWEENEY'S TURN to testify, we had hoped the jury might see him reprise the violent outburst they'd missed during Lillian Pierce's testimony. Alex and I changed our seats to sit directly in front of his sight line, willing our cold glares to agitate him. But he didn't take the bait and came off as a pathetic figure who was possibly sedated.

He brought to the stand his ever-present "prop Bible," as Dad called it, and managed to work up some tears five minutes into his testimony about being bullied by the inmates at his jail. He played the part of a man Adelson had repeatedly described as an "ordinary, reasonable man," who loved Dominique, and though heartbroken when she "dumped" him, believed her when she said they would reconcile.

At that Alex and I managed to catch Sweeney's attention for him to see us mouth the words "Lie, lie, lie."

ALL THAT WAS LEFT was for the opposing attorneys to make their final case to the jury and ask them to deliver a verdict they believed in their hearts to be just.

Barshop reminded them of Sweeney's two earlier attempts to strangle Dominique to death until he finally finished the job. His task would have been easier if Barshop could have cited Sweeney's history of violence toward other women, or if the jury had heard Lillian Pierce's testimony and seen Sweeney's volatile reaction to it. The only hand the prosecution had left to play was to make Dominique real to them: she was a talented actress on the rise whose bright future was forever silenced, a girl who loved her older brothers and who looked after her ailing mother, and the daughter of a father who called her Little Miss Muffet from the day she was born. He told them of her lifelong love for animals of all shapes and sizes, how Dominique once worked at the San Diego Zoo feeding baby condors with a beaked glove to make them think she was their mother. Then he told them about her trademark habit: bringing home stray dogs and cats wherever she found them. The house was full of strays, and each time she came back with a new one, her mother would protest, but only halfheartedly. The only stray Mrs. Dunne wished Dominique had never brought home was John Sweeney. He would be the stray that killed her daughter.

In closing, Barshop read a letter that Melinda had found while cleaning out the house on Rangely. It was written by Dominique to Sweeney, but whether she sent it or if he ever read it, we would never know.

I am not permitted to do enough things on my own. Why must you be a part of everything I do? Why do you want to come to my riding lessons and my acting classes? Why are you jealous of every scene partner I have? Why must I talk about every audition when you know it is bad luck for me? Why do we have discussions at 3:00 a.m. all the time, instead of during the day? Why must you know the name of every person I come into contact with? You insist on going to work with me when I have told you it makes me nervous. Your paranoia is overboard . . . You do not love me. You are obsessed with me. The person you think you love is not me at all. It is someone you have made up in your head.

At the end of Barshop's reading, Adelson leapt from his seat and pointed at my brother.

"Your Honor, Alex Dunne has tears in his eyes!" he cried out, presuming the judge would agree that the sin of his emotion would prejudice the jury. By then Alex had had enough.

"I can't go back there anymore," he said to me as we left the courtroom. "I can't be where Sweeney is."

We buckled up for what we expected to be a brutal closing from Adelson, and he was as advertised.

He found a way to again describe Sweeney as an "ordinary, reasonable person" three times, stealing from the playbook of corrupt politicians who believe if an accusation is denied enough times, it will eventually be believed.

"This was not a crime," he told the jury. "This was a tragedy," a lie he'd been hammering home since the start of the trial. By now I had learned the hard way that in the judicial system, perjury is a crime, but when a lawyer lies for his client, it's perfectly legal.

He told the jury that what Dominique and Sweeney once had was "that old-fashioned thing: romantic love." If he quoted Kahlil Gibran again, I thought I would leap off the bench and grab his throat. Instead he managed to do something even worse: he quoted made-up dialogue as if it were something Dominique had actually said:

"I, Dominique, reject you, John Sweeney," he cried out. "*I lied to you!*"

At the break, Dad sidled up to Adelson and whispered in his ear, "You piece of shit."

Adelson turned on his heels so fast his toupee shifted, and ran back to the bench to tattle to the judge.

When Dad told Mom what he had just called Adelson, she said, "That was very stupid, now you'll get kicked out of the courtroom."

"If the judge calls me up, I'll lie and say I didn't say it. Everybody else is lying. Why shouldn't I? It's his word against mine."

When Dad told Barshop what he'd done and asked if he would be kicked out of the courtroom, Barshop smiled and said, "He can't kick the father of the victim out of the court on the last day of the trial with all the press present," but then added, "don't do it again."

THERE IS AN ADAGE about jury deliberations that the quicker they reach a verdict, the worse it is for the accused, but the longer they take, the better their chances for a lighter sentence or even acquittal. Our will to remain positive was tested every day as the jury deliberated.

I tried to burn off my anxiety by taking long runs with Harry. Despite his leg, he kept pace with me along the stretch of beach in Malibu, but when bathers saw his flopping, useless limb, they assumed I was forcing my seriously wounded dog to run alongside me. Every twenty feet or so, we'd pass a voice crying in outrage, "That dog is injured, stop making him run. That's animal cruelty!" Harry found it as hilarious as I did.

On the fourth day of deliberations, my car broke down, and Charlie had to drive me to set. He'd never seen Harry, and a practical joke came to me that still ranks in my top ten.

When he arrived to pick me up, I told him how annoyed I was that the night before I'd run over Harry in the driveway.

"*What?* Did you kill him?"

"No, of course not. I just fucked up his leg a little."

"Where is he, let me see him."

"Harry! Get out here," I called, and when he appeared with his flapping appendage, Charlie cried in alarm.

"Oh my God! This is serious. We've got to get him to a vet right away."

"No, I don't want to be late for set. But I think I can reset the bone."

I took Harry's leg and bent it so far forward it touched his nose.

"Stop that, you're going to hurt him!"

Harry was in on the joke, and I swear he was smiling.

"Maybe the bone will set if I bend it the other way." And I did, until the leg reached the side of Harry's head.

Charlie screamed again, but then it dawned on him that Harry was panting with his tongue hanging out, feeling no pain at all.

"Wait, what the fuck?" he said as Harry went up to lick his face.

That was the last good laugh I'd have for some time.

I DIDN'T KNOW when Charlie dropped me off at the Fox lot that the jury had reached a verdict. The protocol is for the bailiffs to give notice to the media before it's delivered so they will have enough time to set up their cameras in the back of the courtroom.

Oblivious that Barshop had called my family and they were rushing to Santa Monica, I was shooting a scene with Keaton, Glynnis O'Conner, and the legendary Maureen Stapleton. Maureen, who was hilarious as my mother, had known my parents since Dad had been her stage manager when she did a *Playhouse 90* episode. I had enormous affection for her, and when she asked how my parents were holding up, I told her everything.

As the crew set up to shoot a different angle, I returned to my trailer and was surprised to see Mark Metcalf waiting for me.

"They reached a verdict," he began.

"Just now? Why didn't anybody tell me the jury came back?"

"There was no way to reach you in time, and Nick and Lenny knew you were working."

"So what? Why didn't—"

"Listen to me," Mark interrupted, "the jury found him not guilty of second-degree murder but—"

I leapt so high in joy my head hit the ceiling. "Thank God!" I cried out until Mark put his hands on my shoulders to calm me.

"Griffin, you misheard me. I said *not guilty* of second degree. He was found guilty of voluntary manslaughter, which means—"

I knew what it meant and I did the math in my head. Six years and automatic release after three for good behavior, which means he'll get out in . . .

My brain hurt, and I couldn't have added two plus two with a gun to my head.

Mark finished my thought. "He'll be out in two and a half years."

"I don't believe what I'm hearing. How are my parents?"

"They are back at the house. Griffin, I gotta tell you, your dad did something incredible."

"What?"

At that moment the PA banged on my trailer door.

"Griffin, needed back on set" came from the other side.

"Listen," I said to Mark, "I don't have a car. Can you wait for me?"

"Of course."

I stepped onto the deco set where the actors and crew were ready to continue the scene. Keaton took one look and pulled me aside.

"What's going on?" he said.

I told him about the disastrous verdict and got no further than that before he got up and went to Amy Heckerling, the director, and said, loud enough for all to hear, "Okay, we're calling it a wrap. Griffin has to get home."

What he did that day remains one of the kindest things anyone has ever done for me.

Mark raced me back to Mom's house, which I hadn't seen so crowded since Alex and I arrived on the night of Halloween, ten months earlier. Doris Tate and our loyal supporters from Parents of Murdered Children were there, all the friends who had come to the trial every day, and my parents, who both pulled me into a long hug.

"You should have seen Nick," Melinda told me, with my father standing next to her. "He was incredible."

As she gave the recap, everyone gathered around to add missing details.

"When the verdict was announced, Adelson yelled out, 'I'm ecstatic,' and then he embraced Sweeney. He acted like he'd just got Manson off," Melinda said, forgetting that Doris Tate stood only a few feet away.

"And then, as if one victory wasn't enough, that fucker Adelson immediately appealed for probation," said Charlie.

"Did anyone notice that Mrs. Sweeney wasn't jumping up and down?" asked Lisa.

"Then Katz excused the jury," Melinda continued, "telling them that even though other people might agree or disagree with the verdict, they must not doubt their decision."

"That's because he knew when the press finds out about Lillian Pierce, a rain of shit is going to land on his head," said Charlie.

Melinda plowed on. "And then Katz told them that justice had been served and thanked them on behalf of the attorneys and both families. That's when Nick totally lost it."

Alex also missed the whole episode, but nonetheless looked proudly at our father as he picked up the thread from there.

"I couldn't believe my ears," Dad said. "I've never been so angry in my life. After all those weeks of sitting through this travesty, I couldn't take it anymore. 'Not for our family, Judge Katz!' I shouted. Lenny put up her hand to calm me, but I was too possessed with hatred to stop myself. My outburst enraged Katz, who said, 'You will have your chance to speak at the time of the sentencing, Mr. Dunne.'

"'It's too late then,' I yelled back.

"Katz threatened to have the bailiffs remove me from the courtroom, and I said, 'You have withheld important evidence from this jury about this man's history of violence against women. We're leaving your courtroom. It's all over here.' And then I got Lenny and all of us walked out."

"The room was in stunned silence. You could have heard a pin drop," added Melinda.

I'd missed it. I never got to see my father stand up for what was right in the face of utter defeat. But then again, I never got to see him go behind enemy lines to save a wounded soldier, so I wasn't entirely surprised.

A rain of shit did indeed fall on Katz's head. Papers around the country reported about the suppression of key evidence from

Lillian Pierce. KABC radio ran an on-the-hour editorial blasting the verdict. Letters to the editor from outraged readers, as stories of John Sweeney's history of violence against women became public knowledge, filled the newspapers. The *Herald Examiner* published a front-page article about the case: "Heat of Passion: Legitimate Defense or a Legal Loophole?" The foreman of the jury gave an apologetic interview saying they would have convicted Sweeney of second-degree murder had they known the facts. Judge Katz's dreams of appointment to the Supreme Court of California were dashed.

On November 10, the day of Sweeney's pro forma sentencing, picketers protesting the verdict, the judge, and Ma Maison marched on the courthouse steps in Santa Monica. Courtroom D was filled to capacity. Extra bailiffs were needed to stand in the aisles and eject the unruly, which only added to the already tense atmosphere.

According to a victims' bill of rights called Proposition 8, Changes to Criminal Proceedings Initiative, the survivors of the murdered have the right to make a statement at sentencing to plead with the judge for the maximum sentence. The family of the convicted also have the right to plead for a lighter sentence. Mrs. Sweeney begged for the court's mercy in her statement, describing her life as a battered wife and the trauma it caused her son. My family's compassion for her never wavered. I got up and presented Katz with a petition of a thousand signatures protesting the verdict and demanding the maximum sentence. As I spoke, I death-stared Sweeney, but his eyes wouldn't meet mine, instead looking down at the table, where his Bible, which he'd probably never read a page of, faced him in judgment. Both Mom and Dad spoke, but we knew the whole exercise was pointless and just wanted to get it over with.

Before announcing the sentence, Katz delivered a shameful

and cowardly about-face. My father would later recount in *Vanity Fair* how the judge now rejected the argument that Sweeney had acted in the heat of passion.

> "I will state on the record that I believe this is a murder. I believe that Sweeney is a murderer and not a manslaughterer. . . . This is a killing with malice. This man held on to this young, vulnerable, beautiful, warm human being that had everything to live for, with his hands. He had to have known that as she was flailing to get oxygen, that the process of death was displacing the process of life."
>
> Judge Katz then addressed Sweeney: "You knew of your capacity for uncontrolled violence. You knew you hurt Dominique badly with your own hands and that you nearly choked her into unconsciousness. . . . You were in a rage because your fragile ego could not accept the final rejection."
>
> He said he was appalled by the jurors' decision over Sweeney's first attack: "The jury came back—I don't understand it for the life of me—with simple assault, thus taking away the sentencing parameters that I might have on a felony assault."
>
> He called the punishment for the crime "anemic and pathetically inadequate." Having got the verdict we felt he had guided the jurors into giving, he was now blasting them for giving it.
>
> He went on and on. It was as if he had suddenly become a different human being. However, all his eloquence changed nothing. The verdict remained the same: manslaughter. The sentence remained the same: six and a half years, automatically out in two and a half with half a year served.

YOU WOULD THINK that a sudden death within a family would bring them closer together, but you would be wrong. One study found that 80 percent of couples divorce after they lose a child. The outliers to that statistic were my parents, who almost seemed to fall back in love after the loss of their daughter.

"Do you know how much you have changed?" Mom once asked Dad while they were watching the news after a day in court. She meant since he'd been sober, self-exiled in Oregon, and was now the man she wished she could have leaned on when they were married. His penchant for gossip and name-dropping, which once annoyed her, she now found amusing, and they talked about the old days, a time when she was most unhappy, as if they were Edenic.

"Lenny, you remember the summer Rudolf Nureyev and Margot Fonteyn stayed with Roddy McDowall at the Malibu Colony and you all invented that line dance?" I overheard Dad ask from the other room.

"We called it the Madison. It became the sensation in every gay disco in New York."

If there was a subtext that her ex-husband might very well have danced it with other men, I couldn't tell.

They laughed about the night David Selznick had a heart attack at his dinner party and said to his guests as he was wheeled out on a gurney, "Thanks for coming. Hope you had a lovely evening." Or the time their friend Sharman Douglas, daughter of the US ambassador to the Court of St. James and famous for making grand entrances, arrived at their beach house on an elephant. Or the not-so-pleasant memory of when Frank Sinatra, who had a long-standing crush on my mother, paid the maître d' of the Daisy fifty dollars to slap Dad across the face in front of her. "What was that guy's name?" Nick asked.

"Kurt something. I remember he ran after us in the parking

lot and cried. He said he was scared and needed the money. We never set foot in there again."

"Frank always had a crush on you. God, I still hate that man."

THERE IS LITTLE RESEARCH for how often extended families turn on each other in the event of the sudden death of a relation, but if there were, my parents and the Didion-Dunnes would have been a case study.

John and Joan timed their return from Paris with Quintana to the day of the sentencing. The animosity between my father and his brother reached new heights with every passing day John stayed in Europe. Even my allegiance had shifted during the trial, and it angered and hurt me that John never once checked in with my mother or me to see how we were holding up. But my pangs of neglect paled in comparison to Alex's and Melinda's since the day Patrick Terrail's orchid had arrived while Dominique was on life support, stoked further by the unfounded rumor that John and Joan continued to dine at Ma Maison even after the restaurant hired a cocounsel to defend Sweeney.

The orchid from Patrick Terrail was a mere ember compared with the barn burner Alex had in store for John and Joan the day of the sentencing. While everyone at Crescent Drive was still doing a postmortem about the last day of the trial, Alex grabbed Melinda, and they sneaked out of the house. She disguised herself behind sunglasses and covered her hair with a scarf, while Alex drove to an unfashionable florist in a neighborhood where they were sure not to be recognized. Always game for adventure, Melinda went inside and told the florist, in a thick Slavic accent, that she wished to buy an orchid and have it delivered. She filled out the address to John and Joan's house in Brentwood, paying extra for same-day delivery outside the florist's radius. Putting down a phony return number, she wrote the sender's name and filled out a card according to Alex's instructions.

When the orchid arrived in Brentwood, John and Joan had probably unpacked and fixed themselves a stiff drink after their long flight. They signed for the delivery and opened the accompanying note. It read, "Victory Is Ours, Love, Patrick Terrail."

When Alex told Dad and me what he'd done, my heart almost quit.

"You didn't" was all I could say.

"That is so fucked up." Dad scowled, though the laugh that followed contradicted his disapproval. That made Alex snicker, which made me giggle, setting the three of us into fits of cackling we were helpless to stop. Did I mention we were insane?

DAD HAD TO RETURN to New York to write the article Tina Brown had commissioned for *Vanity Fair*, and get back to his novel *The Two Mrs. Grenvilles.*

Before catching his flight, one of his last errands was to return Dominique's VW Bug to Crescent Drive. (The sight of our middle-aged father tooling around LA in a teenybopper's car with the top down never ceased to amuse Alex and me.) The final errand on Dad's list was to say goodbye to Lenny.

Mom was in bed watching *Good Morning America* when Dad came into her bedroom. He sat in her wheelchair and watched the program with her until his cab honked its arrival.

"I'm proud of you, Len," he said, taking her hand.

"I'm proud of you too," she replied, meaning it, but never taking her eyes off the morning anchor on television. These moments of detachment toward those she loved were involuntary, and we would come to understand them as an early sign that her MS was advancing to its next stage.

In the last years of my mother's life, she moved back to her birthplace of Nogales, and by then the disease had robbed her of her ability to speak. She could choose to listen, but it was painfully difficult to carry on one-sided conversations, and Alex and I found that the only way we had a chance of making her smile was if we were drunk or stoned just enough to no longer be inhibited by her silence. Dad, now decades sober when he visited her in Nogales, had no such problems. He would sit in her wheelchair, which she now rarely used, and tell her stories that actually made her laugh, a brass ring he grabbed with ease that usually eluded Alex and me, as hard as we tried. He delighted her with inside scoops on whatever murder case he was now covering for *Vanity Fair*, which often involved people on either side of the law they had known in years past.

Dad didn't know he had this superpower the day he competed for Lenny's attention with *Good Morning America*, and found his farewell, after all they'd been through, wholly dissatisfying.

After Dominique's trial, Alex stayed in LA to be with Mom, even though he noticed, as did we all, that our defeat in court had somehow strengthened rather than weakened her health.

She had grown very close to the members of Parents of Murdered Children, but as grateful as she was for their presence during the trial, she'd grown frustrated that their sole focus was only to offer *emotional* support to victims' families. Mom was more interested in legislation that would create statutes to protect the rights of victims. Her closest friends in the group, Marcella and Bob Leach, could not have agreed more. They decided to form their own group, called Justice for Homicide Victims.

Marcella's daughter from a previous marriage was named

Marsy, and like Dominique, she had been murdered by her boyfriend. But unlike Sweeney, Marsy's killer had been freed on bail. Neither the court nor law enforcement had bothered to warn Marcella, who would learn the truth days after her daughter's murder, when she saw the ex-boyfriend at her local market. He followed her through the aisles, taunting Marcella until she fled in fear. When she called the police to report his harassment and complain that she hadn't been told he'd been freed on bail, she learned that the state of California had no obligation to tell her, or even to notify her when he'd been released from prison after serving his sentence. Correcting that wrong would be the first amendment that Justice for Homicide Victims would include in a bill of rights called Marsy's Law. In the years that followed, Marsy's Law would be passed in twenty-three other states.

I stayed in Los Angeles another week to attend an elaborate wrap party for *Johnny Dangerously* on the 20th Century lot. An entire soundstage was set dressed as a Prohibition-era nightclub, with floozies and gangsters hired to serve appetizers. It was a riotous celebration, only to be interrupted when I saw Joe Shapiro, the co–defense attorney for Ma Maison, standing near a singer, crooning "Toot, Toot, Tootsie! (Goo' Bye)." Harold Ramis, a director and lovely man I would come to know, brought him as a guest without realizing his role in our trial or my part in the film. I had a security guard throw Shapiro out of the party, and as he was being escorted off the lot, the cast I'd spent months with in fits of laughter surrounded me with love, and we danced the night away.

NOT LONG AFTER I returned to New York, John and Joan sold their Brentwood home and moved to a French Renaissance–style building called Alwyn Court in Midtown Manhattan. The outside of the late nineteenth-century building was carved with intricate terra-cotta ornamentation, and inside there was an octagonal courtyard with painted murals by the artist Richard Haas. Dad still lived in a studio apartment facing an airshaft, and the three hadn't spoken since Dominique was laid to rest.

My closeness with John and Joan picked up where it had left off, though none of us discussed the trial. We knew our relationship would combust if John dared lecture that we "should have taken the deal," or if I told them I thought their hiding out in Paris showed a lack of support when we needed it most. The season of the trial was still too raw for me to rehash, and I much preferred John's morning calls about a recent op-ed, or his expression of glee over a disastrous review of a film he and Joan had turned down writing the script for.

I spoke just as much to my father and played the hapless role of Switzerland, never choosing favorites when dining separately with either party. If I had dinner with John and Joan at Elio's, their usual haunt, Dad would call the next morning to say, "I hear you were seen with John last night," as if I were a Nazi collaborator. For the millionth time I would remind him that my friendship with his brother was independent of him, and that his fight with John was his own.

In March 1984, *Vanity Fair* published "Justice: A Father's Account of the Trial of His Daughter's Killer." Dad's debut article about our legal odyssey and Sweeney's light sentence caused such national outrage that Judge Katz was demoted to a lower court. Tina Brown knew from the moment his piece was submitted that Dominick Dunne had more than one story to tell, and she made him *Vanity Fair*'s star reporter. Every cover story of his thereafter caused the magazine's sales to soar. My father's success in John and Joan's domain was another subject left unspoken during our dinners at Elio's.

I must admit that when the article was published, I wasn't thrilled. It felt like an invasion of our family's memory of a terrible time, and I thought his sharing our sorrow with the world distasteful. I was both happy for him and troubled that our tragedy made him a celebrity.

Over time, the piece became a bible I'd share with anyone I thought might become part of my life. "You won't know anything about me until you've read this," I'd say before handing over the article. I now regard what my father wrote to be a powerful indoctrination of what a family, privileged or not, might experience when thrust into the justice system for the first time. At great cost, my father found his voice as a writer, and I believe my sister did just what was asked of her in her final moments, when he whispered in her ear, "Give me your talent."

Not long after Dad's piece was in *Vanity Fair*, I was perusing the issues of other magazines at my local newsstand and saw that John had a byline in the latest *Esquire*. Even when I struggled with dyslexia, I'd loved his writing from an early age, well before I could understand the complex ideas in his wife's cryptic sentences. John's handcrafted obscenities and venomous portraits of politicians, studio heads, news anchors, and blowhard reviewers who dared criticize his wife's books were hilarious, and inspired me to one day cultivate the dark Irish humor I'd inherited from his generation into my own work.

John was especially admired for his crime reportage, until his brother eclipsed his reputation for writing about sensational murders in the upper classes. A favorite of my uncle's articles was a devastating and empathic piece for *The New Yorker* about the murder in a small midwestern town of a young transgender man named Brandon Teena, which was later to be an important source for the film *Boys Don't Cry*. John was one of the few reporters covering the trial in Nebraska who recognized that the violence against Brandon was a hate crime, and just the beginning of what is now commonplace warfare against the LGBTQ+ community.

I opened the issue of *Esquire* to John's piece and dived in. It was an essay about his process of writing, how a book can sometimes be born of a sentence that comes to mind and then sticks around. In this case the sentence was "When the trial began, we left the country." He went on to say that five months after he thought of that sentence, his niece had been murdered. Then, as an afterthought he wrote, "I do not understand people who attend the trials of those accused of murdering their loved ones. You see them on the local newscasts . . . I watch them kiss the prosecutor when the guilty verdict is brought in or scream at those jurors who were not convinced that the pimply-faced defendant was the buggerer of Jimmy and the dismemberer of Johnny."

It was clear he was mocking us for being so gauche as to attend a murder trial to honor my sister, to make her presence known to the jury, to remind them that there were people who loved her. Our trial received a great deal of press, and after the verdict, my mother and father used the media to express their outrage at having been betrayed by a judicial system they once believed in. Everyone who followed the trial was in awe of my parents' composure and dignity throughout the process—everyone, it seemed, except my uncle.

I raced to my IBM Selectric but had to smoke three cigarettes in rapid succession before my hands stopped trembling enough to hit the keys. Firing off missives intended to inflict damage came naturally to my father and John, and alcohol often sharpened barbed insults not easily taken back, but I was sober, and eager to draw the pint of blood I was after. Pent-up rage since he'd fled for Paris flowed page after page, with accusations of schadenfreude that Sweeney was given a light sentence because we didn't take a plea deal John had convinced himself he'd orchestrated for our benefit. I called him a coward for leaving town, for distancing himself from us just so he could still get a good table at Ma Maison. I never really thought he went back there, but was on a roll and figured it might be more hurtful if I said he did. I expressed pride for my parents during the trial, and that he had traded his cheap description of "people who attend the trials of those accused of murdering their loved ones" for the love and admiration I once had for him. "I hope your glib words were worth it, because they will never be forgotten or forgiven."

John was a master of epistolary assaults toward friends he'd fallen out with, or anyone he felt might have slighted him, and Joan always advised him to put the letter in a drawer to read the next morning before sending. I recalled and neglected her advice as I dialed a messenger for rush delivery of what I had just written.

John's response to my letter arrived by his own messenger two hours later. Email was years away, so this messenger business was a tad dramatic, like writing in feathered quill for pistols at dawn demanding satisfaction. John's opening salvo was to call *me* the real coward for not airing my grievances in person instead of hiding behind a nasty letter sent by messenger.

He went on to explain, unapologetically, that he didn't abandon us but left the country to protect Quintana from being called as a witness. What was less convincing was when he said the offending sentences in *Esquire* had nothing to do with our family, and only a narcissist actor would think so. (At least he didn't say I was a bad one.) The insult was a swing and a miss, and I took his denial as a silent admission of regret. At the end of his two-page single-spaced invective was a curt salutation and below that, a handwritten PS: "While we are throwing accusations around, maybe you can answer this: who was the woman in the dark glasses and scarf who sent Joan and me an orchid with that horrible note? I went to the florist in Culver City and the woman gave a false address and phone number. If you're not behind this, I believe you know who is."

His last sentence broadsided me with shame. I had completely forgotten about Alex and Melinda's vengeful act, and though I didn't participate, my silence made me a collaborator. My first impulse was to call John to beg forgiveness, but I decided to ring Alex in California instead. I read him my letter, which thrilled him because I'd finally joined his outright loathing of John. Then I read his reply, during which Alex muttered, "Liar, he's a fucking liar."

"Stop interrupting and wait for the end."

"Sorry, go ahead."

I never got past "who was the woman in the dark glasses and scarf who sent Joan and me the orchid" before Alex cried out, "Oh my God, what have I done!"

"I know, it's bad, we gotta fix this."

"*I* have to fix this. I'm getting on the first plane tomorrow."

Alex went straight from JFK and met me in front of Alwyn Court. I had told Joan the day before that Alex and I would like to come over, and we set a time. She didn't even ask the reason for the visit. Joan opened the door to the apartment and wordlessly led us to the living room, pointing to a sofa. John was seated farther away and didn't greet us, preferring to watch as if we were confessors on the other side of an interrogator's one-way mirror.

Alex got out no more than his first sentence before he was overcome with racking sobs. His apology was incoherent, but the few words we heard, like "shame" and "unforgivable," got the meaning across. Joan joined him on our couch and put her arms around him. Alex cried himself out into her shoulder, leaving a stain of tears on her cashmere cardigan. John remained in the corner, unmoved by his nephew's mortification. When there was nothing more to be said, Alex and I hugged Joan goodbye. I nodded to John, keeping my distance, fearing any sudden moves might set him off into punching either one of us. Alex, though, never one for reading the room, approached him for what he hoped might be a hug, but when he saw the malice in John's eyes, considered himself lucky to shake a reluctant hand.

If Alex's flight to New York was to achieve his uncle's absolution, then the mission was a failure. But walking away from Alwyn Court, he seemed lighter on his feet, and I realized he didn't prostrate himself before them for their benefit, but to confess to an act of cruelty that was beneath him and the moral code he vowed to live by. What was important to him was not the result of his confession, but that he went into the lion's den to deliver it. The audience Alex had with John did nothing to improve their relations, though both would unconvincingly deny there was any ill will toward the other.

Alex and John might have found a separate peace, but my attempts to get Dad to reconcile with his brother failed miserably. He knew I spoke to my uncle most mornings, and if John had a bit of gossip I thought might interest Dad, I'd share it and say where it came from.

"John said that? . . . Huh," was all he offered. Then he would tell me some juicy bit of info, knowing I would share it with John.

"Nick told you that? . . . Interesting."

I became a medium channeling messages from one to the other through the spirit of gossip, believing each tidbit brought them closer together, but I was as delusional as Neville Chamberlain.

One day while Dad and I were strolling down Madison Avenue, we saw John and Joan headed in our direction.

"Keep walking," Dad muttered.

If I thought our crossing paths without a word would be awkward, stopping to say hello proved far worse. It was obvious they wished we'd walked on by as well. As John and Dad stared each other down like a couple of gunslingers, I grasped for talk so small I even brought up the weather. The tension was unbearable, and after about thirty seconds Dad walked off, leaving me alone with only an apologetic shrug to offer on his behalf.

As it turned out, it would take two heart attacks to break the spell of antipathy that held Dad and John in sway for decades.

John always had a "weak ticker," as he called it, that had to be carefully monitored. In the last year of his life, he was sitting in the waiting room of his cardiologist when my father walked in. Neither were aware they shared the same doctor and they covered their mutual surprise with curt nods before Dad found a seat on the opposite side of the room and picked up a magazine. After a moment, still pretending to read an article, he heard John ask, "When was yours?"

Dad put the magazine down and said, "Two years ago. I was being given anesthesia to have a cyst removed and got so terrified I had it right on the operating table."

John chuckled and said, "You always were scared of hospitals."

"And losing control."

"Yeah, that too."

They looked at each other for a beat, neither sure what to say next, until Dad asked, "What the fuck are we doing?"

That set them off roaring with laughter, and Dad got up and moved to an empty seat next to his brother. They never stopped talking until the nurse interrupted to say, "Mr. Dunne, the doctor will see you now." The two old men looked at each other.

"Which Dunne?"

The nurse looked confused. "Either one?"

The brothers did a "you go, no you go" exchange for a bit, and when one of them finally got up, the other said, "I'll wait."

"Okay, but then I'll wait for you, and we can get a coffee after."

"Deal."

From that day forward they talked on the phone every single morning, until the night John suffered another heart attack and dropped dead at his and Joan's dining table. They talked about whose marriage was in the toilet, or what arbitrage crook was going to jail. They talked about whatever movie got a shitty review in the *Times* that Friday and reminisced about their childhood on Stone Drive in Hartford. They talked the morning Quintana was put in the hospital, desperately ill from septic shock. When John, crippled with worry, cried and cried into the phone, Dad rushed uptown to be with him.

As shocked and saddened as Dad was to lose a brother, he remained ever grateful that his heart attack had placed him in that waiting room with John. What he regretted, he told me once, was that they didn't mend things sooner. I'm not an "I told you so" guy and just kept my mouth shut.

Twenty-Six

Amy and I saw a short film called *Vincent* that preceded a Disney feature neither one of us can remember. The story was about a child possessed of dark fantasies who believes he is Vincent Price, and the director, Tim Burton, actually got Mr. Price to narrate it.

Amy has a gift for thinking outside the box, and as we left the theater, she said, "You know, whoever directed that short movie might be right for *After Hours*." Her first out-of-the-box idea for a director had been Martin Scorsese, not known for his sense of humor, especially after the recent release of *The King of Comedy*, which was a box office failure and entirely misunderstood at the time, though it would find its audience decades later. From Amy's experience working with Marty on *Mean Streets*, she knew how funny he was, and believed he'd appreciate the dark humor of the script.

Our lawyer was a lovable rogue right out of *Guys and Dolls* named Jay Julien, who also represented Marty, so getting him the script was easy. The problem was he was about to leave for

Morocco to prep *The Last Temptation of Christ* and wouldn't be available for at least a year, so we set a meeting with Tim Burton at the commissary on the Disney lot, where he worked in the animation department.

Tim had read the script beforehand, many times it seemed, because he had presented us with storyboards illustrated in the style he would be famous for: haunted characters with skinny arms walking down creepy hallways that fluttered with bats. I assumed the drawings were made with one of the many pens that leaked ink from the front pocket of his short-sleeve shirt. His vision for the movie was brilliant and light-years from anything we imagined *After Hours* could be.

But raising money for an oddball movie with a first-time director, starring someone without a box office name (me), was difficult and took time. So long that in the meantime, Marty had just been fired from his first attempt to direct *Last Temptation* for cost overruns, and the production was scrapped. *After Hours* was on the top of a pile of scripts he read on his flight home from Casablanca and the movie he decided he'd like to make next. Besides finding Joe Minion's script hilarious, he liked that it had to be made for a price, because at that point in his career, he needed to prove to studios that he was still capable of making a film within a tight budget.

Jay called us at Amy's apartment, which we used as our office, and we listened on different extensions as he announced, "He loves the script, so it looks like you two are going to make a Martin Scorsese picture!"

His enthusiasm was met with dead silence.

"Hello?" he said, as if he'd lost the connection.

"Yeah, we're here," Amy said.

"This isn't the usual reaction I get from producers when I tell them Marty wants to direct their movie."

"No, it's great," I began, then paused.

"We are already down the road with Tim Burton. You know that, Jay," Amy said.

"Yes, and it's been what? Six months?" Jay asked, knowing full well the answer.

"Well, there's that company that's interested in putting in a hundred grand," I reminded him.

"They're a schlock outfit. I can make a deal with any studio in town if you have Marty."

We told him we'd think about it but had to speak to Tim first.

Tim met us for lunch in the Disney commissary, and he brought along a miniature, painstakingly handmade model of one of the sets. The detail and imagination that went into it were brilliant and couldn't have made us feel worse. Tim knew something was off when we stared at his masterpiece like a puppy we'd have to put down.

"So, a funny thing happened yesterday," I began, though Tim could tell it would be far from funny.

Amy took the reins and reminded him that we had first given the script to Scorsese, and that he had become suddenly available and was interested in doing it.

Tim interrupted to say, "Wait, are you telling me Martin Scorsese wants to do this script?"

"Uh-huh," I said, and in a cowardly way added, "but we didn't tell him yes or anything."

"If Mr. Scorsese wants to make this film, I respectfully withdraw from the project. I would never stand in the way of anything he wants to do," Tim said with more force than we'd heard from him before.

Amy and I still felt like scumbags but somehow knew that sooner rather than later Tim's unique vision would find a breakout audience. A month later, Warner Bros. hired him to make the hit film *Pee-wee's Big Adventure*, which came out around the same time as *After Hours* and grossed far bigger box office. The studio sent Tim and me across the country to promote our films, and sometimes I would be picked up at an airport in a Warner Bros. limo that had just dropped him off to catch a flight. On one of our overlaps, he left behind a little hand-drawn picture of a bug-eyed child waving hello from a graveyard, on a card that read "Happy Trails, Griffin," so there were no hard feelings on his end, but there remains an unfulfilled curiosity on our part about what Tim Burton might have done with *After Hours*.

I WAS TWENTY-NINE YEARS OLD, starring in every frame of a Martin Scorsese picture that I was also coproducing. I'd dreamed of one day being an actor in a starring role for a prestigious director, and after years of rejections that tested my faith, it would be natural to assume I could now look in the mirror and sigh with relief that I'd finally made it.

Of course, when you're that young, it doesn't work that way. I worked my ass off on that picture and never learned so much, about not just acting but also filmmaking, but I reasoned the opportunity came along because it was my place in line, with far more movies to follow. A kid in his twenties doesn't walk around feeling "grateful" when times are good; that comes later, when you've truly had the shit kicked out of you and can't believe you've been given a second chance. I was too young to understand gratitude for living the dream, and if I did, my performance would never have been free or spontaneous.

Marty was like an older brother to me, too young to be a father figure, but wise enough to tutor me in the history of cinema.

Throughout preproduction and filming, he'd hand me clunky VHS tapes, the technology at the time, of films by Rossellini, Bresson, Kurosawa, or Bergman, always referring to each director with the same line: "This is a guy you should know about."

The only thing he asked of me before the start of shooting was that I not have sex until the picture wrapped. He wanted Paul Hackett, my character, to carry the tension of a young man who hadn't been laid in so long that a subtext of unrelenting sexual frustration would come through in every frame. *Eight weeks*, I thought. *Big deal, I can do that.*

In the early hours of our first Saturday shoot, we didn't have time to finish a scene where I'm on a couch with Linda Fiorentino, massaging her exquisite body covered in only a bra and panties. When we broke for the weekend, I was in such a state of arousal I had to remain alone on the couch another fifteen minutes to let my erection die down.

Let's just say that that Saturday night I met someone in a club called Area and had what Carrie called "a fucking accident," where you get drunk, fall down, and fuck 'em.

When we picked up the scene on Monday, I massaged Linda, not like the trembling, sex-starved twerp I'd been on Friday, but with the flirtatious moves of Pepé Le Pew.

"Cut!" Marty barked after one take. "Griffin, come here!"

I followed him off the set to where he cornered me against a wall.

"Did you get laid?" he demanded.

My shame almost brought me to my knees.

"Yes, I did, Marty, I'm so sorry."

"I expressly asked you to refrain from sex."

"I know, but I had a fucking accident."

"A *what*?"

"Never mind."

"You bet never mind. Never mind the scene, never mind your disrespect for me, and never mind your lack of self-respect. You've fucked up the whole picture. I don't think I can finish it now. I'm going to send everybody home."

"No, Marty, please! Let me just try it again. I'll be better, I promise."

Marty might have been bluffing, but the lesson he taught me was that the terror on an actor's face can sometimes look just like months of pent-up lust. The scene continued without a hitch.

TO OUR COMPLETE SURPRISE, *After Hours* opened to mixed reviews. My ultimate disappointment was when the film critic Pauline Kael, who I'd dreamed might one day mention my name in her *New Yorker* column, called me a "second-rate Dudley Moore." The film would not be crowned a classic until the early part of the twenty-first century.

The reception in Europe the following year was a different story. We'd been accepted into competition at the Cannes Film Festival, and while I couldn't wait to go, Muammar Gaddafi was less enthused and threatened to place bombs on all flights bound for Europe. Word spread that his most tempting target would be 747s full of movie stars headed to Cannes. That didn't deter me in the least, but Marty, Amy, and every cast member thought it best to sit it out.

The only person I could persuade to join me was my close friend Mitch Glazer. Mitch's one condition was that we not fly to the airport in Cannes but to Geneva, because even Gaddafi had nothing against the Swiss, and then take trains from there to Cannes.

The Warner Bros. travel department was baffled about how to get us by train from Geneva to Cannes. It took three track changes in three different cities over eight hours, sometimes going miles north, instead of south toward France. That detour led us through a toxic mist still wafting from Chernobyl, which had melted down just weeks earlier.

"You'd rather die of lingering cancer than a quick painless explosion?" I yelled at Mitch in a train filled with goats and chickens being led to market by local farmers. I could have killed him.

When we pulled into the station at Cannes, we were met by an equally baffled press corps who aggressively wondered why we took so many trains to reach the most famous film festival in the world. When they realized action stars like Schwarzenegger and Stallone would be no-shows, I was no longer confounding, but a hero they dubbed "the bravest American." At a restaurant along the Croisette, Gérard Depardieu, whom I'd never met, threw his arms around me as the rest of the patrons burst into applause.

When I checked into the hotel, I gave them my tuxedo for pressing, but days later and only twenty minutes before the start of the premiere, I noticed it hadn't been returned. The front desk apologized, but the dry cleaner had closed for the night and there was nothing they could do. "Perhaps tomorrow would be convenient for monsieur?" The closed-circuit television in my room showed the last of the guests climbing the red carpet, and even in my schoolboy French, I understood the commentator's irritation when he kept asking, "Où est Griffin Dunne?"

I paced my room in just a bow tie and a shirt, taking no delight in the irony that Paul Hackett's misadventures continued to follow me even after I'd made the movie. These "you're never going to believe what just happened" moments have taunted me all my life. It's why Amy thought of me for the role and Marty couldn't imagine anyone else after picking up on my chaotic vibes. But it can be tiresome to constantly be in stressful situations that an unseen audience finds hilarious. If, when putting my room service tray in the hallway in only my underwear, the door locks behind me, I swear I can hear a laugh track. The twenty dollars that blew out the window of the taxi at the beginning of the movie is something that actually happened to me in the back of a Chicago cab. I had hoped making *After Hours* might exorcise these laugh track moments of my life, but to date, no such luck.

My tuxedo crisis was solved by Claude, a bodyguard armed with an Uzi, whom the festival hired to shadow me my entire stay. (It's unlikely Gaddafi had his sights on killing "the bravest American," but they were taking no chances.) Claude gathered a couple of gendarmes to break into the dry cleaner and rescue my tux. Mitch and I were then hustled into a limo with a motorcycle escort that screeched to a stop in front of a desolate Palais. I bolted up the empty red carpet and followed the sounds of an impatient audience, clapping in time for the movie to begin.

The crowd must have felt I was worth the wait, because when the film ended, they gave me a thunderous ten-minute standing ovation. It was an out-of-body experience to see thousands of people cheering and blowing me kisses in a shot that panned from the mezzanine below to the balconies above in full 360. Their adulation continued for so long that I became embarrassed and wondered if there was a protocol to bring the ovation to an end. The answer came from a woman who yelled from several rows back in a thick French accent, "You must leave now! We cannot leave the theater until you do."

I was the first out the door, followed by a mob of fans that

Claude kept at bay, his Uzi poking out from his blazer, and then was shoved into the back of a waiting car that was instantly surrounded by girls who wouldn't let us pass. They pressed their faces against the window and banged their palms so hard on the glass they turned beet red. I thought of Bob Dylan in *Don't Look Back* facing the same frenzy in his limo after a concert and remembered how bored he seemed by it all. How the fuck could anyone find this boring? A little scary maybe, but certainly not boring.

At the after-party, I met a French starlet who loved my work so much that she wanted to show her appreciation back at my hotel. I thought, or hoped, maybe she would leave after doing what she came to do, but instead she just rolled over and quickly fell asleep. All those hours of being worshipped had left me feeling wired and empty. The evening had undoubtedly been a triumph, but it was spent with total strangers. There was no hugging with Marty, no "Do you believe this shit?" looks with Amy during the standing ovation, only praise from people in languages I couldn't follow but nodded as if I did.

I got out of bed, desperate to speak with my mother. This time when I reached her, unlike most of our phone calls, she turned down the television to give me her complete attention. The tuxedo mishap had her in stitches, she was amazed that I had a bodyguard, and she fell silent when I told her about the ovation and cheering that went on and on.

It took her a moment to speak, and through the receiver I heard her try to maintain her composure.

"I'm so proud of you, honey. And Dominique would be too," she said.

I thought the same thing, and that if Dominique were alive, she would have come with me, Gaddafi be damned, and it would have been my sister I was hugging when the film ended. We might both have had movies in the same competition, who knows?

"I miss her so much, Mom," I said.

"I know you do, honey, me too."

Twenty-Seven

With stardom in my sights, I worked like a mad scientist concocting formulas for how to best fuck it up. "Self-destructive choices" was how my high-octane agent described my decisions before leaving his powerful agency to follow a fledgling agent to his tiny firm. (That agent later abandoned me to become a real estate agent.) The agency he lured me to was run by a frosty old German lady named Vera Veidt, who I thought was married to Colonel Klink from *Hogan's Heroes.* When we met, I attempted to charm her with a "small world" anecdote about the time I mistook Otto Preminger for her husband.

"You are confusing the TV hack Werner Klemperer with my father, Conrad Veidt, a brilliant actor who starred in *The Cabinet of Dr. Caligari.* You should get your Germans straight, young man."

Not a great start at an agency I was to leave after a month.

I lost the ability to make sensible choices about what movies to appear in, or which to turn down. I followed up working with Scorsese by making a humorless comedy with Madonna called *Who's That Girl*, which was a reviled box office disaster. I turned down starring in *Sex, Lies, and Videotape* because Dustin Hoffman was signed to do a movie Amy and I were to produce called *Once Around.* Dustin was notoriously fickle about committing to movies and had taken to calling me, not the director, Lasse Hallström, every morning to talk about his character and be reassured that he had made the right choice to work with us. If I left to act in *Sex, Lies, and Videotape*, he might have walked and killed the picture. As it happened, Dustin did indeed walk, to be in *The Merchant of Venice*, and James Spader starred in *Sex, Lies, and Videotape.* We were developing a script called *White Palace* that I was confident I'd star in, but as my stock dropped after *Who's That Girl,* James Spader's rose after winning best actor in Cannes for *Sex, Lies, and Videotape*, and he got the part in the movie I produced instead of me.

It was a period in my life when I felt unworthy to work on challenging material with directors I admired. That I was drunk when running into many of those directors didn't inspire their confidence either. In the mideighties, booze and blow were social accessories, so to stand out as someone who partied too hard took a lot of work, but I managed to get that reputation anyway.

Sometimes Dominique's murder played a role in my decision-making. One time, while stone-cold sober, I was having dinner with a director who hoped to woo me to be in a movie I needed no convincing to agree to do, as the part and the script were perfect, but I played hard to get because that's what movie stars are supposed to do. But then, as we were getting to know each other, he casually mentioned that he had mob contacts and almost hired a hit man to take out his wife during a messy divorce. He could tell by my expression that his small talk hadn't gone over well.

"Did you think telling me you were going to have a woman killed would impress me?" I said.

I left him in the restaurant before our entrées were served.

Since Sweeney's light sentence and our family's humiliation in the courtroom, I felt as if my luck had run dry and I had only more misfortune awaiting me. Mom's declining health rarely strayed from my thoughts. If the phone in my apartment rang after midnight, I'd jump out of my skin, expecting to be on the next plane to see her in the hospital or at her funeral.

If a midnight call wasn't about Mom, I'd assume it was going to be more bad news about my brother. Alex's mental health had worsened since the trial, and heavy drinking exacerbated his mania. His increasingly erratic behavior came to a head at Mom's fifty-fourth birthday party while I was in New York. He was bouncing off the walls, knocking over drinks, and babbling so incoherently that Mom feared for not only him but herself. She asked Charlie and Michael Lerner, a trusted friend of Alex's, to check her son into UCLA's psychiatric ward. Charlie and Michael knew he wouldn't go willingly, so after making arrangements for his admittance, they invited him to a party in Westwood, where the hospital was located. Alex was game, and dived into the back seat of Charlie's car, eager to party down. He didn't realize what was happening until he entered the lobby of the psych ward and was restrained by two white-clad attendants who bum-rushed him into the locked facility. Alex's screams of betrayal as he fought back still ring in Charlie's and Michael's ears to this day.

I flew out to UCLA, where Alex was mandatorily detained for the next forty-eight hours. They had him heavily medicated, and when he begged me to get him out of there, thick threads of saliva clung to the corners of his mouth. There was a hearing down the hall where, as a family member, I was to go before a judge to give my consent to have him committed.

"You gotta get me out of here, Griffin. I don't belong."

A doctor entered the room to say the judge was expecting me.

"This is all up to you, Griffin. You have the power. *Please* don't do this." I nodded ambiguously and said I'd be right back.

I stood before the bench of a scaled-down courtroom that looked like the set of Judge Judy's daytime tribunal. The judge asked if I was willing to keep my brother incarcerated for further evaluation. I thought of Alex's last words, the webs of saliva in his mouth, and scanned the documents pushed toward me to sign. The judge had to repeat the question twice before I finally answered.

"I can't do it," I said over and over. "I can't do it, can't do it, can't do it." He was released that day.

MY FATHER'S FAME was on the rise as my brief moment in the sun continued to dim. One year *Women's Wear Daily* referred to him as the father of Griffin Dunne, and two years later they called me the son of Dominick Dunne. *The Two Mrs. Grenvilles* was a breakout bestseller, and his articles in *Vanity Fair* were the magazine's most eagerly read and discussed. I was proud he'd at last achieved his dreams, but would audibly groan when he'd rehash Dominique's murder on the countless talk shows where he was now a fixture. His addiction to alcohol had been replaced by a craving for publicity, granting interviews to anyone from even the lowliest rags.

"I get that you have to plug your books, but do you have to talk about Dominique every time?" I forced myself to ask. "It's very upsetting to Alex and me."

"What do you want me to do, kid? They're journalists. It's their job to ask me, and I'm a journalist, so it's my job to answer."

All of this coincided with Sweeney's release after his brief stay at a medium-security prison. He soon found a job as chef at a restaurant in Santa Monica called the Chronicle. The day my mom found out, she asked Charlie to take her there. He wheeled her inside and she summoned the manager to say, "Do you know that the hands that are cooking the food for your customers strangled my daughter?"

The manager claimed innocence and sputtered a few more unsatisfactory explanations, until Mom cut him off to say, "We'll be back," and left the restaurant.

Soon after, Parents of Murdered Children and Dominique's friends picketed in front of the Chronicle with placards that read things like THE FOOD YOU'RE ABOUT TO EAT WAS COOKED BY A MURDERER. Their demonstration got him fired but didn't keep him from being hired somewhere else.

A few months later, I heard Sweeney next got a job in the kitchen at the Bel Age Hotel. Not long after, I happened to be seated next to the owner of the hotel on a flight to Los Angeles. This was in the days when passengers used to speak to their fellow travelers, and after a lengthy conversation on an assortment of subjects, he mentioned that he owned the Bel Age. I turned ashen and he asked me what was wrong.

When I told him what the chef in his restaurant had done to my sister, he was horrified; he had no idea. We exchanged numbers, and he told me he would take care of it the moment we landed. He called me that afternoon to say that because Sweeney had admitted in his job application that he was a convicted felon, the hotel couldn't justify firing him and would be open to a lawsuit if they did. The hotel's owner was a good man and genuinely apologetic, so I assured him we wouldn't be picketing out front because there was nothing he could do about it anyway.

A week later he called, ecstatic to say that Sweeney had

punched a busboy, which gave the hotel manager cause to fire him. I felt bad for the busboy but was grateful he took the hit for making Sweeney's life just a little more miserable.

More months passed, and just when we thought Sweeney was out of our lives, Dad showed me a letter he'd received at *Vanity Fair.* It was from a man in Seattle whose daughter was dating someone named John Maura, who looked like the John Sweeney Dad had written about, but the new boyfriend insisted it wasn't him. The father thought he was lying but had no way of proving it. He was at a loss about what to do and hoped my father could help him find out the truth.

Dad called Anthony Pellicano, a famous LA private eye who would later go to prison for wiretapping but at the time was happy to track down the man who'd killed Dominick Dunne's daughter. In less than an hour he found out that John Sweeney had changed his name to John Maura and was living in Seattle. By the time Dad told the father that Sweeney and Maura were the same person, his daughter had already fessed up that she knew. She was in love with Sweeney and insisted that he'd learned his lesson and would never hurt a fly. That he was a different person. The father was beside himself because the more upset he was toward his daughter, the closer she became with Sweeney.

The two fathers talked for a long time, and when Dad hung up, he felt terrible that the man couldn't talk sense into his daughter. I asked for the father's number to see if I might give it a shot.

When the father answered, I introduced myself and asked to speak with his daughter. He obviously thought she might listen to someone her own age, because without a moment's hesitation, he called out, "Honey, telephone, it's for you."

She picked up on a different extension. I'm afraid I don't

remember her name, but she deserves one, so for the sake of our conversation, I will call her Cathy.

"Hello, Cathy, my name is Griffin Dunne, and my sister's name was Dominique Dunne. Did you ever hear that name?"

"I don't think you should be calling me, so I'm going to hang up."

"No, wait. Just listen to me for five minutes. You don't have to say anything, but please just listen."

She didn't hang up, so I launched in. I told her about the two times Sweeney tried to strangle Dominique before he killed her.

"His last name is Maura, not Sweeney," she corrected.

"It's Sweeney, and he changed it for a reason."

"He said he changed it because the Dunne family wants to have him killed."

"That's not something we would ever do, and he knows it."

"He said what happened to your sister was a mistake. John didn't mean to hurt her and swears he would never lay a hand on a woman again."

"Let me tell you about his other 'mistakes' before he even met Dominique."

I told her about Lillian Pierce, whom he had hospitalized twice, once for six days, once for four. Cathy didn't make a sound as I described in vivid detail Lillian's broken nose, punctured eardrum, and collapsed lung.

"Men who beat women don't just stop being violent. Their rage won't allow them. And not just women. Did Sweeney tell you he lost his job in LA only a few months ago for beating up a busboy?"

When it took her a long time to say "No," I could tell I was getting through.

"Look, I understand why you are calling, and I'll think about it, but I really have to go," she said, clearly wanting to get off the phone.

"That's all I ask, Cathy. Just think whether you really want a guy who calls himself John Maura in your life. Think about how he took my sister's life. Think about what he did to Lillian Pierce. Thank you so much for listening to me. I know it wasn't easy."

Cathy's father called a day later to say she'd broken it off with John Sweeney Maura, and thanked us both for our help.

"It was Griffin who did it," Dad said. "Your daughter might not have listened to me."

Yes, it was me. I did that. And if given the information, I'd track down every woman Sweeney ever had so much as a conversation with. But by the late eighties, I stopped keeping track of Sweeney, or his girlfriends, or where he worked to get him fired. Lugging around all that hate had become debilitating, and to my surprise, over time, it kind of burned out on its own. My body wanted to self-heal before I did and detected my hate as a cancer that would eventually kill me unless my own cells rebelled against it. People far more enlightened than I am say that forgiveness is a choice that frees us from the bondage of hate, and that to forgive is the purest form of love. I choose not to forgive or forget, and as long as I'm no longer bound by hate, I'm happy with the quality of love I have for my family and friends, even if it falls short of its purest form. I wish only the worst for Sweeney but am most content that he rarely crosses my mind or intrudes on the memories I cherish of Dominique. I can let go of the hate, but will never let go of missing her. That is my choice.

Twenty-Eight

The lead actor in a movie is listed as "number one" on the call sheet, which is a daily bulletin distributed to the cast and crew informing them of the scenes they should be prepared to shoot. In 1989, I was number one on the call sheet for a movie so terrible, it would be years before I'd get my name up there again. While the film was a near-fatal blow to my career, it indirectly led to the single greatest decision in my life.

The career-killing movie I perversely signed on to was about a man who talks to his penis, called *Me and Him*. The penis, of course, talks back, gratefully off camera, in a voice only my character could hear. Being number one on the call sheet, I had penis approval and total control over what my member should sound like. In a dreamworld, I wanted my dick to sound like Jack Nicholson. The casting director approached him, and for about ten minutes Jack actually considered prerecording all the penis's lines before wisely turning it down. We settled on an actor with a gravelly voice who was available to be on set every day, leaving room should my dick and I decide to spontaneously improvise.

Rebecca Miller, the daughter of Arthur Miller, and later a gifted writer-director in her own right, was hired as my love interest. The author of *Death of a Salesman* read his daughter's talking-penis project and forbade her to be in the movie for her own good. The actress who replaced Rebecca would play a far bigger part in my life than just being my costar.

When Carey Lowell was cast, our offscreen affair began the first week of shooting. After the picture wrapped, she went on to be a Bond girl in *License to Kill*, and I pined for her until she returned from Europe, and when she did, we picked up where we'd left off and fell truly in love.

Three months into our bliss and reckless lovemaking, I accidently got Carey pregnant. This unplanned event was so early in our relationship that neither of us was sure how we felt about it. I rented a house on Martha's Vineyard for long walks on the beach to talk over our options, of which there were only two: terminate the pregnancy or have the baby. Carey and I were still getting to know each other, but were undoubtedly in love and worried we would feel differently if we didn't love each other enough to have a child together. Though if we had the baby, did we know each other well enough to handle the radical change to our relationship, which was perfect as it was? I was thirty-four and she was twenty-eight, and though still young enough to have children with other partners, both of us feared we'd never find anyone as suited as we were for each other. Carey not only was beautiful on the outside, but inside possessed a DNA I found wildly attractive. She was raised in Colorado by a family in which not one member was a drunk, killed themselves, had mental illness, or got murdered. So far, the only tragedy in Carey's life was when her great-aunt had died in her sleep at the age of ninety-three. If we were to raise a child, those were the kinds of genes I wanted, to counterbalance some of my own.

On our last day on Martha's Vineyard, we sat in the kitchen quietly drinking our first coffee of the morning.

"I want to do it," I said out of the blue.

"I was just about to say the same thing."

"So this is real?"

"This is real," Carey said, and then pointed to her belly. "Besides, something tells me it was never up to us. This kid wants to be born whether we want it or not."

I hadn't met Carey's parents nor she mine, but both parties were beside themselves with joy. We had decided for their sakes to get married before the child was born, so first I went with Carey to meet her parents in Denver, and then soon after, we went to LA to introduce her to my mother. She'd already met Dad in New York over dinner at "his table" at the 21 Club. After Carey excused herself to the ladies' room, he'd pointed his finger in her direction and said, "Now that . . . is a *class act*!"

Carey's parents and sisters were as loving to each other as a family in a fifties sitcom. Jim Lowell's girls called their father Jimmer, appropriate for a guy who looked my age but was actually twenty years older and twice as fit. During our stay, Jimmer and I hiked two of the 5-Peak Traverse mountains outside of Boulder. Carey's dad was a geologist, and hoping to impress him, I had read John McPhee's tome on geology, *In Suspect Terrains*, beforehand, which was scientifically way over my head. But the way Jimmer described the strata of shale we ascended was easy to grasp, and his fascination with formations beneath the earth's surface was contagious.

Next stop on Carey's and my whirlwind pregnancy tour was

the house on Crescent Drive. I had prepared her not to take it personally if my mother seemed distant and more interested in watching television than talking to either of us.

Mom could not have been more present, and even turned off the television when we entered her bedroom. Her excitement at being a grandmother was apparent, and I felt proud to have done something that made her so happy. After discussing our not wanting to know the gender of the baby until it was born, and possible dates for our wedding, Mom's expression suddenly shuttered with sadness.

"Oh, Griffin, I didn't want to tell you until you got here, but Panda died."

I hadn't noticed till then that her cat was missing from her lap, where Panda always rested. I could only imagine how brokenhearted Mom must have been, but since she typically kept sorrow hidden, imagination was all I had to go on.

"Oh no," Carey said. "Was she the cat that picked the flowers for you?"

"Yes," Mom said, pointing to a crystal bowl with rosebuds floating in water. "Those are the last ones she gave me."

"Now, Griffin," Mom said, sounding all business, "I need you to do a rather unpleasant task. Panda is in a freezer at the vet's, and I need you to go there and then bury her in the rose garden outside my window."

I'd never been able to look at that window without picturing Sweeney's face banging on the glass, but I said, "Of course, Mom. I'll go first thing in the morning."

"No, I need you to do it now. Panda has been there for three days."

Incredibly, the vet who'd cut the rubber band off Sunijet's

paw still worked there, and if he remembered me from that day, he gave no sign. I'd told Carey about all of Dominique's pets, but left out the part about almost killing one of them.

Panda was inside a garbage bag and hard as a discus when the vet handed her to me from the freezer. I could feel by her shape that she was curled up just as she had always been when sleeping on Mom's lap.

Back at the house, I grabbed a shovel from the garage, and Carey looked on as I dug a hole next to a rosebush high enough for Mom to see from her window. Then I laid Panda to rest.

"Griffin," Carey said, "she's still in the garbage bag. You can't put her in there like that."

"I know, but I can't bring myself to look at her."

"I got it," said my future wife as she gently untied the knot to the bag.

Holding a frozen dead cat in her arms, she placed Panda back in the hole.

"Welcome to the Dunne family," I said.

Thank God she laughed.

MY FATHER QUICKLY DISPELLED any illusion that Carey and I had a say in our own wedding. This was his moment. We let him pay for it, from the invitations on Smythson stationery, to the venue, to the menu he haggled over with a wedding planner who was a doppelgänger for Marty Short, years before he would star in *Father of the Bride*.

As Dad studied the menu the wedding planner was pitching, Carey and I witnessed a tense standoff between two men of similar age, dubious sexual orientation, and completely different ideas of what accounts for "class."

"I don't see my chicken potpie listed," my father said in a tone not unlike the one I heard him use with the salesman at Tiffany's when I was a boy.

"Well, yes, Mr. Dunne. I did give that some thought. But as we have a salmon, a beef, and a chicken paillard, it just felt like putting a hat on a hat, so I decided to cut it."

"But I said . . . I wanted chicken potpie."

"Yes, I remember that, Mr. Dunne, but I've been doing this for many years and just felt—"

"Well, *I'm paying for this*, and when I say I want chicken potpie at my son's wedding, I want *chicken pot fucking pie*!"

A fourth entrée and second poultry dish was quickly added to the menu.

It would not be cruel to say, because Carey would be the first to admit it, that she waddled down the aisle with a belly so fecund that no one would have been surprised if she'd suddenly popped out a baby right on the altar. The clergyman we'd asked to marry us was an hour late, so in a sudden-death move, it was decided that Earl McGrath would perform the duties. Uncle Earl was already stoned, but to calm his nerves, he downed three vodkas in quick succession.

"No fucking jokes! Play it straight for once in your life," Dad barked at him, ignoring how Earl's hands shook as he refilled his glass.

To our dismay, the clergyman showed up just as we were shoving Earl into place to marry us off. The chaplain legitimized the ceremony but lacked the stoned, outrageous delivery we would have preferred from Earl. He wished the two of us a bright future, which was odd, because he gave no mention of the third person in Carey's belly.

Alex was my best man and stood beside me, still beaming

with the same excitement he felt since the day he learned he'd be an uncle. I could already picture him telling the baby magical stories he'd make up off the top of his head, and the collages he'd painstakingly scissor from magazines to hang in his or her room. Our baby had no idea how much love would be coming its way from Uncle Alex.

Dad gave a rapturous toast, and Mom caught up with old friends like Howard Erskine, her beau before Dad stole her away to marry in Nogales. I hadn't seen her so happy in years. Suzanne Lowell, Carey's mother, even buried the hatchet with Dad for sending out the Smythson wedding invitations with his name as the headliner, ignoring protocol that the bride's parents be listed first.

After the ceremony, when the last guests were leaving, I talked my pregnant bride into saying good night to Mom, who had left earlier and was staying blocks away at the Carlyle. I was high from the evening, and stoned from Earl's joints and the flowing champagne.

Carey and I placed ourselves on either side of Mom's bed while she watched television, hoping to distract her with a rehash of our triumphant wedding.

"Did you have a good time?" I asked.

"Uh-huh" was all she offered, her eyes never leaving a rerun of some seventies sitcom.

"You seemed to be having a really good time," I said desperately, trying not to notice that Carey was dying inside for me.

"Yes, it was very nice."

Mom clearly wanted the conversation to end and be left alone, so I kissed her on the cheek, her eyes still never leaving the sitcom, and we shuffled out of the room and into the hallway to summon the elevator.

"Well, that was a mistaken way to end the evening," I said, hoping not to let my sadness dampen our wedding night.

Once Around, the movie Dustin Hoffman ankled, as they say in the trades, and the one I sacrificed for *Sex, Lies, and Videotape*, was back on track when Richard Dreyfuss and Holly Hunter recognized the unique voice of the script's writer, Malia Scotch Marmo, and wanted to work with Lasse enough to sign on to the picture.

After Carey's and my brief honeymoon in St. Barts, Lasse, Amy, and I scouted locations and settled on Raleigh, North Carolina. During a tour of the city, I asked our guide from the state film commission, "How are the hospitals here in Raleigh?"

He had a tiny panic attack, as if he'd forgotten an important location we desperately needed and just blew North Carolina's chance to be in a movie from Universal Pictures.

"Is there a hospital scene in the script? How did I miss that? We have wonderful hospitals in Raleigh that we'd be happy to empty so you could film without disturbance."

"That's very kind of you, but I'm asking for me, not the production. My wife will be having a baby during the shoot."

I called Carey that night from my hotel to say the hospital with the best reputation for maternity care was UNC Rex Hospital. I kept waiting for Carey to worry about having a baby in an unfamiliar city, but she never did.

"Our child's birth certificate is going to say she was born in North Carolina. How exotic!" she said, laughing.

"Or him."

We didn't want to know the gender but decided on James if it was a boy, after Carey's father, or Hannah if it was a girl, because we both liked *Hannah and Her Sisters.* During Carey's first ultrasound, we could have sworn we heard the nurse point out "his" heart, and both of us groaned in frustration because we distinctly had said we wanted it to be a surprise. The nurse vigorously denied saying "his" heart, insisting she had instead said "its" heart. We chose to believe her to keep the mystery going, but were pretty sure we were having a "Jimmer."

Our first stop when I returned to Raleigh with Carey to start shooting was UNC Rex Hospital so we could meet her obstetrician. A kid wearing a white lab coat introduced himself in the waiting room and asked us to follow him. I thought how cute it was that the hospital let the candy stripers dress up like real doctors. We were led into our new obstetrician's office and assumed he'd join us shortly, when the kid took a seat behind the desk.

Carey and I shared a confused glance.

"I'm sorry," I began. "You're Dr. Worthing?"

"I'm Dr. Worthing."

"I don't think I have ever seen a doctor so young before," I ventured.

"You are not the first to tell me that," he said with a laugh. "But I can assure you I am highly experienced and only look young. I'm thirty-three years old and have delivered many, many babies safely into the arms of their mothers."

"I'm thirty-four," I said pointlessly.

While on set, I must have checked my beeper every five minutes. I made Amy call it several times a day to make sure it worked. Psoriasis had come and gone most of my life, but now with the stress of waiting, it flared all over my body worse than ever. Richard Dreyfuss, who for some reason never liked me, would slap the scalp flakes off my shoulders and say, "That's disgusting, man." He was by then sober, and I was always tempted to remind him of the night he snorted coke off a Bob's Big Boy statuette at Carrie Fisher's after his shitty review in *Othello*.

In the house we rented in Raleigh, I had a recurring nightmare that I'd taken our newborn to the supermarket and then, not realizing it, I'd left it behind in a shopping cart in the parking lot. Still trapped in the dream, I'd leap out of bed to go back to the supermarket, until Carey calmed me down.

"You're going to be a great father," she'd whisper when I got back in bed. "Nothing like that is ever going to happen. When our baby is born, she will be impossible to forget."

"Or he."

"Or he."

Despite her confidence in me, I still lost wallets and passports, missed flights, showed up at parties on the wrong date. Not great traits, I secretly worried, for a grown man expected to raise a child.

MY BEEPER WENT OFF at two in the morning on April 8, 1990. It was on my nightstand, and when I grabbed it, I saw Carey standing in the living room with a phone in her hand.

"I know how long you've been waiting for that thing to go off, so I thought I'd give you your money's worth," she said. "My water broke. We gotta go."

Everything seemed to be going smoothly until it wasn't. The contractions were getting closer, the shooting pain in Carey's back was relieved by an epidural, when suddenly a monitor started to beep wildly, causing looks of concern among the attending nurses. Dr. Worthing, who was absent at the time, rushed into the room.

"What's happening?" Carey and I both asked.

Worthing quoted gobbledygook from a *Merck Manual*, and the only words we understood were "breech," "cervix," and "caesarean."

"Caesarean!" Carey moaned. "I don't want to do that. I wanted this to be natural."

"I'm afraid we have no choice, Carey," said the doctor. And then to the nurses: "We have to wheel her into surgery right away."

As I hurried behind Carey's gurney being rushed into the operating room, I had an unsettling thought: *Doogie Howser is going to kill my wife.*

The staff outfitted me in a paper gown and hairnet and placed me at the foot of Carey's bed. The anesthesiologist had already put a nitrous mask over her mouth that put her out cold. A curtain was drawn over the lower half of her body to spare me seeing the scalpel open her belly. My mother had had five caesareans. Alex, Dominique, and I were the only survivors. Carey was a healthy, corn-fed Colorado girl who'd hardly had a cold before she met me, before I'd infected her with my crazy-pants genes.

There was an opening in the curtain that I parted, determined to see exactly what was being done to Carey. I watched the doctor casually push aside her intestines like sausages at a deli counter. I didn't see how it was possible he'd get all that back inside her abdomen in the right order.

Dr. Worthing knew the alternate names we had for our child, and that ever since the first sonogram, we were convinced we were having a boy, but when he pulled out a shiny, wet, red object and held it up for inspection, the doctor said, "Well, it looks like he's . . . he's . . . a HANNAH!"

"That's exactly what I secretly hoped," I said.

"You want to cut the umbilical?" he said.

"Hell yes!" I thundered, bounding up to greet my daughter.

The nurses wiped Hannah down, and Dr. Worthing handed me an instrument to cut the cord, which was surprisingly difficult.

"Oh, Carey," I said to Hannah's sleeping mother, "I wish you could see this."

Once the cord was cut, a nurse swaddled her in a tiny blanket and handed her to me to hold for the first time.

"There is a room across the hall," Dr. Worthing said, "that we keep for fathers to be with their newborns until the mother wakes up."

The room was dark, save for a night-light in the corner that was just bright enough to illuminate every feature of Hannah's face. She lay content in my arms, as if she'd finally arrived at the place she was meant to be. We looked at each other for the longest time, until her gaze wandered up toward something unseen that had entered the room. I felt it too. A presence had joined us, and I knew at once it was Dominique. A rush of warmth washed over me, and maybe over Hannah, too, because she made a tiny sound that might have been her first giggle, or could have been her way of saying hello to her aunt.

"Oh, Dominique," I whispered, "look what I have. Isn't she beautiful?"

ACKNOWLEDGMENTS

I struggled to come up with a title for this book, but I always knew the subtitle would be *A Family Memoir.* Before I ever wrote a word, I called Alex, who has long since recovered from his struggles with mental illness, is happily married, and now divides his time between Oregon and Los Angeles, to get his blessing.

He said, "You can write whatever you want about me, just make sure it comes from a place of love." I have taken that direction to heart and extended it to the friends and family whose spirits I felt so strongly while writing the book. Alex is the only surviving member of my immediate family and my first acknowledgment, but if it's possible to acknowledge the dead, I want to thank my parents, Dominique, John, Joan, and Quintana for letting me bring them to life in my office each day as I wrote. Their presence was so vivid that the pictures of them on my corkboard actually shimmered with light. When my work on the book was complete, I mourned their losses all over again.

I was a fan of John Burnham Schwartz's novels long before I

ever dreamed he would be my editor. He taught me so much about the craft of writing, and more than once saved me from myself. ("I don't think you want to tell the reader *that*, Griffin" would be written in the margins of his edits.) We had a lot of laughs over more than a few martinis and I hope we work together again soon.

I want to thank John's assistant editor, Helen Rouner, for talking me off the ledge the numerous times I thought I'd deleted entire chapters and for patiently explaining Word's byzantine prompts that helped me find them buried deep in my laptop.

For at least a decade, the legendary agent David Kuhn has badgered me to write a memoir. "You have a book inside you, and when you write it, I want first look," he'd say, and I'd shrug as if I'd give it some thought. In fact, I had been secretly cobbling pages together, and when I had a neat stack, I sent them to David and was delighted by his reaction and the confidence he had in me as a writer. He is not only my brilliant and tenacious agent, but a trusted friend who gives me great advice. I also want to thank his associate Nate Muscato and everyone at Aevitas Creative.

Alexandra Styron and Susanna Moore wrote exquisite memoirs that influenced and inspired me to write my own. They are also close friends and early readers who offered notes that were both tough and encouraging. I gave the book to another great writer, Scott Spencer, whose friendship I exploited to push my first draft on to the next level. To not give an early read to Amy Robinson, with whom I had produced seven movies, was unthinkable, because I have relied on her opinions for over forty years. My cousin Annabelle Dunne, who has become as much a sister as Dominique had been, was trusted with the first family read, and her laughter about the antics of our relatives, most of which took place before she was born, always anchored my confidence. Had Dominique lived, she would be almost sixty-five, and I often reflect with a smile and a twinge of sadness how close the two of them would have become.

I want to thank Zonia Pelensky for her unflagging support from the moment I began this book. She'd heard all the stories long before I wrote them. My affection and gratitude for her know no bounds.

As difficult as it was to attend the trial, my family entered that courtroom every day surrounded by friends who protected us in a halo of love: Brooke Adams, Bryan Cook, Melinda and Lisa Bittan, Liz Heller, Kit McDonough, Erica Elliot, Denise Dennehy, Mark Metcalf, and of course Charlie. I also want to thank everyone from Parents of Murdered Children, who tried to prepare us for the worst, and comforted us when it was worse than we imagined. Though the verdict was not the outcome we hoped for, my family always admired how our district attorney, Steven Barshop, put his heart and soul into the trial to get us the justice we deserved.

Random but heartfelt thanks to the staff at the Georgian Hotel in Santa Monica, where I finished this book in a room overlooking the beach house my father rented in 1959, Don Carleton, our family historian Sigrid Maitrejean, Debbie Rosten, Michael Keaton, Shelley Wanger, Susan Traylor, Boaty Boatwright, Kevin Falls, Carrie Malcolm, Mitch Glazer, Gabriel Byrne, Yana Romano, Ted Griffin, Happy Massee, Octavio Gomez, Fisher Stevens, Carey Lowell, and the pride and joy of our lives, our daughter, Hannah.